Marvin Richardson Vincent

God and Bread with other Sermons

Marvin Richardson Vincent

God and Bread with other Sermons

ISBN/EAN: 9783743353909

Manufactured in Europe, USA, Canada, Australia, Japa

Cover: Foto ©Lupo / pixelio.de

Manufactured and distributed by brebook publishing software (www.brebook.com)

Marvin Richardson Vincent

God and Bread with other Sermons

GOD AND BREAD

WITH OTHER SERMONS

BY

MARVIN R. VINCENT, D.D.

PASTOR OF THE CHURCH OF THE COVENANT, NEW YORK

NEW YORK
DODD, MEAD, AND COMPANY
1884

COPYRIGHT, 1884,
BY DODD, MEAD, & COMPANY.

ELECTROTYPED AND PRINTED
BY RAND, AVERY, AND COMPANY,
BOSTON.

To

The Congregation of the Church of the Covenant

This Volume,

Published at Their Request,

Is Affectionately Inscribed

By Their Pastor.

CONTENTS.

		PAGE
I.	God and Bread	3
II.	Does it Pay?	21
III.	The Single Need	39
IV.	Facing God	59
V.	Light and Loyalty	77
VI.	The Ordered Steps	97
VII.	Fidelity and Dominion	115
VIII.	Extra Service	135
IX.	The Pride of Care	153
X.	The Plough and the Kingdom	173
XI.	Joy and Judgment	189
XII.	Silent before God	207
XIII.	A Leper's Logic	227
XIV.	Prayer and Panoply	247
XV.	The Daysman	265
XVI.	The Lesson of Ripeness	285
XVII.	Strength, Victory, and Knowledge in Youth	305
XVIII.	God and the Times of Ignorance	323
XIX.	The Promise of Incompleteness	343
XX.	Only a Little While	363

I.

GOD AND BREAD.

I.

GOD AND BREAD.

"But he answered and said, It is written, Man shall not live by bread alone, but by every word that proceedeth out of the mouth of God." — MATT. iv. 4.

HOW shall we live? Multitudes of people are asking that question to-day with peculiar earnestness. The man who could give a satisfactory practical answer would be regarded as the greatest of all public benefactors.

But why do not men go to the Bible for an answer? For one reason: because many of them, at least, assume that the Bible has little or nothing to do with their every-day affairs. It does very well to preach from, to read sometimes on Sundays, to furnish fine sentiments and apt quotations; but in the pushing, open-eyed world of business, in the atmosphere of capital, stocks, bonds, business-combinations, panics, it is as much out of place as a fifth-century hermit would be on Wall Street.

Then, again, if they do chance to consult the Bible, they find such astonishing answers, so utterly at variance with the principles by which they have been accustomed to live, that they quickly shut the book, saying, "Fanciful! Impracticable!"

This text, for instance, offers an answer to the question, "How shall we live?" It strikes out, in a sentence, a theory of living. How generally that theory has been accepted we can see for ourselves without looking very far. It has stood on record all these centuries: yet the cry, "How shall we live?" is as clamorous as ever; and the great mass of society is living by quite a different, indeed, an *opposite*, theory.

To understand Christ's theory as here propounded, we must examine briefly the story of Christ's temptation, with which it is connected.

After having fasted for forty days, our Lord was visited by the great tempter of mankind. He was weakened by hunger; and his hunger may have been aggravated, as has been suggested, by the very appearance of the stones which strewed the ground, and which in that region have the shape of little loaves of bread. Satan began his assault by urging Jesus to use his divine power in changing these stones into actual loaves, and thus to appease his hunger. It was a very plausible temptation. "Here thou art, the Son of God, the powers of heaven at thy command. Why shouldst thou suffer from a vulgar, human need? It should be no hard thing for thee to make a loaf out of a stone. If thou *be* the Son of God, command that these stones be made bread."

Now, this temptation was aimed at Jesus *as an individual*, and as *the head and representative of a kingdom*. Addressed to Christ as an individual, it was intended to make him commit himself to the admission that his life could be sustained only by *external and visible means*. If Christ had yielded, he would have said, in so doing, "Bread is *indispensable* to the support of life. I can live only as I shall have bread. I shall perish if I do not have it."

But suppose the tempter had quoted Scripture, as he did a little later, and had cited the story of the manna in the wilderness, and had clinched that with those verses of the seventy-eighth Psalm: "He rained down manna upon them to eat, and had given them of the corn of heaven. Man did eat angels' food: he sent them meat to the full." Suppose he had said, "As the Son of God, do you profess to be more scrupulous than God himself? *He* wrought a miracle for his hungry children: why should you hesitate to do the same for yourself?"

Our Lord's answer included this very case, and was pointed directly at it; since his words are a quotation of Moses' words to the Israelites in his review of their history. God's intent in the miraculous giving of the manna — a *new, special thing*, created for the special need — was to show the people that their life depended *directly upon him*, and not upon ordinary means of support. Cut off, as they were, from their accustomed food, they should, nevertheless, be fed, and drink abundantly, through God's special bounty. They should not starve because the wilderness did not furnish the products of the Nile valley, not even if it were utterly barren. There was a purpose in God's giving them an unfamiliar article of food, and in giving it through unfamiliar channels. Their own exertions had nothing to do with their subsistence, beyond gathering each day's supply at their tent-doors. The nature of the supply left no room for them to boast of their own enterprise or prudence in their journey through the desert. Hence Moses says, "He humbled thee, and suffered thee to hunger, and fed thee with manna, which thou knewest not, neither did thy fathers know; that he might make thee know that man doth not live by bread only, but by every word that proceedeth out of the mouth of the Lord doth man live." [1]

Here, then, the two theories of living are squarely confronted. Satan, as the prince of this world, announces his, and tries to win Christ's assent to it: "*Man lives by bread, and by bread alone.*" Christ replies: "*Man lives not by bread, but by God.*" Man lives by God's gifts, only as God is behind them. Man's *real* support is not in the *gifts*, but in the *Giver*.

What is covered by this word "*bread*"?

It covers *the whole visible economy of life*, — all that range of supplies, helps, and supports upon which men usually depend to keep themselves alive, and to make life comfortable and enjoyable. It covers the whole economy of food and drink, clothing, shelter, ministry to the senses, to power, respectability, and worldly honor. The world's commonly accepted theory is, *By these things we live. We cannot get on without them.* Do you need to be told how widely that theory prevails in soci-

---

[1] Deut. viii. 3.

ety to-day? For what are the mass of men spending their energies? For food and raiment and position, — for the abundance and *superfluity* of these things. Not for shelter merely, but for *costly* homes. Not for competency merely, but for *wealth*, and *vast* wealth; the plain inference being, "We cannot have too much of such things: a man's life *does* consist in the abundance of the things which he possesses."

Now, I am not blind to men's natural and pardonable anxiety about such things. Food and raiment and home are parts of *God's own economy of life* in this world; and Christ himself says, "Your heavenly Father knoweth that ye have need of all these things." But I am speaking of the false position in which men put these things, — of their tendency to *separate* them from God, and to seek to live by them *alone*. While Christ says, "Your Father knoweth that ye have need of these," he forbids men to hold them *alone* or *first* in their thought. Something is to take precedence of the *gifts*, and that is the *Giver*. The gifts are to be sought *through* the Giver. Men often seek food and raiment without reference to God, and often in ways *forbidden* by God: whereas Christ says, "Seek God *first*, seek to be under his rule, seek to be right according to his law, and the food and raiment will come with these." The kingdom of God *includes* bread; and hence, in the Lord's Prayer, immediately after the petition, "Thy kingdom come, Thy will be done," comes the prayer for daily bread.

Man lives *by God*, in direct dependence on God. God may use, and does commonly use, natural means for man's support; but God is not *limited* to these. Men think he is. When these means disappear, they think all is over. But they forget that these things derive all their power to sustain and to delight from God. It is God alone that gives any value or efficiency to these. Men say that the secret of life is to be in right relations to the world. God says, "You are in right relation to *nothing* until you are right with me. You are nothing at all,—not so much as that red leaf driven by the wind, which lies now over a gold-mine, and now on the roof of a hovel; nothing, save as I uphold you, and send you your food, and give it power to nourish you, and to please your palate. Dainties are no better than chaff if *I* do not impart their quality. Let me withdraw my hand, and see what they will do for you."

The very structure of the body asserts that man was intended to eat and drink. The earth was commanded by God to bring forth fruit for the service of man. The facts of heat and cold and tempest suggest clothing and shelter. If man lives in a spiritual economy, he also lives in a *natural* economy, to which he is plainly adapted by his Creator, and which is as plainly adapted to meet his conditions. But Nature everywhere points beyond herself. The nature of man points up to God. If that is first which is natural, it is only first in order of *succession*, not of *importance*. If the physical life of the babe precedes the intellectual and moral life of the strong man, the intellectual and moral life is none the less the *higher* stage of being. If God so arranges the physical life of man that it is sustained ordinarily by food, it is that the physical life should suggest the higher life of the soul, and the bread the *Giver* of the bread. Why, in ordinary matters men recognize this principle clearly enough, that, ultimately, the great forces on which they depend for the common transactions of life are not material. A cable despatch comes to you across the Atlantic. You know that it passed over a wire; you know that it was borne by an electric current; but you also know that neither wire nor current nor telegraphic key is of any avail until a *human mind* brings them into combination. The cable will not carry messages of itself. You do not for a moment think that iron and fire and water only carry you over the rails from New York to San Francisco. Mind and will must adjust and apply these agents. No more will bread avail without God. Behind all this physical economy, to which bread is the visible minister, are the divine Mind and Will, creating and adjusting the human organism and its minister alike. Every thing depends on that divine Mind and Will.

And in proof of this, God has now and then put men in places where the physical ministry failed, and has shown them, that, if need were, he could sustain their life without it. Moses was with him on the summit of that barren mountain for forty days, nourished by no mortal food. Elijah travelled in the strength of a single meal for forty days. God has only to say "Live," and man lives, and continues to live whether there is bread or not. Says Jeremy Taylor, "If the flesh-pots be removed, He can alter the appetite; and when our stock is spent, He can also lessen the necessity: or, if that continues, He can drown the sense of it in a deluge of patience and resignation." And Wesley writes, —

> " Man doth not live by bread alone:
> *Whate'er thou wilt,* can feed.
> Thy power converts the bread to stone,
> And turns the stone to bread.
>
> *Thou* art our food: we taste thee now.
> In thee we move and breathe.
> Our bodies' only life art thou,
> And all beside is death."

But I have said, that Christ appeared in this temptation as the head and representative of a kingdom: whatever rule or policy he might adopt for himself would give the law for his followers.

If, then, our Lord had yielded to this first temptation, he would have committed himself to the *bread-theory* as the law of his kingdom, no less than of his own life. He would have said, by changing the stones into bread, "As *I* cannot live without bread, so *my kingdom* cannot thrive so long as men's worldly needs are unsupplied. My administration must be a turning of stones into bread. It must make men happy by at once miraculously removing all want and suffering from the world, and inaugurating an era of worldly prosperity."

We know that this has not been Christ's policy. He abjured it in this answer to Satan. He did, indeed, mean that a time should come when the wilderness and the solitary place should be glad; but that was to be the result of *holiness*, of the subjection of society to a King, the girdle of whose loins should be righteousness. This is what Christ asserts, that *society*, no less than man as an individual, *truly* lives only as it lives by dependence on God. Social prosperity is based on *righteousness*. It would be possible to test the matter on a small scale. Suppose that a man of immense wealth and grand administrative power should have a little town of a thousand people given to him in charge, with absolute authority to rule it, and to develop its resources in his own way. Suppose the man to say, "Yes, I will make this people as happy as a community can be. I will build comfortable homes for those who are poor. I will give each of these poor families a competence. I will educate all these ignorant ones. Poverty and squalor shall disappear. The sanitary arrangements shall be perfect. There shall be no foul pools to breed miasma. There shall be pure water and good ventilation." If the plan embraced nothing more, the man, however in earnest and philanthropic, would be doing precisely what the Devil wanted Christ to do. He would have the power — which to those poor people would be as good as miraculous — of changing bodily misery to comfort, stones to bread. His theory would be the bread-theory, prosperity through the supply of physical need. Do you think that would be a happy community? Do you think that a society which should recognize God nowhere would be a peaceful, well-ordered body? Do you think that good homes and good food and ventilation would keep out passion and greed, or do away with depraved appetites? No. Culture would only refine selfishness. Competency would furnish greater power for mischief. Natural differences of talent and energy would assert themselves, and call out the envy which attaches to such differences. The members of that community, in short, would be no happier with bread, and without God, than they were without either God or bread, and would be infinitely more dangerous. The bread-theory is the radical weakness of communism, in that it contemplates only the adjustment of outward conditions and the satisfaction of natural appetites. There must be, as we all know, a material basis in society, just as there must be an underground foundation for a palace. That is not first which is *spiritual;* but when you look down into an excavation, and see great foundations laid, you say, "A house is to be built here. That foundation means a house, or it means nothing." So, if civilization is only a matter of material forces, of steam and electricity, of telephones and sewing-machines, of drainage and ventilation; nay, if it add to these, taste and culture, libraries and art-galleries, and leave out God and conscience, and faith and worship, — it is only a *foundation,* daily emphasizing the lack of its superstructure.

Civilization, without God and righteousness, is mere *cellarage*. The community which lives by bread, without God, does *not* truly live.

History repeats itself. In these modern days one finds himself rummaging the pages of Gibbon and Tacitus and Juvenal. Look at those old empires which lived by bread alone; by riches so enormous that it seems as if God had determined to give money a chance to do its best; living by power so vast that there were no more worlds to conquer; living by pleasure so prodigal and so refined and varied that the liveliest invention was exhausted, and the keenest appetite surfeited. Babylon, Rome, Antioch, Alexandria, Carthage, — to-day you dare not open to your children the records of the inner life of these communities. You almost hesitate to read its fearful summary in the first chapter of Paul's Epistle to the Romans.

And what of ourselves? what of this nineteenth-century civilization in America, to go no farther? What is our measure of progress? Has this civilization advanced in the measure in which it has woven rich stuffs, carved statues, painted pictures, wrought cunningly in gold and ivory, and written with grace and power? Other and earlier centuries have these to show as well as we. In many of these things we still take our lessons from them. No, truly. When the civilizations of the world sent their representative products to Philadelphia, the true key and test of that vast exhibition of human achievement were in one little case — where the word of God, translated into the various tongues of the earth, was spread before the spectator. Just so far as the principles of that book are behind and beneath the material display, does it mark a *real* progress. The nation, like the man, lives truly, only as it lives by God, and not by bread alone. I look back to the barren mountain of the temptation. I see, rising before the eyes of the weak and exhausted Son of man, the vision of the kingdoms of this world and their glory, vested with the witching glamour of satanic sorcery. I hear the stupendous offer of the whole mass of the kingdoms which know not God, with all their pomp of art and learning, of fleets and armies, all on the simple condition of accepting the law of life by bread instead of life by God. And that picture is lifted up to-day, amid the crazy rush of the exchange and the crash of falling fortunes, as a silent reminder that the world's great pattern of life chose life by God, — though there went with it the desert, and Gethsemane, and the cross, and the long, sad centuries of the growth of righteousness, — rather than life by bread, with its quick and superficial triumphs, and the gilded glory of Satan's kingdom. Through all time, until the kingdom of God shall have fully come, his voice will make itself heard above the roar of traffic and the whirl of dissipation, — "Thou shalt worship the Lord thy God, and him only shalt thou serve."

And suppose bread fails. Suppose the body literally starves, and the man *dies*, as we say. Is Christ's theory disproved? By no means.

Christ's choice led him to the cross, and many a follower of his has been forced to choose between the bread-theory and death. When God says that man shall *live* by his word, he means by "life" far more than the little span of human years, with their eating and drinking and pleasure and gain-getting. This utterance of the world's Redeemer assumes the fact of immortality. If not, the theory of life by God is branded; and there is nothing for us but the bread-theory: "Let us eat and drink; for to-morrow we die." To live by the word of God is to share the eternal life of God. The bread-life is but the prelude and faint type of this. It gets all its real meaning and value from this. Human life is nothing if it does not foreshadow the larger life of eternity: and when the lower physical life fails for lack of bread, the man does not cease to live; he only begins to live, and to prove that if man cannot live by bread alone, he *can* live by *God* alone.

Here, then, we have Christ's theory of life, individual and social. Man lives by God's gifts, but not by the gifts *only*. By bread, but not by bread *alone*. Bread is nothing without God. Bread gets all its power to feed from God. Bread points away from itself to God. Bread has a part in the divine economy of society; but it comes in *with* the kingdom of God, under its law, and not as its substitute.

In such disturbances as those of the past week, it is well that men take heed lest their anxiety should throw them upon Satan's bread-theory, and divert them from the counter theory of life by God. We cannot, being human, be entirely free from care. At any rate, we *are* not. But this we *can* do, by God's help: we can keep it constantly before us, that our life, after all, is not in these material things. The loss of the material gift does not carry with it the loss of the divine Giver. The man who lives by bread *alone* has nothing when bread is gone. He may run down the whole line of his reserves, and find nothing which is beyond the possibility of disaster. But you who live by God, when you reach back to what lies behind bread, find the best of your treasure, which moth and rust cannot corrupt, nor thieves break through and steal. Face the question to-day; it is a good time, in the presence of these hard tests. What is my theory of life? Is it Christ, or Satan? Is it bread *alone*, or bread with God? Ask yourself, "Where is my heart fixed most of the time? Is it on God, as my life? or is it on my stocks and securities and ventures?" And, ere you answer the question, call up the words of your Lord and Saviour, "Where your treasure is, there will your heart be also." The practical working of the two theories is written down in lines which he that runs may read. Before you is the picture of the Man of Sorrows, who had not where to lay his head, reviled and spoken against, walking by his hard road to the garden and to the cross, and yet deliberately choosing to live by God rather than by bread; and you see the choice vindicated by the peace and poise of that life, by the enthusiasm of its faith, by its heavenly joy in its work, by its ever-growing power over the life of the world, by the adoration and love and praise daily wafted towards it from millions of souls: and all this while the worldly dominion he refused has proved a vanished shadow, while the old empires have gone down in ruin, and their pleasures have turned to a corruption which is an offence in the world's nostrils. The old city which rang with the cry of "Bread and the Circus!" is only a monument now. The tourist wanders over the Palatine, and peers down into the choked vaults of the Cæsars' palaces; and the antiquarian rummages where Nero's fish-ponds gleamed, and climbs along the broken tiers of the Coliseum, from which the culture and beauty and fashion of Rome looked down with delight upon Christian martyrs in the fangs of tigers.

As you look on this picture, surely you will take fresh heart; surely you will win a new faith in Christ's theory; surely you will not dare, with the glory of that life before you, to take the baser theory of the prince of this world, to choose the life which is by bread alone! You have seen more than one man who lived by bread alone find his theory of life fail. You have seen him, when bread failed, go down, down, heart-broken, dishonored, ruined, reputation gone, conscience stained, honor blighted, manhood wrecked, *nothing* left; but you never saw, and you never will see, such a catastrophe befall a man who lived by God. When the silver and the gold are gone, he has the God who holds the treasures of the earth in his hand. He has manhood untainted, his best self untouched, and round him the strong arm of Him who says, "Cast all thy care on me. I will never leave thee, nor forsake thee."

II.

DOES IT PAY?

II.

DOES IT PAY?

"For what shall a man be profited, if he shall gain the whole world, and forfeit his life? or what shall a man give in exchange for his life?" — MATT. xvi. 26.

"COMMONPLACE is contemptible," is the verdict of modern culture. Not of *modern* culture only: the Athenians, we are told, were equally impatient of it, and spent their time in nothing else but either to hear or to tell some new thing. But is this a true verdict? Stone pavements, for instance, are very commonplace to us; so much so, that we have ceased to be conscious of them, and walk or ride over them all day long without a thought of what we are treading on. When the street is torn up, when we come to a muddy gap in our accustomed track, we wake up to the fact, that, in a city, stone pavements count for a good deal. Nobody takes notice of lamp-posts; they are very commonplace: but let the lights go out all over the city, and we begin to find out how large a part they play in our convenience and safety. The fact is, that the best things in our lives are the commonplace and familiar things, — the senses, health, home, reading, and writing. It is often the highest praise of a thing that it has become commonplace. A thing which has no value does not pass into common use. The best thing that can be said of bread is, that everybody uses it.

So of texts of Scripture. Certain texts carry a flavor of novelty, while others are household words. Our text to-day is one of these latter. I suppose every preacher in Christendom has preached upon it some time or other. It is more than doubtful if any thing new can be said about it; and yet that is the best reason for preaching about it: for this text is to Christianity just what the solid ground is to our business and building, just what bread is to our living. It is a shaft that opens down into the very heart and centre of the gospel, and branches off under the whole Bible. No reader or preacher of the Bible can escape the truth it tells. He must run against it if he reads the Bible at all.

What, then, is the truth? It takes the form of a question of value, — a question which, in some shape, interests us all. It is thrown into the setting of the market-place. All life is a bid for something, — that something, whatever it be, which each of us calls his end or object in life. That something we want; and for it we are willing to pay a price, — our labor, our pains, our best thought, our temporary rest and comfort sometimes. I seem to see the great market in the fresh morning. The young, vigorous forms, and the bright, eager faces are pouring in at the gate.

There is one thing up at auction, though there seem to be many. It is the world. Here one cries up honors! — literary, military, civic honors, — praise of men, flattering of crowds, flaming paragraphs in the newspapers; social honors, — homage to beauty, society at your feet. Here is a rival vender. Pleasures! what infinite variety! appeals to every sense, suited to all tastes; coarser wares for the coarser grained, and subtler enjoyments for the æsthetic; pleasures of meat and drink, pleasures of luxurious ease, pleasures of artistic study; the wildest excitements, the most delicious languors; pleasures of color and of sound and of perfume, — all going, going cheap! In another corner, wealth! close beside it, power! The world is on sale. Do monks and puritans tell us it is a "fleeting show"? Ha! it is a good world, full of good things. And the silks and jewels rustle and sparkle, and the banners wave, and the trumpets sound, and the gold chinks, and the sweet odors rise in rich steams, and the air is laden with sweet harmonies, and glowing with lovely hues. A good world, and going so cheap too! something within the reach of everybody: who will buy? Do you wonder that young eyes grow brighter, and young cheeks flush, and young hearts beat quicker? So much for youth, especially. Why, the world is for youth. Hope, love, pleasure, — they are all for youth. I seem to see, in the midst of that eager throng, one who appears far more interested in the buyers than in the wares. With a wonderful blending of majesty, affection, and sadness, he scans the young traders as they crowd round the booths. And now I see him lay a hand — a hand with a strange mark on it — upon the shoulder of an eager youth, who is crowding forward, and bidding high and eagerly; and, as the youth turns impatiently, he gazes into his face with a look which seems to go down to the deepest secret of his heart, with a love which disarms resentment, and says, "Wait a little. There is time enough to buy here. One question only: that thing which you want, and for which you have just bidden so much, what shall it profit you?"

I have only thrown into a kind of allegory what is actually going on. I have merely used a fancy to carry a fact. I want you to see and feel the fact, if you will, the fact that the world is bidding for your homage, your allegiance, your love, your energy. It is a fact that the world appeals to you to accept its rules, its customs, its modes of thinking, its ends of living. It is a fact that the Lord Christ says to every one of you, "Suppose you get it. Suppose you make it all yours, all the kingdoms of the world and the glory of them, — what good is it going to do you? You are about making a bargain: of course you want to make a profitable one. Well, what shall it profit you if you gain the whole world, and lose your own life?"

Notice, then, what our Lord tells you in this text. First, *that your choice of a principle and end of living involves an exchange.* You get nothing in life, good or bad, without cost. You know very well, that, if you are to succeed in business, you will do it at the cost of leisure and ease and amusement. You must work when you would rather rest. You must stay in the hot, dusty city, when you would rather be among the cool hills, or down by the breezy sea. If you would succeed in medicine, you must conquer your natural repugnance to disgusting sights and odors. If in literature, you must shut yourself up with books, and toil while others sleep. No man ever leaped into a success of any kind without cost to himself. Success is always paid for with some coin or other. Do you expect you will win *moral* success, spiritual victory, on any other terms? Is this grandest and highest of successes going to be poured into your lap as a free gift, for nothing?

Secondly, look then, at the nature of exchange in this particular case. What do you pay, supposing you buy the world? You have passed many a shop in cities, in the window of which you have read, "price fixed." The vender would have you know that you need not try to beat him down. He will take so much, and no less. If you want the article, take it at that price: if you do not care to pay that price, let it alone. That exactly represents the case here. If you buy the world, you pay a definite price for it, a price from which there is no discount to the most favored buyer; and that price is *your life*. You see our Lord is not merely putting a supposed case, a bare possibility, as if it might possibly happen that a man should do so monstrous a thing as to lose his life for the sake of the world: he states it *as a principle*, a universal fact, that the man who takes the world takes it at the price of his life. For you will notice that the text is only the conclusion of the statement in the previous verses, about which there cannot be any doubt. "Suppose a man wants to come after me," says our Lord. "He pays for the privilege this price; namely, that he denies self, and takes up the cross. Suppose a man wants to keep his life, his worldly, selfish, lower life; to live for self, as we say; to keep his pleasures, his pursuits, his studies, under the economy of this world. He can do it. He can save that life, but only at the expense of his real life, his better, Christlike self, which Christ stands ready to develop in him. He that would save his life shall lose it." If the neat, smooth, wheat-corn should say, "This form of life is good enough for me: I prefer to remain as I am. I do not like going into the dark earth, and parting with my identity," all that could be answered would be, "Very well. Remain as you are; only, the price of your remaining is the forfeiture of that higher, more beautiful form of life,—the bearded stalk with its multiplied grains." The higher life is at the expense of the lower. "Except a corn of wheat fall into the ground and die, it abideth alone." If it bring forth fruit, if it would save the lovelier, richer life, it must lose the other form of life. If a man wants his shoulder free of the cross, he can have it so; only, he forfeits whatever good comes of being Christ's disciple. The two things exclude each other. You cannot have

Christ and self too; you cannot follow Christ, and be crossless; you cannot live partly in the higher, and partly in the lower, life: you must choose between them; and, whichever you choose, you pay for it with the other.

Here, then, is Christ's fixed price, — *Your life for the world.* He states it to you here: he hears you bid for the world, and he asks you, "What then? Is it a good purchase? If so, you ought to be able to tell why." You pay what seems to me an extravagant price for a piece of land, and yet there may really be no extravagance about it. You may have special reasons for desiring that situation, — reasons which make it more valuable to you than it could be to any other man; only you can surely give those reasons. You can surely show that you are getting your money's worth. So Christ says to you, "You pay your life for the world. It is a high price, but doubtless you can give a reason for paying it. How shall you be profited if you gain the world and lose your life?"

Will it not be well to stop, and examine the value of this purchase before the bargain is concluded? And please to note, that, in what I shall have to say about it, I shall appeal mostly to your own observation and experience. I shall go into no guesses nor speculations. But let me first say, that you may be none the less a purchaser of the world if you do not go to the length of our Saviour's supposition, and gain the whole world. You need not be rich nor powerful nor luxurious to be worldly, and to exchange your life for the world. You may be as ignorant and as rude in your life as a Hottentot, and as poor as Lazarus, and yet have gained the world and lost your life. For this is not merely a question of the things which you acquire by your exchange: it is a question of the law under which you put yourself, of the moral quality of the end which you seek. It was not Lazarus' poverty which carried him to Abraham's bosom, nor Dives' riches which put him on the other side of the gulf. It is possible for you to be quite as worldly in poverty as in wealth, in weakness and obscurity as in power. It is enough that you choose to follow the world's rule; that you find your pleasure, whatever it be, in going the world's way; that you live, in short, for just such ends, and in just such relations to your fellowmen, as you would if there were no such thing as God and heaven, love and unselfish ministry.

But suppose we go to the entire length of the Lord's words. Suppose you gain the *whole* world, every thing the world has to give you. I submit to you first, that you have gotten something *perishable*. Suppose you should buy a beautiful flask of some precious cordial, with the understanding that there was a secret leak in the flask which you could not find nor stop, and through which the precious liquid was slowly trickling away. Would you not be deemed a fool? Yet you buy the world with this certainty. Grant that its pleasures are ravishing, its sights and harmonies bewitching: you know as well as I do that they cannot last. The world is at the feet of your beauty, young woman. Are you willing to look to-day into a mirror which shall show you the face of thirty years hence? The world praises you, young man. Do you not know that the world will soon tire of you, and kick you aside for a new object? Do you not know — you may easily know, for the thing is all through history — that the very men who sing "Hosanna!" to-day, will cry "Crucify him!" to-morrow? Drip, drip! The golden cordial is going. The clock strikes one! A drop gone. Two! Another drop. Three! Another. And so on round the dial, only to begin again. The world is passing away. Men and women are growing old before your very faces. Your purchase has this quality, at least, — *it will not last.*

But I submit to you further, your *interest* in it will not last. I know it does not seem so now. You are so full of burning zeal to grasp the world that it seems as though your desire would never cool. But "the world passeth away, and *the desire of it.*" The fascination of the world is largely in your zest for it. The richest banquet has no charm for you if you are sick or surfeited. But you see for yourselves that the zest for the world passes away with the world. There were certain things which you longed to have and to do when you were boys and girls; you are not very old now, but you do not care for those things any more: and that weakening of desire is going on all the time. The time comes to all men when they say, "I have no pleasure in them." The pleasures of youth require the vigor and the freshness of youth. The time comes when the strong man's ambition begins to droop, and he does not kindle at the call of fame. The time comes when the honored and praised man becomes indifferent to honor and praise, and only asks the world to let him go on his way in quiet. You have purchased, in short, something which *you will cease to desire.*

And yet, ceasing to desire is not satisfaction. Your ceasing to desire will not be the feeling of the man whose appetite is sated, but rather of him whose food has become loathsome. And I say of your purchase, *It will not satisfy you.* Did you ever achieve any worldly success, or win any worldly prize, that you did not want something else beside? Why, open your eyes, and look about you. All round you are men and women who have gained the world. The world is all before them where to choose. They can gratify their tastes; they can eat and drink whatever the world's markets or gardens furnish; they can command every pleasure for the eye; they can travel when and whither they please; and yet they wander listlessly about, not knowing what to do with themselves,—now in Europe, now on the Nile, now in Asia, going from scene to scene, from gallery to gallery, from spectacle to spectacle, all the while possessed and driven by a consuming restlessness. Or they are in business. The man has gotten his million: he wants another million, and then another. He has gotten his position, but there is another man a step higher than he. Alexander had conquered the world: there was no more to conquer, and he wept. You have purchased something *unsatisfying.*

But still further. You have gotten something *dangerous.* Men would laugh to see you buying a pair of fetters or handcuffs in the market, but that is just what you are doing. You think you are buying something to possess: did it ever occur to you that it might possess you? You are buying the world as a servant: did it ever occur to you that you might change places, and that the world might become master, and a hard one at that? "The wages of sin." But it is a master, and not a servant, that pays wages. No doubt of it. When you buy the world, you buy a master at the price of your life. A terrible mistake, to find that you have paid your best, your all, for slavery, when you thought you were buying freedom. Do you think that is a morbid fancy? Nay: see for yourselves. Any thing that is necessary to a man is his master, is it not? Did you never see a man whose whole thought and life had been concentrated on money-making, and who could not rest when he wanted to, could not live without the excitement of the money-market? Did you never know a man's honesty mastered by the love for gain? Did you never know a man who had fed himself on the world's praise, until, when his banquet was withdrawn, and men forsook his shrine for that of another popular idol, his manhood drooped and shrivelled, and he became a disappointed, snarling misanthrope? Did you ever know a more relentless, masterful demon than that which drives the woman whose chief end in life is social position? A dangerous thing this purchase! The selfish man is a suicide: his lower self kills the higher. A man takes on the measure of his aim. He who aims high is the nobler, even though he miss his mark. His arrow will fly higher aimed at the sun, than when aimed at something on his own level. You see and know for yourselves that one who lives for low, sensual ends is lower and meaner in the quality of his manhood. Dangerous! you know what masters drink and the passion for gaming become. Dangerous! there is a life going on in certain circles in this city, which veils itself under social proprieties and elegances, but which is aptly described by the term "fast." A continuous whirl of feasting and spectacles and carnivals, which is undermining some of the brightest youthful promise, and blighting some of the best young manhood and womanhood of this city. Do you know what the end of that will be? Some of you have seen Couture's great picture, "The Decadence of the Romans," in the gallery of the Luxembourg at Paris,—a picture of a luxurious hall, where a frenzied orgie is at its height, a carnival of drunkenness and wantonness. A drunken youth, with a wreath in his tangled hair, sits upon a pedestal; while a reeling boy proffers a dripping goblet to the marble mouth of a statue. The old Roman dignity is gone from the brutalized faces of the revellers, which contrast sadly with the noble features of the statues of the old Roman worthies ranged round the hall, and with the sad faces of a group of thoughtful-looking men who are quitting the scene. And what is perhaps as significant as any other feature is, that the faces of this picture present a surprising likeness to faces which one sees every day in the streets of Paris, and that the models for this wreck of human nature are furnished by the painter's own city. It is a truth not told by Paris only. It has been told over and over again, as one city after another — Antioch, Corinth, Rome, Sybaris — has gone over the precipice. It is the story of the inevitable end of fast life and of fast society. You buy a *dangerous* thing when you buy the world.

And, once more, you come to the line at last, and pass over. You and I do not know much about that future world: speculation amounts to little. The word of God is reticent about details; and all that we do know, we know from that Word. But from that Word we do know something of the moral conditions of the future life. About one thing there cannot be any doubt; and that is, that the only thing we carry over the line with us is *ourselves*. What we are goes nakedly into that world, without any of the disguises or deceptions with which circumstances invest character here. "We brought nothing into this world, and it is certain we can carry nothing out." Whatever price you pay for the world, you leave the world behind you when you pass the gate of death. If, then, that is all you have gotten, what do you carry into the next world? You have given your life for the world. You cannot give it, and have it too. The world has passed away, and you go to face God — *with what?* The only thing that has any hold on the future is the Christ-like self, trained in the school of faith and self-denial and ministry; and if you have not that, if you have parted with that for the world, what have you? What shall it profit you if you shall have gained the whole world, and lost your life? I give you Christ's teaching, not mine. He knew both worlds. He has told you the solemn truth betimes, that you might not find it out only when the mischief was done; and if, when you get into that new life, this truth shall come to you as a new discovery, rest assured it will bring pain and anguish with it.

Christ asks you this morning, "Does it pay?" He appeals to fact, to your observation, to your common sense. Does it pay? Is it a good bargain? "What shall a man be profited if he shall gain the whole world, and forfeit his life? or what shall a man give in exchange for his life?" Or let another evangelist give you the same truth in his way: "For what is a man profited if he gain the whole world, and lose or forfeit *his own self?*" Is it a good bargain? — a world that passes away, a desire that passes away; an unsatisfying world; a world that carries in itself the seeds of danger and disaster; a world that proves a hard and cruel master, and gives slavery instead of freedom. All this for a life inspired and guided by Christ, a life in communion with heaven, a life rich in helpfulness and love; a faith which conquers the world, and makes you superior to its chances and changes and sorrows; a hope of eternal rest and eternal life,—is it a good bargain?

My young friends, I would save you from this fearful mistake. Christ would save you; and therefore his call is strong and urgent to you to-day: "Seek ye first the kingdom of God and his righteousness." You tell me there is much good in the world, much that may rightly be enjoyed; that God made the world to be used. That is all true. God did make the world for you to use and enjoy, but under his direction; and it may be well for you to remember, that, setting aside all considerations of the future life, you will make the most of the world by following Christ. You will make the world your servant, instead of your master. You will enjoy its lawful pleasures without a sting, instead of being ridden and driven by it as by a demon. The alternative of this fearful purchase we have been considering is before you. Christ stands beside you in the market-place, and asks what it will profit you to gain the world and lose yourself, and then says to you, "Follow me! Yes, along the way of the cross! yes, leaving self behind! but my yoke is easy, and my burden is light: you shall find rest unto your souls; you shall not walk in darkness; you shall not want for the best of society. Lo! I am with you alway, even unto the end of the world." Self may die, but the world will be the richer for the fruit of a ministering life; and beyond is rest, reward, heaven.

III.

THE SINGLE NEED.

III.

THE SINGLE NEED.

"But the Lord answered and said unto her, Martha, Martha, thou art anxious and troubled about many things: but one thing is needful: for Mary hath chosen the good part, which shall not be taken away from her." — LUKE x. 41, 42.

MARTHA was determined to provide a fine entertainment on this occasion. She was doubtless a notable housewife, and, not unnaturally, a little proud of it; and she had with her, to-day, her dearest and most honored guest, and was bent on setting before him her best, and in her best style. So there was much anxious discussion, we may suppose, about what dishes should be prepared, and not a little worry about their being properly cooked and served, and that the honored guest should have what might please him most. It was a loving impulse on her part, and our Lord did not fail to appreciate it. All natures do not express their affection in the same way. What a blessed fact it is that our Master and Judge sees the love behind the differences, and tolerates the differences for the love's sake!

Mary, though her quiet sitting at Jesus' feet was in strange contrast, apparently, with Martha's bustling activity and worry, showed, on other occasions, that she was not indisposed to active ministry. It was Mary who brought the flask of spikenard, and anointed the Lord's feet at that same table; and the words in this story seem to indicate that she had been assisting Martha in her preparations before Jesus came: but her finer spiritual instinct discerned that there was a better way of entertaining him than by feasting him. Custom in all ages, I know, has prescribed a feast as an appropriate way of honoring a guest; and in one sense it is so. You give a man a mark of your confidence and respect by inviting him to your table; but you do not, after all, if you will think of it, show him the highest mark of respect by inviting him to a splendid and formal banquet, assuming that he is best entertained by the gratification of his appetite. You pay him a higher token of your regard when you invite him to partake of your informal family meal; taking him into your private life, and assuming that he cares more for your society than for your fare. Mary, I repeat, discerned this fact, with a loving woman's quick perception; and so she was less anxious than Martha about the details of the feast. She had done all that she thought necessary for comfort and decency; and she valued her guest enough to desire to get something more out of his visit than the mere pleasure of seeing him eat, or the gratification of having him praise her viands. Call it a kind of selfishness, if you will; indeed, Martha had no hesitation in calling it so: it was nevertheless true, that Mary was bent on enjoying as well as entertaining her guest. Surely we are all selfish to that extent. She knew the blessing of Jesus' presence in the house. Are there not some Marys to-day, who, if he should come into their houses, would well-nigh forget altogether to lay the table, in their eagerness to hear the words of him who spake as never man spake? Let us hope so, at least; because there can be no doubt that Mary's attitude was the more pleasing of the two to the Lord, that her spiritual instinct was keener, and her spiritual fibre finer, than Martha's. The Lord's gentle and affectionate rebuke of Martha, — so gentle, so playful I had almost said, as to rob it of its sting, — and his commendation of Mary, set that beyond question, and give us our lesson to-day, — " Martha, thou art anxious and troubled about many things: but one thing is needful: for Mary hath chosen the good part, which shall not be taken away from her."

In the first place, observe that Christ's words imply no disapproval of active service as against a contemplative or meditative life. It has been a favorite fancy to make these two characters typical, — the one of the active, and the other of the contemplative, life; but the fancy is not borne out by fact, nor is it the contrast between these two that is present to the Saviour's mind. It is not Martha's *activity* that he is rebuking, but her *anxiety* and *distraction*. He who went about doing good, and who said, " My meat is to do the will of Him that sent me," was not the one to rebuke active ministry. The point of his rebuke lies in enforcing the pursuit of one thing as against many things. Martha is distracted and bustling about many things: Mary has chosen one thing, — a good part which shall not be taken away from her, — and that thing alone is needful. It may have been that the peculiar form of the expression grew out of the feast itself. Martha has provided, with much worry and care, many things to eat. To sustain life, only one thing is absolutely needful; or, as some read it, "There is need of few things, or of one." Be this as it may, the lesson is plain: the life of the soul depends on one thing; the whole energy of the soul should be concentrated upon that.

That accords with the Saviour's teaching elsewhere: "Leave all, and follow me! seek first one thing, — the kingdom of God!" The man in the parable, when he had lighted on the hidden treasure, concentrated all his desire and all his fortune on that one field; and, selling all that he had, he bought it. The pearl-merchant, who was seeking many goodly pearls, at last sold every thing for one wonderful gem. All the law is summed up in one word. Now, if we will only think of it, we shall see that just that simplicity is what we are seeking everywhere. Wherever we have a variety of facts or details to deal with, we are not satisfied until we find some law or some principle, some one thing which includes them all. We see the stone fall to the ground when it leaves our hand, and the planets held in their orbits. We are delighted when we can group these two facts, apparently so unrelated, under the one law of gravitation. When work involves a multitude of details requiring a multitude of separate forces, we aim to find one single force which will take up all the others into itself, and do their work. Suppose a man who had never seen a great machine-shop, and who knew nothing of the power of steam or water, were set down in a great hall full of lathes and looms and circular saws, and required to set the machinery in motion: how many men he would call in! how many separate contrivances he would apply to each machine! how he would bustle about from wheel to wheel, from lathe to lathe, now heaving away at a great trip-hammer, now cutting his fingers on a circular saw, now turning round the driving-wheel of a lathe! And at this point the experienced engineer comes in, and laughs as he sees the poor man's perplexity, and says to him, "My friend, all this trouble is unnecessary: only one thing is needful;" and he slips a belt over a drum, and pulls a lever, and behold! the whole hall is in a whirl, — lathes, saws, trip-hammers, all in motion, without a hand on any of them. Or, here is a schoolboy with his arithmetic before him, and a whole page of "examples" to work out: and he takes each example by itself, and tries to think his way through it; trying all sorts of experiments, applying one method to one, and another to another, and getting more confused every minute. Presently the teacher looks over his shoulder at his slate covered with a chaotic mass of figures, and glances at the boy's hot and troubled face, and says to him, "You are taking a good deal of unnecessary trouble. This is not as hard as it looks: only one thing is needful; all these examples are illustrations of one law." And he sits down, and explains a simple principle to the lad; and then the work becomes a delight. The boy has a clew in his hand which leads him straight through the whole labyrinth of figures. He turns from the multitude of details to the principle, and finds that the details arrange themselves, and the answer comes right every time.

So that there is nothing arbitrary or unnatural, or even unfamiliar, in the gospel's summing itself in one thing, and concentrating men's attention on that. It is evident, as we have already seen, that the gospel illustrates this great truth of centralization. It is intensely centralized. Whether we regard it as a system, as a life in man, as a code of laws, as a theory of morals, — from all these points of view, the lines run straight to Christ. As a system, it centres in his person; as a life, in man: its moving forces are love and faith toward Christ; its ultimate aim, conformity to the mind and will of Christ: as a code of laws, Christ is the fulfilment of the law, its perfect illustration; as a theory of morals, it is summed up in obedience to Christ. It keeps this one figure constantly before us. It groups all details round him. God's great gift to the world is Jesus Christ; and with him, he gives us all things. Not that he adds all things to the gift of Christ as another and distinct expression of his love, but rather that Christ carries all other things with him in the nature of the case. The greater gift takes up all the minor gifts into itself — includes them. When a man buys an estate of so many acres, he does not ask for separate titles for the woodland and the pasture and the streams and the mines. He wants one title to the estate. He pays so much; and then, if there is gold or coal or an oil-well on the estate, that is his. The purchase of the estate gives him command of all its possibilities, whether apparent or latent. And so, when God would lead a man to spiritual power and riches by the most direct road, he leads him to Christ. He says: "Receive him implicitly. Only that one thing is needful; the rest follows, the rest is contained in him, all things are in him, — all power, all grace, all wisdom, all spiritual possibilities of every kind; and, therefore, when you receive him, you receive all these things with him." That is Paul's simple logic. "All things are yours because ye are Christ's, all things are Christ's because he is God's; and therefore, in Christ, God becomes yours, and God is all in all." If this be so, shall we be surprised to hear Christ insisting upon the one thing? to hear him say, — "Seek ye first the kingdom of God, and his righteousness; and all these things shall be added unto you"?

Now, this seems simple; but practically it is not so easily realized as we might expect. It is the higher spiritual outlook which reveals this simplicity and centralization of the gospel. When you are set down for the first time in a great and strange city, the streets are a labyrinth to you; and when you strike out into the city, and begin to explore it, you get no sense of system in the arrangement of the streets: you lose yourself in all sorts of by-ways and blind alleys, and your walk is a constant succession of experiments. But when you climb to the top of some cathedral-tower, and look down, the confusion resolves itself. You see the central square or the market-place, and how all the streets have a certain relation to that. So it is the higher outlook, I repeat, which reveals how the gospel is centred. Lower down, it presents great possibilities of confusion; because the gospel, in one aspect, is a thing of infinite details. It is a system framed for life, and for life on every imaginable side, and for application to every possibility of life. It embraces an immense range of duties and attainments. Life along its whole line touches the moral and spiritual kingdom. And when a man confronts the gospel on this side, — and that is the side on which, perhaps, the majority of men approach it, — he is appalled. Like Martha, he becomes cumbered and anxious with the thought of much serving. He does not see that the gospel is any thing else than service, and service touching an infinite variety of details, and service tested by a perfect moral standard. He is occupied with the thought of how he can deal with this mass of details; and it does not at once occur to him that he may get at the details of service by a shorter process, that he may be placed at a point from which the details will all arrange themselves, that he may come under the power of an impulse which will make duty meat instead of drudgery, and carry all duties and all services easily along with it. The sooner that man gets through Christianity as a system, to Christ as a friend and helper, the better for him. Suppose a boy taken from his home at an early age, and sent to school in a foreign land. He has staid there year after year, until his impressions of the faces and voices and incidents of his home have well-nigh faded out. Occasionally some one visits him who has lately seen his home, and brings him messages from parents and friends. The boy is naturally eager to know all about that home. "Tell me how father and mother look. Tell me how large my brother has grown. Tell me how the house is furnished, and whether the trees are still in such a place." And the visitor says, "Your home is a charming place. Your parents are loved and honored everywhere, and their household is ordered with the utmost system and precision: no drones are allowed there. Each son and daughter has specified duties. Every thing must be done on time, and well and thoroughly done." And as such reports reach him again and again, the boy becomes troubled and anxious at the prospect of going home. He is afraid he cannot fit himself to that exact and beautiful system, that he cannot meet all those requirements, that he will bring reproof and displeasure upon himself by inadvertency; and so all the pleasure gradually fades out of the prospect of going home, until he comes actually to dread it, and would rather stay in the far-off land. Home has taken on, in his mind, the character of a well-conducted workhouse. But oh, how little he suspects the joy and expectation and longing which pervade that home in the near prospect of his coming! He cannot see the preparations which busy the mother's hands from morning till night for his welcome and comfort. He does not suspect the father's nervous, growing restlessness as the day draws near for the arrival of the ship. And at last it comes. The carriage drives up to the door: the boy leaps out, and is clasped in his father's arms, and his young head bedewed with such tears as only a mother can shed, and is led into the light and cheer and hilarity of home; and, in a moment, all that dread and anxious care which have been oppressing his heart for months are gone. The atmosphere of love in which he finds himself, a single glance at the faces of his parents, dispel those false pictures of his fancy like a dream. It does not take him long to see that the household *is* well-ordered, that every thing moves like clockwork, that his brothers and sisters are trained to implicit obedience. But those things do not trouble him any more. He sees them all through the medium of his parents' love; and he knows by instinct, that under the shadow of that home, under the guidance of those parents, he will find a place in the home-system, and a round of duties which will be a joy. One look assures him of all possible wisdom for his direction, all possible concession to his weakness, all possible tolerance for his mistakes. He is in his own home, girt round by love, — a happy son. Duty and fidelity will spring as naturally, and will regulate themselves as sweetly, as the growth of a flower.

The first thing with us all, the *one* thing, is to get home to Christ, — not merely to read about him or to speculate about his character, but to get face to face with him. A great many things will take care of themselves then which distract and make us anxious now, and lay us open to the rebuke which Martha received. There is a law of duty, with many provisions and touching many things; but when shall we learn to go first behind the law to Christ himself, and sit like Mary at his feet, and learn the lesson of duty as he shall expound it to us? When shall we learn that duty, in its multitude of forms, becomes a new and a simpler and a sweeter thing the moment it is seen in the light of love for Christ? Oh, how this theory of many things to be done dominates and rides us! how restless and fretted we get under it! so much to do! so much to do! so fearful that we shall not overtake our work! so afraid of our Father's displeasure if our work falls into arrear! each day a wearying strain to accomplish so much! as if Christ were no more than a taskmaster, and our Father's house only a workhouse! We are sincere about it too: we want to do God's will, we want to please Christ; but we get so little comfort out of it! Christian life is a life of duty and of service; but I have yet to learn where, in the New Testament, Christ puts service as a perpetual burden. I do hear him saying, "My yoke is easy, and my burden is light." Somehow I have gotten the impression, in my study of the Gospels and of the life of Christ, that service may be a joy. Even in lower regions, I think we have all known cases of men's enjoying their daily task, going with delight to their studio or their library or their factory; and if one can be happy in these daily tasks, why must the service of Christ be drudgery? It is not so, and the secret and the correction of the mistake alike lie in these words of the Master. We contemplate too many things: we range all along the vast circumference of duty, instead of striking direct for the centre; we live by law, which takes up duty in detail, instead of by love, which masses and carries all details. But one thing is needful, — to receive Christ into our life with all our hearts, with complete self-abandonment. This will change us from slaves into sons. "To as many as received Him, to them gave He power to become sons of God." This will not relieve us of service, but it will make our service the service of sons; and you know, without any words of mine, the difference between the service of a son and of a servant.

Our religious education, and the circumstances amid which we live, make it important that we should give heed to this truth. The word which Christ uses in his rebuke to Martha is the same which he employs in the exhortation: "Be not anxious for your life." It is the word which means *dividing, distracting* care, — care which divides the heart from God; care which pulls us many different ways; care which sets its stamp on our lives, and makes them fussy and turbulent. And the great danger in the religious life of people in a great city like this, is distraction. Duty pulls so many different ways: there are so many calls to help and to achieve, so many shining opportunities of doing good, that it is very easy to foster the Martha type of life here. And then, too, there is, to many spirits, a fascination about doing. They love to be active, and activity appeals to the world as a good thing in itself. The tendency is to look upon a man who is constantly busy about a great number of things as a useful and important man. And the busy man knows that, and his self-importance is flattered by it; and close by this lies the great danger of making activity cover the whole ground of religion, and of sinking the equally important requirements of prayer and meditation and self-examination. And a man who lives by this theory will, spiritually, deteriorate very fast. That saying, "To labor is to pray," is a very pretty little phrase, and carries a grain of truth; but its popular interpretation is, that work is a *substitute* for prayer, which is sheer nonsense. Our Lord was the busiest of men while on earth; but he retired often to the mountains, and to other secret places, to commune with the Father. Again let it be repeated, — it cannot be repeated too often, — the one thing needful in the Christian life, as in the solar system, is, *that it be properly centred;* and as, in the solar system, two forces are necessary, — the one to hold the heavenly bodies to the centre, the other to send them wheeling in space to do their office of enlightening the world and regulating times and seasons, — so, in Christian life, prayer is the centripetal force, holding and drawing the man to Jesus Christ, his true centre: while the impulse to work is the centrifugal force, sending him out along the orbit of holy ministry. These forces must be kept balanced. If a man does nothing but pray and meditate, his life becomes morbid and unprofitable. If he does nothing but work, he loses his hold on Christ, and swings farther and farther from the centre which regulates and warms and enlightens him. He gets out of his true orbit, and becomes distracted amid a multitude of duties lying in other orbits, and is deceived in thinking that he is one of God's lights in the world, when he more resembles an errant marsh-fire. Any thing which breaks the conscious connection of faith and love with Christ is one of those distractions against which Christ so kindly warned Martha, no matter whether it be good work in itself, or even work done in the name of Christ. Much of the work done in Christ's name, if we are to believe Christ himself, will not stand the test of the last day. "Many will say to me in that day, Have we not prophesied in thy name, and in thy name have cast out devils, and in thy name done many wonderful works? And then will I profess unto them, I never knew you."

The intense centring of the life on Christ does

not divorce it from service, as we have seen. It generates service, but it regulates service; nor does it deprive the life of variety. No life is less monotonous than one which is in conscious, close communion with Christ. Paul said, "I determined to know nothing among you save Christ." Yet what a variety and range of activity that life presents; and withal, what a simplicity and exquisite regulation of activity. There is no clashing or confusion of duties. He simply walks day by day after Christ, and the duties meet him in due order. There is no anxiety about strength, even in that sickly and much-burdened man; Christ has engaged to provide for that: there is no trouble about methods; Christ lays them down: there is no fretting about visible success; he is not responsible for success, only for duty. The excellency of the power is of God, not of him; and the key to all this is one thing, — he tells us what it is when he comes to the end, — one thing which he had held all through, while every thing else had been swept away: "I have kept the faith!" and, instead of being cumbered with much serving, we hear him saying to the Philippians, — to whom, perhaps more than to any other church, he revealed his heart, — "I have learned, in whatsoever state I am, therewith to be content. In every thing and in all things have I learned the secret both to be filled and to be hungry, both to abound and to be in want. I can do all things through Christ that strengthens me."

On this, then, let us fix our thought, — one thing

is needful. Christian belief, Christian life, Christian experience, are simple; but to realize that simplicity, either in theory or in practice, they must be viewed from their true centre. If the gospel is approached on the side of mere duty, — the duties which we have to do, the spiritual attainments we have to make, — it is a mass of confusion. If, on the other hand, we go straight to Christ, receive him into our hearts, gather up our whole life into simple, loving, believing consecration to him, keep ourselves by faith and prayer in continual contact with him, always within the sound of his voice, always hearing, pondering, and practising his words, — then the confusion resolves itself, and duty and place and attainment will take care of themselves. We too often act as if God had merely recognized us as his children, and given us the freedom of his house, and then left us to ourselves to work out our life as best we could. That is not God's way. When he makes us his children through faith in Christ Jesus, he assumes the care of our life in all its details. He not only turns us loose in his house: he goes with us into every corner, and shows us its treasures. He not only gives us the freedom of his domain: he assigns each of us his plot of ground, and stands by us while we try to sow the seed and water the growths, and teaches us how to be workers for and with him; and as for our care, all that tends to distract and cumber and confuse us he bids us cast it all on him. Christian life, I say, is simple. It is summed up in one thing, — "Follow me!" It may seem to us that that is a little support on which to cast such a burden and problem as life is to most of us, but we shall do well to try it. Day before yesterday I had occasion to go to the lower part of the city by the elevated railroad; and, as I got out at Hanover Square, I looked down upon the street far below, and a thought something like this went through my mind: supposing that, without any knowledge of the existence and mode of working of an elevated railway, I had been placed on this train while asleep or unconscious, and had awakened at this station, and been told that I must get down to that street. I get out of the train, and find myself on a narrow platform. I look down on either side, and say, "No way down there, except by being dashed to pieces." Instinctively I follow those in front of me. Steps, but the door is shut: no getting down there. I follow still. A door, but it opens into an enclosure. I follow still. Another door, and there are steps which lead me safely and easily down to the street. I might have stood still, and distracted myself with a dozen devices for getting down. I might have gone bustling about, looking for a rope or a ladder. There was only one thing needful, and that was, to follow those who knew the way. So in our Christian experience, one thing is needful, — the part which Mary chose, to hear Jesus' words and to follow him. A good many times in the course of this life we shall be puzzled about how to get up or down or out, sadly puzzled if we think it our business to extricate ourselves; but those many things are not our business. The puzzle will resolve itself in due time if we simply hold to the one thing, — following Christ. When you gave yourself to him, you took him in place of all human skill and wisdom, for every emergency. These things no longer concern you. *He* careth for you, and they may all be laid on him.

The pertinent, practical, pressing question remains. If one thing is needful, if that one thing is a good part, is it yours? Face the question. Where is your life centred to-day? Have you many aims, or one aim? One master, and only one, is needful. No man can serve two. Who is your master? The great object of life is one, — to be like Christ: is that your object, and are all minor objects taken up in that? or is your mind divided between many objects? The claims of the world are many and pressing, and seemingly important; but in the face of the teeming, crowding throng of worldly cares and labors and ambitions, is Christ, saying, "One thing is needful! I am that one thing!" Which voice will you hear?

IV.

FACING GOD.

IV.

FACING GOD.

"I have set the Lord always before me: because he is at my right hand, I shall not be moved." — Ps. xvi. 8.

CONVICTIONS are of two kinds. They are born of emergencies and of experience. The former are instinctive, springing into life full grown: the latter grow and mature slowly. A ship strikes a rock, and begins to sink. The conviction of danger and of possible destruction takes shape at once in the mind of every passenger. This is the conviction of emergency. You are impressed with the amiable qualities of a man; you desire his friendship; you are prepared to admire and trust him: but that is not conviction. After years of intimacy, in which you have proved his powers, experienced his constancy and devotion, have always found him true and brave and pure, you are convinced of his worth. It becomes to you a fixed fact, which you unconsciously assume, as you do gravitation or the succession of night and day. Belief is not conviction, except in the germ. Conviction is faith in fruition, and fruition takes time. Belief may entertain reservations, or hold itself subject to possibilities: conviction knows no reservation. Belief grasps: conviction possesses. Belief may run up into conviction. All well-grounded belief does ultimately. Belief may serve a temporary purpose while conviction is maturing, just as the cable serves while the bridge is being built. All that is real and valuable in belief ultimately passes into conviction, and is taken up into it. As a young Christian, you believed the Bible to be the word of God, and the only infallible rule of faith and practice. You believed it on authority, on the testimony of your parents and teachers; and that belief was enough to make you accept the Bible as your rule of life, and strive to keep its precepts. But that belief was probably disturbed. Authority was not enough for you. Questions were raised which set you thinking, doubting, and investigating. To-day you believe the Bible, but your belief has grown into conviction. Your belief on simple authority has given place to a deeper sentiment, based on the experience of years, in which the Bible has proved its power to instruct and comfort and enlighten you. I remember going, in company with some brother ministers, to visit an aged clergyman then past his eightieth year. As we bade him farewell, he laid his hand on the Bible, and said solemnly, "*There*, brethren, *there* is our authority: *there* is our guide." A young minister might have said that, and have believed it; but the words would have lacked the emphasis imparted by those long years, and that stormy life wrought out under the guidance and inspiration of the word of God. We all felt that every fibre of the old man's being went into those words.

Our text to-day is the utterance of such conviction as this. When I say the text, I mean the whole psalm; for this text gives the key-note to the psalm. It is not the exclamation of a man to whom a truth has come as a flash: it is the deliberate outcome of a long and varied retrospect. It has a life behind it. The man is convinced that he shall not be moved; that he may safely and heartily rejoice; that in the unseen world, as here, he will be safe and happy: and this conviction is the result of a life in which God has been continually before his face. He is not kindled into confidence and gratitude by a single act of Divine Providence. The providence has extended over his entire life. The Lord has fixed his place in life, and has provided for his support: "The Lord is the portion of mine inheritance and of my cup." What Christ means when he says, "I am the bread of life," David means by the words, "The Lord is the portion of my cup;" and in like manner he speaks in the familiar psalm: "Thou preparest a table before me: my cup runneth over." Moreover, the Lord has not suffered his enemies to deprive him of his portion: "Thou maintainest my lot. Thou preparest my table in the presence of mine enemies." And he has found it not only safe but pleasant to dwell in God's place, and to be fed by God. "The lines have fallen unto me in pleasant places." The portion of territory which God's measuring-line has marked off for him has been a goodly heritage. Nor has he ever wanted for good advice. Jehovah has given him counsel; and with such an experience behind him, we are not surprised to hear him say, "My heart is glad, my soul rejoiceth. This poor flesh of mine must die; but God, who has cared for me all along, will not give me up as a prey to the grave: he will point out to me the way of life. He who has been always with me, will continue to be with me; and in his presence is fulness of joy. He is at my right hand, and at his right hand are pleasures forevermore."

The secret of all this rejoicing and confidence, I repeat, is in our text. David has set the Lord always before him; and this is his reward, as it may be ours. Let us look now more closely at this thought of having God always before us.

It is of the greatest importance what that is which is continually before us. That which is constantly in a man's eye must help very largely to shape him. I have heard a very significant criticism on a certain picture, to the effect, that, though it was a good piece of artistic work, it was not a good picture to *live with*. You would not wish to have hanging up in your sitting-room, and constantly in sight of your children, a picture of Herodias with the head of John the Baptist, or of a crazed mother in the act of murdering her babe. You try to keep pictures of wholesome subjects as well as of beautiful forms before your children's eyes; because you know that they are insensibly educated by familiarity with such things. In an age of few books, men and women learned mostly by the eye. It was not wholly nor mostly idolatry which filled the old churches with pictures. The visitor to St. Mark's, in Venice, may follow for himself the footsteps of the earlier catechumen; passing into the Christian temple through a vestibule of Old-Testament history wrought in mosaic pictures, and then reading, on the walls and domes within, the truths of crucifixion, resurrection, the baptism of the Spirit and the coming of the Lord to judgment, — all arranged in the order of Christian thought. The peasant who passed over the old wooden bridge over the torrent at Lucerne had daily before him, in the painted compartments of the bridge, a reminder of that other stream which all must cross sooner or later. Nature sets her mark on character. If her surroundings are gloomy and savage, they impart a sombre tone to the men who live among them. Men tend to be narrowed or broadened by their daily task. The man who has columns of figures forever before him may easily degenerate into a mere calculating machine. If the thing which is constantly before us is larger and better than ourselves, its hourly presence rebukes our littleness and our badness, and works to assimilate us to itself. If it is worse than ourselves, it draws downward. There was philosophy as well as enthusiasm in the apostle's exhortation to run, looking unto Jesus, and in Paul keeping his eye on the prize of his high calling, and reaching forth to that which is before.

But it may be asked, Is not God *always* before us? can we help having the Lord always before us? Assuredly we can. The Psalmist evidently thinks so. He does not regard it as inevitable that we should have the Lord always before us. On the contrary, he speaks of those who hasten after, or, literally, take unto themselves another God. Both their course and his are matters of choice. He does not say, "The Lord is always before me," but " I *have set* him always before me." His own will, his own act, have had something to do with the matter. He has been at pains to *bring* God into the foreground, and to *keep* him there always. And there is nothing strange in this; because God manifests himself in the world, because every common bush is afire with him, it does not follow that men recognize the fact. There is abundance of sweet music in the world, but there are multitudes of people to whom it means no more than the rumble of the carts in the street. There are men who live all their lives amid the grandest scenery, but who see in it nothing but so much stone and timber: men to whom a great picture is meaningless, and literature as dumb as the pyramids. So, it is not strange if men should not see the God who puts himself before them in his Word and in his providences, in every star and flower and lightning flash. A sense must be educated to see God. The apostle is only stating what is a familiar fact to us in other departments, when he says " The natural man discerneth not the things of the Spirit of God. They are foolishness unto him.

He cannot know them because they are spiritually discerned." It is quite as likely, to say the least, that a man's spiritual sense should be uncultivated and dormant, and give him no knowledge of that vast spiritual economy which touches him everywhere, as that his eye or his ear should be unimpressed by pictures or harmony. A babe has the organs of vision, but nevertheless he must *learn* to see.

This blindness towards God is a fact of history and of common experience. We say, for instance, as we read the history of Israel, that such manifestations of divine glory and power could not fail to impress them: they were so mighty, so terrible, so unquestionable. And yet they *did* fail. The dividing of the Red Sea, and the lightnings and thunders of Sinai, were followed by the frenzied dance round the golden calf. We say that the person and miracles of Christ were adapted to convince the most incredulous; but they did not, as we see: and we hear Christ himself saying, "If I had not come and spoken unto them, they had not had sin: but now they have no excuse for their sin."

Thus, then, God will not be, in any true sense, before our face unless we set him there. It is a matter which involves our determination and effort, a matter of special training and practice. There is a spiritual inertia to be overcome: there is to be corrected the perverse tendency of a nature which sets any thing before it rather than God. That bar of steel does not point naturally to the pole. Balance it on a pivot, and it will point south, east, or west, as the case may be. It must be acted upon from without. It must have magnetic virtue imparted to it; and then, and not till then, will it keep the north always before it. Man is not naturally religious. Naturally he does not point Godward. No quality in him swings him inevitably round towards God. He must be set that way; or, rather, he must set himself that way, under the divine power which comes down upon his will, and magnetizes it, and gives it its eternal direction.

You will observe further, that this having God before the face requires *persistency*. It was not enough to bring God once or twice into the line of vision: he was to be *kept* there. The Psalmist tells us not only of an act, but of a habit: "I have set the Lord *always* before my face." Men often claim that they are susceptible to religious impressions, and are disposed to flatter themselves on the fact; and it is a familiar enough fact, — it would be strange if it were not so, — that God often brings the face of the most unsusceptible man round to him by some display of his power, or by some stroke of his providence. Jonah tried to run away from God, but met him on the way to Tarshish: Balaam turned his back on God and his face toward Moab; but the angel of God met him in a narrow place, where there was no chance of turning back. The impressions which men receive under such circumstances are vivid and truthful: the trouble is, that they do not expand into permanent convictions. When God sets himself before a man's face, it is in order to make the man set

God continually before *his* face. The crisis means an experience. A compass-needle would be to a sailor of no more account than a knitting-needle if it were made to point northward only by some violent shock: it is the fact of its *always* pointing thither that gives it its value.

It is this fact of persistency which gives value to David's saying: what he tells us is the story of a man who has become familiar with an object by long looking. It is not the kind of a story which Jacob would have told the morning after the vision at Bethel, but rather of the kind which Enoch would have told on the eve of his translation, — the story, not of a vision of God, but of a walk with God. When a man has shut himself up to one thing as the source of his strength and happiness, he will find out a great deal about that thing. Robinson Crusoe, when he had once made up his mind that his life must be confined to his little island, set himself to discover its resources, and found in it a multitude of things which he never would have known were there if he had been expecting to sail away in a week or two. In that event he would have used his island only for the food and shelter of the day. That is the way in which many people deal with God: they turn their faces towards him when they have nowhere else to turn. They use his bounty when their own supplies fail. As soon as they have something else to look at, they turn their faces from God; and it does not take much to turn them, either. A silver dollar held before your eyes will conceal the whole orb of the sun. You can shut out an entire landscape with a finger; and it is amazing, likewise, what small things will divert men from God, what a little temptation will shut out an immense range of duty, responsibility, and privilege. Esau was the rightful inheritor of a splendid destiny; but a coarse dish of red lentils shut out the whole brilliant future, and his birthright went for a mess of pottage. Our Psalmist fixes his gaze on God: nothing is to come between God and him. He has taken counsel with his soul, and said unto God, "Thou art my Lord. I have no good beyond thee. I have set the Lord always before my face."

And one who thus keeps God always before him makes discoveries, and many of them. David, in the twenty-seventh Psalm, declares that he has desired *one* thing, and will seek after that; but that one thing evidently includes a great deal for him. It will reveal to him the beauty of the Lord; it will give him opportunity to ask questions of divine wisdom; it will afford him a hiding-place in time of trouble, and a means of triumph over his enemies. Let us, then, note a few of the many things which a man finds in God by keeping him always before his face.

He finds *himself revealed*. In the Shinto temples in Japan the shrines contain no altars, pulpits, or pictures, but only a circular steel mirror. What it means is not known; but it would be no inappropriate symbol in a Christian shrine, to set forth the self-revealing power of the word of God. Nor is the symbol without its warrant in Scripture.

You remember that James draws a picture of a man beholding his natural face in a glass, consulting his mirror for some temporary purpose of arranging his dress or hair; and then going his way, and forgetting all about it. And he puts this picture in contrast with another, of a man stooping down, and looking attentively, and fixing the impression of what he sees, so as to keep it always before his face. This man, who looks steadfastly into God's perfect law, and translates what he sees there into daily practice, this man "shall be blessed in his doing," keeping God always before his face. The Psalmist tells us he receives counsel, and that, not only by way of direct communication, but through the working of his own mind: "I will bless the Lord, who hath given me counsel: my reins also (that is, my heart) instruct me in the night seasons." An inner spiritual wisdom develops in the quiet meditation and communion with God in the night season. "The night season," as some one has aptly said, "which the sinner chooses for his sins, is the hour when believers hear the voices of the heavenly life within themselves." The man who studies God, studies self at the same time; the man who steadfastly follows Christ, learns as much about self as he learns of Christ. Self-knowledge is the hardest kind of knowledge. The thing which is identified with our interest and pleasure is not always the thing which we know best. We shut our eyes to its imperfections; we look at it only on the side where it ministers to our gain or enjoyment; we do not like to pick flaws in the self which we love; we refuse to see that it is fallible and proud, and otherwise faulty: it is ourself, and we stand by it. But when Christ persuades us to deny and lay aside self, he puts self in a position where we can study it from without; where we can weigh and test it by higher standards; where we can set it, with all its greed and conceit and sophistry and littleness, beside the perfect manhood of Jesus Christ, and, in the light of his symmetry and purity, see it as it really is: and hence the Psalmist says, "Thou hast set our secret sins in the light of thy countenance." If we would truly know what kind of men and women we are, we must set the man Jesus always before our face.

Setting God before our face carries with it *a power of growth*. God is not only always before us: he is always *going* before us, and beckoning us to follow. The man who has his back towards God, like one who has the sun behind him, follows a shadow. The Bible, from one end to the other, is full of growth. It is itself a growth. It is a picture of God leading men; and, as we read on, we are impressed with the fact of an advance in humanity. The plane is higher at the beginning of Matthew than at the beginning of Exodus; and, moreover, the New Testament especially thrills with the summons to advance and growth: "Grow in grace." "Forgetting the things which are behind, and stretching forward to the things which are before." "Be no more children; but grow up into him who is the head." "Press toward the mark for the prize of your high calling." Constant contact with true greatness and goodness lifts even a small man. Enoch, who walked with God, must have acquired a divine quality in his manhood. In the very nature of the case, a man who has God always before his face cannot be stationary. A mountain is a constant temptation to climb; and when one has climbed, and caught a view of still higher summits beyond, he is restless until he has climbed them too. The vision of God ever draws us on with sweet and powerful allurement. The more we learn of him, the more we see to be learned: the higher we rise in character, the greater possibilities of character are revealed.

And the keeping of God constantly before the face engenders *hope*. Hope, if we are to believe Paul, is the very atmosphere in which a Christian lives and breathes. "We are saved in hope." The creation is indeed "subject to vanity," but "in hope" that it shall be "delivered from the bondage of corruption into the liberty of the glory of the children of God." There are sufferings of this present time; but God also is in this present time, alike as a fact and a promise of glory to be revealed. Amid the darkness and vagueness which encircled the Old-Testament future, this psalm is like a sweet flute-note amid the crash and discord of a vast orchestra. I know nothing more winning, more soothing, than these verses, which put the whole future into God's hands with such serene trust and sure confidence that all will be well for ever and ever. I have not been moved, and "I shall not be moved;" because the Lord is "at my right hand." Because he is at my right hand, my happiness is secure; for "at his right hand are pleasures forevermore. In his presence is fulness of joy." I shall not wander in the dark and devious ways which lead to death, for "thou wilt show me the path of life." Death and the grave frighten me not: "thou wilt not leave my soul to the unseen world; thou wilt not suffer thy beloved one to see the pit. I have no good beyond thee." Oh, how wonderful that is! No good beyond thee. Thou includest all good; the remotest future will not carry me beyond thee; the march of eternity will not overpass thee; thou shalt still be continually before my face, age after age, as I shall rise and grow and work on ever-longer lines in the atmosphere of heaven, changing, developing, but ever "into the same image, from glory to glory." In this world we are often troubled about the future. Sometimes the shadows fall backward, and cloud all our present with gloom: but it need not be so if only we keep the Lord continually before our face; for then we are going forward to God, and after God; and whatever the future may have for us, it will have God, and that is enough. So Jesus evidently thought when he said to his disciples, "I will receive you unto myself, that where I am, ye may be also." It was enough that they should be with him: they had, and could have, no good beyond him.

To-day, as we approach the Lord's table, we bring David with us. The words of the Old-Testament saint fit into the holy rite, and carry with them a profound Christian meaning. For God ever before the face is a truth of God's economy in all dispensations, — a truth bound up with the fact of a human relation to God. The Christian dispensation brings out the truth with new power, by showing the glory of God in the face of Jesus Christ. The holy sacrament is a constantly repeated admonition to set the Lord — the Lord as revealed in Jesus, our Redeemer — always before our face. Its lesson is, "looking unto Jesus;" looking, as a means to our successful running of our Christian race; and its admonition is pointed in this, — that it emphasizes the *always*, the continual keeping of Christ before us. It is not meant to drag our faces round six times in the year, and to fasten them for an hour on Christ, only that we may turn them away again to the world and its vanities. It does indeed offer us a reminder of Christ; but it reminds us that Christ is not merely an incident of our life, but our life itself. It sharpens the spiritual perception, and brings out the lines of the beloved form more definitely; but it says to us, "Look now, that you may continue to look." Keep the form which faith sees, always before your face. You who come to-day to enjoy this privilege for the first time, take this thought into all your life henceforth: for you can have no weightier thought attaching to this sacrament, than that it is an admonition to you to keep Christ before you in each day's life; as on this day he is set before you in symbol.

V.

LIGHT AND LOYALTY.

V.

LIGHT AND LOYALTY.

"Jesus answered, Are there not twelve hours in the day? If a man walk in the day, he stumbleth not, because he seeth the light of this world.

"But if a man walk in the night, he stumbleth, because the light is not in him." — JOHN xi. 9, 10.

THE disciples were dismayed when Jesus proposed to go to Bethany to visit Lazarus. A Jewish mob was no trifle, and it was only a little while before that the Jews had sought to stone Jesus for what they counted blasphemy. They were orthodox but ferocious, and would not hesitate to murder him.

Hence the disciples remonstrated against his exposing himself again to these fanatics: "Master, the Jews were but now seeking to stone thee; and goest thou thither again?" They spoke for themselves as well as for him. Thomas evidently expected that the journey to Bethany would result in death to him and to them.

Jesus takes this opportunity to explain to his disciples the great principle on which he himself worked; and, to commend this principle to them, he puts it in a figurative way. If a man walks in the daytime by the light of the sun, he walks intelligently and securely. If he tries to walk in the dark, he stumbles, and goes astray. I walk in God's light, which shines on my path during the time he has fixed for my ministry. Wherever that light shines, I go, regardless of every thing but the light. So if you, my disciples, have this same divine light in you, and follow it, you will be as men walking in the daylight. Your path of duty will be clear. Without that light, you will be as men walking in the dark, — stumbling, and meeting disaster. You will have no clear or consistent ideas of duty, and your practice will be as confused as your ideas.

We are thus led up to the question of the simplicity of duty. Somehow duty has come to be, to many of us, a very complicated matter; and possibly our conceptions of it have tended to a little haziness. That duty presents problems, every one of us knows; but it is a fair question, whether the problem always lies in the *duty*, and does not sometimes lie in *us*. It is a fair question, whether we do not often complicate the problem by adding factors of our own. It is a fair question, whether the haziness is not sometimes in our eyes, and not in the moral outlines which God draws. Christ asserts the possibility of the light in us being darkness. The oculist will tell you there is a blind spot in every eye. Possibly, when we think that *God* has made duty obscure, we have brought the duty into line with the blind spot.

As a matter of precept, duty is simpler than

perhaps we give it credit for being; for, if duty is to be a thing of universal obligation, it must be simple in the nature of the case. To make it a matter of subtle casuistry, of painful research and nice balancing, would be, at best, to limit it to a very few, and to make moral outcasts of the rest. The Jew of Christ's day made it just that. He had gotten into a muddle over the moral law; but the muddle was in him, and not in the law. The law was so simple and clear that Christ threw it into two great principles; and Christ came not to destroy it, not to supplant it, but to clear it of the rabbinical rubbish with which the Jew had overlaid it. The fresh simplicity of our Lord's teaching was like a strong, wholesome breeze sweeping away cobwebs, and laying bare the original simplicity and directness of the old code.

But, after all, our thought to-day does not turn on the simplicity of the moral law itself. Men stumble none the less because of this simplicity. Christ, in our text, does not put the blame of the stumbling on the law or on the complication of duty. It is not the geological structure of the stone which makes the man stumble: it is darkness or blindness. As men stumble who walk in the night, and stumble because they do not walk in the twelve hours of sunshine; so, morally, men stumble because of moral darkness in themselves. "He stumbleth because there is no light *in him*." Our Lord here asserts that a divine light is given to men to guide them to duty, just as the sun is given to enlighten the way by which they travel, or the work which they do; and that that light is placed by God himself in the man himself, just as the sunlight is set working through the human eye to produce vision. Hence he says elsewhere: "The lamp of thy body is thine eye: when thine eye is single, thy whole body also is full of light; but when it is evil, thy body also is full of darkness. Look therefore whether the light that is in thee be not darkness. If therefore thy whole body be full of light, having no part dark, it shall be wholly full of light, as when the lamp with its bright shining doth give thee light." When a man sees two trees where there is only one, or a crooked line where there is a straight one, or prismatic colors in a house that is white, we do not blame the structure of the tree or the drawing of the line or the painting of the house. We say, the man's vision is diseased. A sound moral vision recognizes duty under every shape, and takes its measure. Hence the truth of our text is, that the recognition of duty, and the practical solutions of its problems, lie in the principle of loyalty to Christ. A divinely enlightened conscience and an obedient will, not only push, but lead. They prompt to duty, but they also define it. "I am the light of the world: he that followeth me shall not walk in darkness, but shall have the light of life." In other words, he shall be enlightened as to how to live. The light shall shine upon the path of right living, and the path of the just shall prove to be as the shining light that shineth more and more unto the perfect day.

Let us look, now, at the illustration of this truth in the incident of our text. Going to Bethany involved a question of duty for Christ. God was to be glorified in his son's victory over death, and the faith of the disciples was to be strengthened thereby. The obligation was laid upon Jesus to go to Bethany then.

And to one who had no thought but to do the will of his Father, the case was very simple. No question was possible. There was that plain duty to be done, and the light shone full and clear upon the way to Bethany.

But the disciples, in their natural timidity, put another element into the question, which complicated it: that was, the element of personal safety. "If you go to Bethany you will be stoned, and possibly killed." It is easy to see, that, if Jesus had entertained this suggestion, his mind would have been diverted from the plain duty before him. A new question would have been raised, which God had not raised at all. God's commission said nothing about danger, stoning, or death. It was simply to go to Bethany, and to do what was to be done there. Every thing else was excluded; and so long as Jesus was true to the principle of simple loyalty in his own breast, so long as he refused to entertain any thought beyond that of implicit obedience to God's command as it stood, his course lay out in the clear light. It might bring him into peril, but the course itself was plain. If he meant simply to do right, the decision presented no difficulty: if he meant to save himself, then the question became full of uncertainties, and weighing of probabilities. From the moment of admitting that consideration, he would have walked in darkness.

What an expounder of duty that element of singleness is! How much meaning there was in our Lord's expression, — "A *single* eye"! How much easier and simpler a man's walk and work are when he sees an object in its oneness, than when his diseased eye doubles it! Is not singleness of purpose an element of all the heroism of which you know? Was there ever a great general whose thought was divided between victory and personal safety? Would the six hundred ever have passed into history if they had stopped to weigh the probabilities of mutilation and death? The familiar poem puts that singleness powerfully: —

> "Theirs not to make reply,
> Theirs not to reason why,
> Theirs but to do and die."

The men who have moved society have moved under that principle of self-abandonment, seeing nothing but the end to be won. No man whose thought was divided between himself and his object ever succeeded as a moral reformer, or as a helper of the wretched. When a physician enters upon his profession, he does so with the knowledge that he must ignore contagion. That makes his duty very simple, — to relieve disease and pain wherever he finds them. The moment he begins to consider whether he may not expose his own life to fever or cholera, his usefulness is over. When Luther stood before the Diet at Worms, he had a terrible danger to face, but a very easy question to solve. His most significant words, as it seems to me, were, "I can do no otherwise:" the expression of a loyalty which could entertain no other thought along with a plain issue of duty. Had he thought of imprisonment, papal ban, papal favor, or death, Christendom would not be ringing to-day with the name of Luther. That inability to do any thing besides the one right thing carried the Reformation.

And this singleness is the very essence of Christian service, on Christ's own testimony. Its first law is, Deny self, — treat self as though it were not; follow me. It is not always easy to follow Christ; but the way, at least, is plain.[1] A greater difficulty arises the moment that the question becomes one of compromising and adjusting between Christ and self. A man gets no divine help in the solution of that question, because Christ refuses altogether to entertain it. The command to take up the cross is the command to throw down self. The shoulder of self will not bear the cross. Self and the cross exclude each other. The only way in which self can ever be adjusted to the cross is

---

[1] "For the object of religion is *conduct;* and conduct is really, however men may overlay it with philosophical disquisitions, the simplest thing in the world. That is to say, it is the simplest thing in the world, as far as *understanding* is concerned; as regards *doing,* it is the hardest thing in the world. Here is the difficulty, — to *do* what we very well know ought to be done." — MATTHEW ARNOLD: *Literature and Dogma.*

by being nailed to it. Any other mode of adjustment is as impracticable as the squaring of the circle. The vital question in all cases of duty is not *the nature* of the duty, but *the fact* of duty, and your and my attitude toward the duty. To what does the duty appeal in us? Does it appeal to a settled principle that duty is to be done always and everywhere, because it is duty? or to a principle that duty is to be done under certain circumstances, when it does not conflict with desire or self-interest? If the appeal is to the former principle, then, though the duty itself may be hard, it is not hard to know whether it ought to be done. It is enough that it is duty. No man can ever walk in darkness who accepts that principle. The largest element of difficulty is removed from the case when self is forbidden to raise the questions of hard or easy, safe or dangerous. Self always makes greater difficulties than God does.

Duty is a fixed fact, to be taken as it is. It does not adjust itself to us; we must adjust ourselves to it: and that is a great deal easier, hard though it be, than to shape the duty according to our notions. There is a nebulous mass far off in the depths of space, — a tangled skein of stars, appearing to the eye like a volume of thin vapor. The problem before the astronomer may be very difficult of practical solution, but the nature of the problem is simple and clearly defined. He is to resolve that mist into its component stars, and to find out, if he can, the number and relative position of those stars. If he is bent on bringing the facts which his telescope discovers into harmony with some theory of his own, he complicates his task at once. The stars will not change their size or their position because of his theory. If he would know the facts as they are, he simply takes what his telescope gives him. Then every thing depends upon his telescope. Let some careless or malicious hand crack the lens, or incrust the mirror with a film, his observation results only in guess-work: but, with his lens and mirror clean and rightly adjusted, his eye penetrates the veil of mist; and he brings back from the infinite spaces tidings which enrich the records of science. So, when men look at duty through loyal and obedient hearts, its lines come out plainly and sharply. Let self put a film over the spirit, duty remains unchanged. God's will must be done, but the man sees only a mist. That filmed eye raises more and harder questions than the duty itself. Duty is not complicated by elements of danger and self-sacrifice: the complication comes out of our refusal to see these elements as parts of duty, out of our fruitless attempt to see duty at some point from which the danger and sacrifice shall disappear, out of our determination to convince ourselves that any thing which involves danger and sacrifice cannot be duty. When the engineer sat down before the mountain which divides Italy from Switzerland, and decided that his railroad must go straight through that mountain, he had a difficult task indeed, but a simple one. His railroad must go under that mountain; and you see, that, in addressing himself wholly to that solution of his problem, he at once got rid of a thousand questions as to the practicability of other routes, and the possibility of getting round or over the mountain. His task was infinitely simplified by his fixing upon a definite course, with all its difficulties. He could concentrate all his ingenuity and skill on overcoming the difficulties.

I take it no one ever had so clear a perception of the hardness and agony which his mission involved as Christ himself had; so clear and vivid, indeed, that his humanity more than once recoiled, and cried, "Father, save me from this hour. If it be possible, let this cup pass from me!" And yet the closest study of Christ's life reveals not a shadow of hesitation or doubt about following the line of duty. His step is as firm toward Bethany, where he knows that the Jews may be waiting to stone him, as when he is going to the sweet retirement and hospitality of Mary's and Martha's home. Whether duty points to Zaccheus' feast or to Calvary, he walks with equal decision. He goes to the cross saying, "The Scripture must be fulfilled." He comes back from the dead saying, "Thus it behooved Christ to suffer." Sometimes as we look at this firm, constant walk of our Lord, we are moved to say, "Would that duty were as plain to me as it seems to have been to him; would that I could move forward without hesitation as he did." And then we go on to reason that this may not be; because Christ was so superior to us, and possessed of divine knowledge. But we are wrong there. Whatever Christ was, he was a man; and duty was no different a thing to Christ than it is to us; and Christ not only tells us in our text the secret of his own clear perception and unfaltering pursuit of duty, but gives us the same secret for our own use: "If a man walk in the day, he stumbleth not, because he seeth the light of this world." The case was not that Christ knew the nature and bearings of duty better than we do (though that is true), but it was that Christ walked in the light of simple loyalty to God, under the simple rule that God's will was to be done; refusing to admit into his mind any question but this: "Is it, or is it not, the will of God?" The motto of his life is given by himself at Jacob's well: "My meat is to do the will of him that sent me, and to finish his work." Living by that principle, he walked in the light. His eye was single, and his whole body was therefore full of light. He admitted no question of stoning or crucifying. He knew that duty involved loneliness and hatred and homelessness and persecution and crucifixion; but it was enough that it was duty. And hence it is that his life, while it is the most tremendous tragedy in history, ranging through the whole gamut of human experience, marked by an infinite variety of incident, is the most purely simple, clearly cut life in all its relations to duty of which we have any knowledge. This singleness of eye, this principle of absolute loyalty to truth as truth, and to duty as duty, relieved his life of a thousand elements of perplexity and hesitation which confronted other men. As a straight road carries one past a multitude of thickets and bogs and stony places, even though the road itself may be rough; so Christ's path, though it was a rough way, and led to Gethsemane and Golgotha, carried him past all questions of policy, — questions of making a good appearance, questions of the good opinion of the world, of wealth, of worldly position, — past all the endless perplexities which wait on the effort to compromise between God and the world, all those things, in short, which are the torment of nine-tenths of the world to-day, and which make duty, even to so many Christians, a sphynx's riddle.

Now, look at a contrast to this straightforward, clear course of Jesus at Bethany. Take an Old-Testament case, — Saul at Michmash. The matter of duty there was as plain and simple as at Bethany. God had said to Saul, "Do not move the army without sacrificing to God; do not offer sacrifice yourself, but wait till Samuel comes." Saul had only to wait till Samuel should come, whether it were seven days, or seventy; and if he had fixed his mind on that single point of duty, his course would have been as plain as the sun in heaven. There were indeed other considerations, but not for *him* to discuss. Obedience to that naked command involved apparent trouble and disaster; but God had said nothing about these, only "Wait." But Saul admitted those other considerations. He would not walk in the light of that simple duty. He admitted the possibility, that circumstances might justify him in disobeying God. And the moment he did that, you see how his course became complicated. What a multitude of hard questions crowded upon him. The enemy was concentrating, the soldiers deserting: a decisive blow must be struck. He was burdened at once with the solution of all these difficulties, instead of having simply to wait. True faith and simple loyalty would have left all these matters in God's hands; but Saul had not true faith and simple loyalty. He assumed the functions of a priest, he sacrificed to the very God he was disobeying; and his presumption cost him his kingdom.

In short, the life of obedience to God, while it bears the cross, and includes danger and self-sacrifice, is simpler and easier than the life of worldly policy and self-interest. The selfish life always walks in darkness, though it often prides itself on its astuteness. The loyal, unselfish principle of duty carries with it a power of revelation. If duty is merely a question of circumstances, then every new set of circumstances raises a new question and a new difficulty. If duty, on the other hand, is a matter of absolute obligation under *all* circumstances, then the whole mass of such questions and difficulties is disposed of at a blow. In the most confused whirl of circumstances, Christ's true follower knows his way.

And Christ's teaching and example in this matter are valuable to every age. To none more than to this, when the selfish and politic principles of the world seem to be pouring like a flood over the lines of Christian duty. In an age which tends to moral compromise, this principle which illumined Christ's way ought to be sharply defined and emphasized in the consciousness of every Christian. If there is a word to be spoken for truth and righteousness, even though it recoil upon the man who speaks it in abuse, or in social or political or religious ostracism, he must none the less speak it; looking not at the recoil, but at the truth and the righteousness. If there is a protest to be made by example against social looseness and corruption, the loyal Christian cannot be in doubt about what his duty is, though he may shrink from the hardness of the duty itself. His way lies straight before him. It is an easier way than the path of compromise. Almost daily, practical issues arise in our lives which bring us face to face with this teaching of Christ; issues where the only light we can get will come from a loyal and obedient heart: where, the moment we step out of the line of light which streams straight from God's Word, we are in darkness and confusion. I repeat it: we simplify life and duty, we clear up and dispose of a multitude of hard questions, by taking, as our fixed, immutable principle, duty, always and everywhere. Suppose duty costs reputation, popularity, ease, social approval: it is none the less duty for that reason. Christ does not mean to save us cost. He gives fair warning of that. He does not promise that the man who walks in the light shall have an easy walk. He promises that he shall not stumble: but Christ did not stumble because he was crucified; Stephen did not stumble because he was stoned; Paul did not stumble because he was imprisoned and beheaded. Each of the lives over the cross, the stone, the prison, walked straight to its goal; and their track lies out in the light as a lesson and a warning to every one who would live a true, loyal, faithful life. The stumbling begins the moment we let in any other consideration than that of duty. Darkness and confusion come in with these. The stumbling would have been in Christ accepting Satan's offer of the kingdoms of the world, in Stephen keeping silence; in Paul making terms with Nero and with the Jewish leaders, and saying smooth things to the debauchees at Corinth, and to the philosophers at Athens. If a man adds to his life by avoiding the danger that lies in the path of duty, that added life is no gain. It has no divine blessing and no divine guidance. Such life is not God's gift: it is filched by him who wins it. Reputation, popularity, security, won by evasion of duty, are not gains. They shine in a false and transient light, and they will soon lapse into darkness. The light shines steadily to-day over Bethany, — light which gilds the door of every closed tomb. Better that Christ should have gone in the face of the stones than that the world should have missed the lesson of the resurrection and the life. The light of all the ages centres in the cross. Better all that agony than that the world should have missed a Saviour. Better the light and glory and honor, in which Christ and his apostles and the good and true of all time stand enshrined to-day, than if they had shirked the cross and the scourge, the prison, and the sneer of the world.

But remember that this steadfast, light-giving principle in the soul is not a matter of mere human resolve. As I have often told you, no radiant, life-giving life is ever generated by a mere code of laws, or by mere strength of resolution. Christ is in the soul as an inspiration, and not merely before the eye as an example. The single heart is formed only by the living contact of God's spirit. The single heart is the pure heart; and no amount of resolution, no library of moral treatises, no portrait-gallery of holy examples, can of themselves purify the heart. That is the work of God's transforming spirit alone.

And once more remember, that though Christ, in setting you on that well-lighted track of duty, does not allow *you* to take account of the hardness, *He* takes account of it. He has been over every inch of the ground himself: he has felt the rending of the thorns, and his feet have been bruised by the same stones which bruise yours. You cannot live a life so hard that Christ has not lived a harder, you cannot make so great a sacrifice that Christ has not made a greater. He does not push you out on straight lines of hard duty to walk alone. He goes before. His word is, "Follow me!" And all along that line he walks close to you, even as he promised, when he said, "Lo, I am with you alway." Only keep the eye on him, follow him anywhere and everywhere, and you cannot go wrong: you cannot get into darkness in questions of duty. He is a strict but a tender master; and on the way in which he leads you are not only crosses and thorns, but light and love and sympathy and peace, and, at the end, heaven.

"Deem not that they are blest alone
   Whose lives a peaceful tenor keep;
For God, who pities man, has shown
   A blessing for the eyes that weep.

There is a day of sunny rest
   For every dark and troubled night;
Though grief may bide an evening guest,
   Yet joy shall come with early light.

Nor let the good man's trust depart,
   Though life its common gifts deny, —
Though with a pierced and broken heart,
   And spurned of men, he goes to die.

For God has marked each sorrowing day,
   And numbered every secret tear;
And heaven's eternal bliss shall pay
   For all his children suffer here."

VI.

THE ORDERED STEPS.

VI.

THE ORDERED STEPS.

"The steps of a good man are ordered by the Lord: and he delighteth in his way.

"Though he fall, he shall not be utterly cast down: for the Lord upholdeth him with his hand." — Ps. xxxvii. 23, 24.

THAT first step of your little child, — what an event it is! After the child has grown into a strong and hearty boy, his walking does not interest you in itself, but only in its direction, which often menaces his safety or that of your household treasures; but now the single step is a thing of profound meaning. One, two, three, — each time your eye is on the little foot, and your hand ready to catch the tottering form at the first symptom of a fall. Never again will single steps have such interest for you. And yet why not? In manhood, no less than in infancy, single steps are significant. You find it out sometimes in disagreeable ways. One step in the dark carries you off firm footing into an open trap, or down a bank. The first step down a wrong road is the beginning of troublesome, and possibly dangerous, wanderings. The first wrong step, — how many men have looked down a dismal perspective, and have seen it like a footprint of fire! The first step to honor or fortune, — how much meaning it has after the honor or the fortune has been won!

Now, Scripture holds to the emphasis upon the single steps. The word "walk," as you know, is constantly used by it to express the course and method of a man's life: "Enoch walked with God." "Thou shalt keep the commandments of the Lord thy God, to walk in his ways." "Walk while ye have the light." "See that ye walk circumspectly." These are a few instances out of scores. Walking is a matter of steps; and, in God's training of men, he directs their attention to the single steps rather than to the course of their lives as a whole — to the details of the life, in other words, rather than to the life at large. This is the first truth of our text: *God orders, arranges, establishes, the details of his children's lives.*

There is a practical wisdom in this. We speak contemptuously sometimes about a man of details, as if he were an inferior sort of man; but really very few of mankind have the ability to grasp large masses of work, and succeed only by doing work in detail, a piece at a time, each day's duty in its day. And the man who can give details over to somebody else, and devote himself to the larger aspects of his business, is no less dependent upon details than before. He is at the top of the ladder, but the top rests on what is below. He had to climb the steps to the top.

There is also a profound philosophy in this. The principle has a very wide reach. The boy who saves penny after penny in order to make up his dollar, is working on a line which goes out through all the universe. His little economy is an outcome of the great truth that God moves masses through details. When the attraction of gravitation acts upon that cannon-ball as it flies through the air, and gradually draws it to the ground, the attraction is exerted, not upon the ball as a mass, but upon each separate particle. When water, in obedience to its law, flows down a steep, the force which draws it down to its level acts upon each separate drop. Thus, then, the particles of the cannon-ball do not fall to the ground because they are included in the mass. The particles make the mass, and the mass falls because of the force exerted upon the separate particles. The drops make up the current. There is a current because the attraction draws every drop to its level.

This law of matter is a law of morals, a law of providence, a law of divine economy: the greater is reached and moved through the less, the mass through the detail. Character is an accretion, an aggregate. A man is what the *details* of his life are, whether in his business life, his intellectual life, or his moral life. He receives great impulses in all these spheres, but all these impulses work out their result through detail. See the illustration of this in the history of Divine Providence as we have it in the Bible. One of the most common of popular delusions is, that God is always and only busied with great things; and yet in the

Bible he is constantly dealing with details. He is explaining a servant's dream; he is providing for a little castaway babe in a bulrush basket; he is furnishing water to a thirsty crowd of people; he is dictating a code which goes into every item of eating and drinking and cleansing; he is giving directions about fringes and embroideries, about blue and scarlet curtains, about the patterns of the priests' dresses, and the knops and flowers in the temple architecture.

The case is no different when he becomes manifest in the flesh. Christ's life and work are full of detail. Now he is coming out to comfort some poor fishermen in their lonely toil, and to fill their nets with fish. Now he is caressing little children, again noting a poor widow's little coin dropped into the treasury, or talking with a wretched woman by a well, or supplying wine for a wedding, or bread and fish for a hungry multitude.

The same thing appears in Christ's preaching. He tells men how to live; but he says nothing about great, far-reaching plans of life. His talk is rather of living by the day, and letting the morrow take thought for the things of itself. He treats of our talk, yet not of our studied discourses and elaborate orations; rather of our ordinary communication, our words, our common affirmations and denials: and by these he tells us we shall be justified or condemned. He comes to reveal God to us: but his speech is not about the God of vast designs and transcendent power; rather of one who paints each lily of the fields, and feeds the birds, and marks the sparrow's fall, and numbers the hairs of our heads. He teaches men their duty to society: but he says nothing of great schemes of beneficence; rather, he cautions us against harming the little ones; bids us visit the sick and the prisoner, and give the cup of cold water to the wayfarer; to speak a kind word for an angry one, and to meet the blow with forgiveness. And, when he promises reward, he sums up the achievements of the best and greatest in these words, — "Thou hast been *faithful* over a *few* things."

Thus you see one law — the law of the steps — running through physical and moral nature alike. Gravitation and Providence observe the same principle. God regulates the mass through the particles; society, through the individual; the individual, through the details of his life. Men, with their joys and sorrows and infirmities, are not carried down and swallowed up as single drops in a current. Each individual soul in the great sweeping tide of souls, each element in the experience of each soul, is the subject of his divine forces. The drops determine the tide, the steps determine the life; and the life which is led by him is led step by step, and each separate step has its meaning and its relation to every other step. We do not see this. As life unrolls day by day, the duties appear to have so little relation to each other that we receive no impression of design or plan. There seems to be that absence of design even in the Saviour's own words: "The morrow shall be anxious for itself." But that is only in appearance. The steps of a good man are *established;* not ordered each day as emergencies arise, but *pre-arranged.* The plan, the pre-arrangement, does not appear when you see that laborer laying a single course of brick or stone; but the architect sees that course as part of his design. We must study history, and especially Bible history, to realize that life evolves itself according to a plan. Look, for instance, at the familiar story of Joseph. The plan is plain enough to us now. We see a meaning and a mutual relation in all the separate events of that history, but Jacob did not see it. He said, "All these things are against me;" while we know, and he afterwards found out, that they were all for him. To Joseph the pit did not mean the place next the throne. The same is true of all history. God moves on such long lines that it takes a good many centuries, with their countless steps of countless men, to work out a design of his; yet that plan bears the footmark of every one of those millions, and its lines are only the lines of those myriad lives.

The steps of a good man, then, are ordered. He does not walk at random. His life is not a series of accidents which some superior power gathers up after a while, as a potter might gather the loose fragments of clay, and mould them into what he could. And really you and I, in our measure, are familiar with the same fact, and act it out. You see in a son of yours promise of intellectual and moral power; and you set yourself to shape that boy's career, and you do shape it, and that by attending to its successive steps. You watch and care for every detail of his training, and the boy's life bears the mark of your ordering. Is there any thing strange in our heavenly Father's ordering the steps of his children? Is not the true reasoning from the less to the greater? "*How much more* shall your heavenly Father give good things to them that ask him."

We talk a great deal of our free choices, our independence, our self-determination; but, if we insist on these, we do not come within the Psalmist's description. It is the steps of a *good* man that are established. I do not say that God has nothing to do with the steps of others; he has very much to do with them: but we are not concerned with that now. The good man of the Psalmist's thought is the man of law, — the man who recognizes the excellence and the rightful claim of the divine law, and who gives himself up to it. The Bible alternative is very sharp and plain. Either we are to be ordered by God, or we are to be self-ordered. If we undertake to order our own steps, we must take the consequences, and relinquish all claim upon God's ordering. I am not preaching to you inflexible fate, but obedience to divine wisdom; not the passive submission of a corpse to a rushing current, but the loving and intelligent obedience of a free will. There are those who seem to think that obedience is inconsistent with freedom, and that a man shows his freedom by revolt against law. They forget that a free will may *choose* to obey another will. If

God has prepared tracks for my life; surely my very freedom of choice empowers me to keep to those tracks: and, to the obedient, loving soul, it is an immense comfort and relief to know that his life moves on prepared lines. I sat one evening in a window looking out on Charing-Cross railway-station, with its trains arriving and departing every few minutes, and its cross-tides of thronging people. A train stood on the track, and the bell rang for starting. In front, through the great archways, I looked out into the misty night. A few stray gleams of light revealed a labyrinth of rails, curving and crossing: above was a signal-stand — a great hieroglyph of green, red, and white lights, shifting every moment; and into this darkness and confusion the engine moved. What was it that made that engineer so quiet and confident? Why was he not disturbed and anxious at the chaos of rails and lights and the thick night beyond? Simply because every thing was laid down for him. He had only to obey the signals, and drive his engine: the track was laid. Other minds had the care and responsibility of the switches and signal-lights: he had only to go forward, and to stop when bidden.

"I do not like the picture," some one will perhaps say. "It leaves me little to say about my life." Well, change the picture if you will. Let the engineer go forth from the station on an engine not fitted to a track. Let him move out into the night, in the consciousness of independence and free choice, to avoid collision and wreck as he can.

Have you bettered the matter any? Are you any better, any more dignified, any more secure, striking out into this selfish world on your own responsibility, and with only your own wisdom? Have ever so much to say about the ordering of your own life, the simple question is, whither your ordering will take you. The area of human life is marked all over with these tracks of individual choice, but unfortunately they are lined with wrecks. There are no wrecks along the lines on which God orders the steps: "He that walketh uprightly walketh surely." "Acknowledge him in all thy ways, and he shall direct thy steps."

The second truth of the text is, that *God is pleased with him who thus lets his steps be ordered.* Literally the words read, "From Jehovah is it that a man's steps are established, so that he hath pleasure in his way." This need not detain us long. It is self-evident that God is pleased to have men walk in the ways which he himself ordains; and his pleasure is not simply in the fact that he is obeyed, not merely in receiving from men the tribute of respect and submission which is his due. We do God a great wrong when we picture him as a creditor whose interest in his debtors begins and ends with their paying their debts. God merges the relation of debtor and creditor in that of father and child. It is a very small part of your interest in your child, that he should repay you for your care of him. In fact, payment is impossible. On the contrary, every thing the child does or says is interesting to you because he is your child. Other children say bright and quaint things, but none of them have quite the flavor of those which come from his baby lips. And when he begins to walk, you are not criticising his walk by the rules of the dancing-master; you are simply delighted in his way, rejoiced to see him growing strong and exercising his limbs: and so it is all the way up to manhood. What he does and says and achieves and suffers has the keenest interest for you, because he is your child. Now, possibly, we find it hard to transfer just that feeling to God; and yet that is the true view of his feeling towards his children. A group of statesmen engaged in the discussion of a treaty would probably give no thought to the group of children playing under the windows of the council-chamber, but God does not look upon men in that way. From one point of view we might justly think, that all the "windy ways of men"—all their rushing up and down, all their hot pursuit and all the objects they pursue, all their striving and wrangling—are to God just what two newsboys playing marbles are to that banker as he walks down the street to negotiate a loan of millions. And yet "God so loved the world that he gave his only begotten Son." It was to just this crowd of men and women, with their little ambitions and their petty strivings, that he looked for those whom he should call and justify and glorify, conforming them to the image of his Son. And therefore God is interested in whatever concerns these children. Every step of that life-problem which you and I are working out is noted by him. No one has so deep an interest in our working it out well. Each undertaking, each acquisition, each trial, each conflict, each victory, — he concerns himself with it; and your fatherly heart never beat with more joy at your babe's first step, or your boy's first prize in school, than does his at each step of ours in the way he has laid down: every victory over self and sin, every honest purpose formed in reliance on him, every forward step in self-mastery, reflects glory on him. He leadeth his children in the paths of righteousness, not for their glory, but for his name's sake. He delighteth in their way.

"Ah!" you say, "I would fain believe myself a child of God. I desire to please him, but my way is not perfect. It is sometimes little better than a series of stumbles and falls: and, instead of being a radiant, strong, white-robed son of God, my garments are soiled with the world's dust, and I am all bruised and scarred; and it seems a cruel satire to tell me that the Lord delighteth in my way."

Here, then, the third truth of the text comes in. Evidently the Psalmist recognizes *infirmity as an element of the good man's walk.* There is a possibility, more than a possibility, of his falling, which the text provides for: "Though he fall, he shall not be utterly cast down: for the Lord upholdeth him with his hand." We may go back again to the illustration of the babe's first walk. There is none which better suits the case. We who call ourselves strong men, who seem to walk so firmly and securely, what is our walk, after all, but the tottering walk of little children? And yet you do not despise that baby's attempts at walking, because he falls over now and then. The falls somehow are taken up in the fact of his walking: they are a part of it. You do not want him to be hurt; you are sorry for him when he falls; you try to keep him from falling; you take him up tenderly, and dry his tears after each fall: and yet, clumsy, tearful performance though it is, you delight in his way. You would rather have him fall a hundred times, — yes, and hurt himself too, — than not have him walk at all. Let us face the fact squarely. There is falling along the path by which God orders a man's steps. It is not that God ordains sin. He does not. But the path which God ordains for a good man lies through this world: and sin is in the world, no matter why or how; and a good man's walk with God consists very largely in a fight with sin. What God pledges is not that the man shall escape all contact with sin in his walk, not that he shall not feel the power and bitterness of sin, not that he shall walk to heaven a perfect, sinless man all the way. The Psalmist prays, "Order my steps in thy word: and let not any iniquity *have dominion* over me;" and, when we turn from the Psalmist to Paul, we find the answer to that prayer: "Sin shall not have dominion over you, for ye are not under the law, but under grace." The promise, therefore, does not cover the fight with sin, but the victory of sin. Even the man whose steps are ordered of the Lord shall know, and know well, the anguish of that fight; but, though Apollyon bring him to the ground, he shall stretch forth his hand, and grasp his sword, crying, "Rejoice not against me, O mine enemy: for when I fall, I shall arise;" and, as he goes on his way scarred but victorious, he shall be a living, walking testimony to the truth: "The steps of a good man are established by the Lord." Establishment does not exclude conflict or fall. It comes about through the successive conflicts and falls and risings again. You and I never have seen a perfect man, we never shall see one: we know enough of men to know that those whom we love best, and think best, and trust most, have their infirmities and their errors; and yet we are not unfamiliar with men who are nobler than their faults. We know of something in those men which lies back of all their faults, which seems beclouded now and then by the dust from their fall, but which, after each fall, rises up again through a mist of penitent tears, and asserts itself as the dominant power in their lives. There is something in the deathless persistence of that power, something in its dauntless renewal of the struggle with sin and self, which makes us reverence that man more than one whose life seems an even-spun thread of rectitude without knot or tangle. One has said of David after his moral fall, "He is not what he was before, but he is far nobler and greater than many a just man who never fell and never repented." Let us beware of thinking repentance a sentiment of a lower grade, or degrading to the man who drops its bitter tears. There is something heroic in the man who looks up to God's ideal of manhood far, far above him, and at himself, lamed and wounded by his fall, and says, "By God's grace I will mount to it." There is something transparently honest and noble about the man who looks his own shame and infirmity in the face, and says to God, "All that thou sayest of its vileness is true to the last word. Thou art justified when thou speakest, and art clear when thou judgest." "Unbelievers," says Carlyle, "sneer, and ask, 'Is this your man according to God's heart?' The sneer, I must needs say, seems to me but a shallow one. What are faults, what are the outward details of a life, if the inner secret of it — the remorse, temptations, the often-baffled, never-ending struggle of it — be forgotten, — struggle often baffled, sore baffled, driven as into entire wreck, yet a struggle never ended, ever with tears, repentance, true unconquerable purpose begun anew."

So the steps of a good man are established, — established in spite of his fall. Walking in the way of God's order brings with it that strong, immortal, unconquerable principle which re-asserts itself after every fall, and keeps the man's face set toward God, and his feet pressing on along the heavenward road. It is a divine principle, the very hand of God stretched forth each time in fulfilment of the promise: "Though he fall, he shall not be utterly cast down: for the Lord upholdeth him with his hand."

From these truths we draw some conclusions of great practical value: —

If God has ordained a way for men to walk in, it is the height of folly to walk in any other way. If a man's steps are established in that way, they must be feeble and uncertain, and ending in a disastrous fall in any other way. If God walks that way with his children, establishing their steps, and upholding them when they fall, those who walk on other roads, walk without his help and strength, and therefore walk in danger. Fancied independence, which chooses its own road and walks in its own wisdom, is a poor compensation for the surety and safety and help vouchsafed to him who commits his way unto God.

If God, as we have seen, orders our ways, step by step, it becomes us to take heed to the details of our lives. If our acts and choices were detached, if the significance of each one began and ended with itself, a single step might be less important. But every step is an element of progress in one direction or the other. Every act, every choice, is a piece which fits into some other piece. Every deed is a link in a chain. You shall go, and stand beside yonder woman at her embroidery, and see her putting in the stitches carelessly, and now and then inserting a stitch of the wrong color; and, on your calling her attention to the fact, she shall say, "No matter, the whole piece will be very beautiful when it is done." You know it will not, for what is the entire pattern but a mass of single stitches? The great outcome of our lives will be shaped by their details. Our lives are not what great crises make them. They are made by those little words and deeds, those daily touches, those successive steps.

If God orders each detail of our lives, ought we not to get great and solid comfort out of the fact? More and more, as it seems to me, his divine discipline turns our eyes from the vague future with its uncertain results, and fixes them on to-day's duty and to-day's privilege. We are distressing ourselves, it may be, about the outcome. There is no need, if we follow God's rule, which confines us to the separate steps. When a traveller in the Alps is ascending an ice-slope where he has to cut steps as he mounts, he thinks of little besides the step he is at that moment cutting. He has a point to reach, a space to traverse; but all that is lost sight of in the danger and difficulty which wait on every step. He knows he will escape destruction only as each step shall be rightly cut, and his foot firmly planted each time. It is a good deal so in this life. It is not a safe journey by any means; but there is this assurance for a child of God who walks it, that each step shall be sure if he only commits his way unto the Lord. And while there is not much comfort to the man who is cutting his way up the ice, there is a great deal for the man who will accept this principle as his rule in life, and concern himself with his single steps rather than with his life in a mass. You say that makes your life fragmentary. Very likely. I wonder if some of us have not to accept fragmentariness, and make the best of it? You have been balked in many of your plans; and your life, perhaps, has been a mere doing of what came to hand; and you have possibly said, "Life is an utter failure. It would not have been so if I could only have carried out my plan." Perhaps not. Perhaps it would have been a greater failure if you *had* carried out your plan. Only, here is Christ, pointing down at a little dead sparrow, and saying, "Not one of them falleth to the ground without your heavenly Father's notice." God looks after fragments, and works through them to make glorious units of his own.

The separate steps! Sometimes each one seems to sink into a quagmire, or to strike a stone. It is hard to walk on in strong faith that they are ordered by the Lord. The little cares and vexations! They seem to be interruptions to the course of the life. No call for patience or self-control in these. And yet suppose these are the very things which go to make up the course of the life. Suppose you wake up by and by to find that you have cast away the blessing which lay hidden in an annoyance. So, then, to conclude, it becomes us to fall in with God's order, and to attach to the separate steps the same importance that he does. If we do, we shall never think slightingly of any act or word. We shall acquire a new sense of the value of each single soul, and shall cease to view men in masses. We shall be led to develop the resources of single points of effort. We shall find more joy and success in our daily lives, and in our worries and disappointments, and amid the temptations to feel that we are carried helpless and uncared for in the mighty sweep of time and change, we shall turn back to the old psalm, and say, "My steps are ordered of the Lord; he delighteth in my way; he upholdeth me with his hand; and if he be for me, who can be against me?"

VII.

FIDELITY AND DOMINION.

VII.

FIDELITY AND DOMINION.

"His Lord said unto him, Well done, good and faithful servant: thou hast been faithful over a few things, I will set thee over many things: enter thou into the joy of thy Lord." — MATT. xxv. 21.

THERE are three great elements of work in the kingdom of God, — quantity, quality, and ability.[1] Quality is a matter of character; ability, of endowment; quantity, of improvement. When we sit down before an artist's picture, we consider his skill as a draughtsman and colorist, and the power of his mind to evolve ideas. These represent his ability. We consider the character of his picture, the lesson it teaches, — whether it awakens pure and high thoughts, or base and sensual ones; whether it is true to the great laws of art. These represent quality. And then we sum up the result, and ask how much of a picture the artist with his degree of ability has made. What rank will it take? Is it a great picture, or a poor picture? The answer to that is quantity.

How do these three stand related to each other

---

[1] I am indebted in this introduction to Professor Alexander B. Bruce's admirable work on *The Parabolic Teaching of Christ.*

in Christian work and reward? For what is reward given in the kingdom of God, — for ability, quantity, or quality? Here we may profitably study this familiar parable of the talents, in connection with the parable of the pounds in the nineteenth of Luke. These two are not the same. Each treats the truth from a different point of view. In the parable of the pounds, we are taught that equal ability implies equal quantity, and that, when ability is equal, quantity determines merit, and, therefore, that unequal quantity is unequally rewarded. The master gave his ten servants a pound apiece. The endowment was equal, the outcome was unequal. One returned ten pounds for his one; another, only five for his one. The first received authority over ten cities, and was, besides, addressed as a good and faithful servant. The other received only five cities, and not a word was said about his goodness or fidelity.

Turning now to our parable of the talents, we find that the endowment, the ability, of the several servants, was not equal. It is represented by the difference between five, two, and one. As in the parable of the pounds, we have a varied quantity in the returns, represented by five, two, and zero. But in the award we notice that the difference between five and two is wiped out or ignored; and that the same reward is given to the servant who brought two for two, as to him who brought five for five. Here, then, it appears that quantity does not enter into the question of award. The same award is given for different quantities; so that we need a third factor in order to determine the principle of this judgment. That third factor is quality, and quality is fixed by the proportion of quantity to ability; in other words, by the answer to the question, Did the servant do all he could with his endowment? Were two talents all the interest of which his capital admitted with the most faithful and diligent use? The award in this parable, then, is based, not on the differences between the returns, but upon the fact common to both returns, that ability had been worked at its highest power, and had yielded the most and best of which it was capable; that both alike bore the stamp of *faithfulness*. To both servants it is said, " Thou hast been *faithful;*" to both, therefore, " Enter thou into the joy of thy Lord." Faithfulness imparts the quality which answers God's test of moral value; and value and award in the kingdom of God turn upon quality, and not upon quantity. Faithfulness spans the differences of ability. No difference of endowment can put one out of reach of that test. It follows endowment down to its vanishing-point, and binds the possessor of an infinitesimal fraction of a talent to raise his fraction to the highest power as stringently as it binds the holder of five or ten talents. The servant with the smallest capital was condemned simply because he did not use it. On the other hand, endowment never rises out of the atmosphere of faithfulness. No measure of ability ever exempts from duty. No amount of brilliancy compensates for unfaithfulness.

Let us now look at a few of the details of the parable which illustrate this principle. Observe, first, that *all human endowment and its largest results are small, measured by the standards of God's kingdom.* To the holder of the five talents, as to the holder of the two, it is said, "Thou hast been faithful over a *few things.*" Human endowment and human performance, the few things, get their significance from their relation to the many things, — the great, thronging facts and principles and laws of the kingdom of God. The most persistent and varied activity and the largest achievement of the greatest man are but small, in themselves considered; but they are points where the vast economy of the kingdom of God — that something which is vaguely indicated by "many things," "the joy of the Lord," — emerges into the region of our human life, and touches it. That which is out of sight is more and greater than that which pushes out into our view. That point of rock which rises out of the hillside is, to the geologist, not merely a distinct stone. It tells him the dip and quality of the great strata under ground which buttress the hills. Obedience, responsibility, duty, work, love, trust, — all that makes up Christian life here, — are sides and manifestations of the unseen, spiritual universe. Godliness has promise, not only of the life that now is, but of that which is to come, — has the promise which one part of a thing gives of the other part. Godliness is a part of the life to come. Godliness is God revealing himself in human character. Follow back godliness, and you come to God. The boy who is learning his alphabet is handling the same elements which enter into the plays of Shakspeare or the dialogues of Plato. He has begun upon literature when he has learned A B C. It is a little thing in itself for him to learn twenty-six letters, but it is a very great thing when you consider the alphabet as the medium of the world's thought. Even so, I repeat, the largest endowment and the largest result are shown by this utterance of Christ to be but as " a few things," but acquiring, nevertheless, a tremendous and eternal importance as integral parts of the great moral economy of God. The man who is administering a moral trust, discharging duties, improving gifts, is within the circumference of that kingdom which spans eternity and the universe; and it is that fact which gives meaning and value to his few things.

This appears further as we consider a second feature of the parable. *Work and accomplishment, in themselves, are trivial, because they do not involve mastery.* Look at our Lord's words: " Good servant, thou hast been *faithful* over a few things, I will *set thee over* many things." The word is habitually used of putting in a position of authority or mastery. Good and faithful people are constantly tempted to identify success with accomplishment, and to think that they fail because they cannot do what they set out to do.. But you observe that God gives no promise of mastery for this world. God is not nearly so much concerned that you and I should accomplish what we purpose as that the quality of our work should be heavenly. Hence it is that he sets upon true and good work, not the seal of *accomplishment*, which is a thing of to-day, but the great moral seal of the eternal heavenly kingdom, which is *faithfulness*. This, and not accomplishment, is what determines its real value. It is a fact of observation, that good men do not always, nor perhaps often, carry out their plans. Often their plans are larger than their lives; often their plans are weaker than their circumstances: and these facts tend to irritate and depress them. They do not see that these temporary failures may lie on the direct line of a delayed success. The greatest success in life is to maintain fidelity, — to be faithful, though the outcome be only a few things. The man who has a great reform to carry through, a great truth to lodge in the convictions of society, has not necessarily failed if he die with society unreformed and unconvinced. He has failed if he has given up trying, if he has lost faith in the truth, if he has let down his ideal. That is disastrous failure. One thing which we are slow in learning is, that the best human work is fractional. The divine whole is greater than any one man, or than any one man's work. We of this age are carrying out something which our fathers left incomplete, and we in our time shall leave something for our children to carry out. "Other men labored," says our Lord, "and ye have entered into their labors." Abraham filled his place grandly; he was the father of the faithful: but the divine economy of faith was not completed in Abraham. Paul was needed to supplement Abraham, and the saints of the nineteenth century to supplement Paul; and the men of faith of the twentieth century will supplement those of the nineteenth, and add something to the outcome of their life and work. The men of the past, so the writer to the Hebrews tells us, "had witness borne to them through their faith;" but he says also that "they received not the promise." Faith did not issue in full fruition. God "promised a better thing for *us*, that they should not be made perfect apart from us." In other words, we are necessary to their perfection. Their work, their moral ideals are carried on and developed by us, and so the development goes on from century to century. Therefore, human work, Christian work, does not issue in mastery here. Even the few things may be too much for the servant. The mastery comes only by way of reward.

And yet the parable very clearly shows us that *faithfulness is on the direct line of mastery:* "Thou hast been *faithful, therefore* I will make thee *ruler*." Fidelity tends and leads up to mastery. Success is a thing of stages and aggregations; and it is of vastly more consequence that the man should be rightly pointed, set in the direction of a larger, *divine* success, than that he should achieve what he undertakes here. If there is no larger, purer, more spiritual kingdom than this, there is no such thing as real success. If there *is* such a kingdom, and if the earthly sphere of Christian life and work is a part of it, then the success may well lie beyond the line of our human vision, and be too large for our little inch-rules. The great principle holds, — fidelity leads up to mastery. You see it illustrated daily. You see the faithful journeyman advanced to the foremanship, the plodding student become an authority: you see men of moderate ability becoming powers in business or in manufacturing, by steady devotion to one thing. The thing itself may be small; their perseverance magnifies it: and they themselves grow into the ability to handle larger things through their fidelity to the smaller interest.

We notice again, that *fidelity to the few things carries with it the promise of fidelity to the many:* "I will set thee over many things." In that promise, you observe, not power, but confidence, is emphasized. The idea of a trust is carried up from the lower to the higher plane. Delegated *authority* is a trust no less than delegated *duty.* All through the New Testament, Christ insists that endowment means, first of all, *responsibility.* Rule is trust. The man who cannot be trusted is the man who must not rule.

Now, the popular idea is, that moral responsibility is concerned mostly with great things. But keep in mind the truth we have been illustrating, and which lies at the root of this parable, — that all human action gets its quality and meaning from its relation to the kingdom of God. From this point of view no act is insignificant, no neglect safe, no violation of trust trivial. Christ strikes at the root of the popular error. Fidelity has nothing whatever to do with the magnitude of the trust. That truth is written in black lines on the moral history of humanity. The story of Eden, whatever else it may teach, asserts God's insistence on fidelity to a *small* trust. The conditions imposed on our first parents were not complicated nor burdensome: they were but to let one tree alone. That simple condition they did not meet. Put in trust with the tree of knowledge, they betrayed their trust; and is it too much to say that the loyalty which could not bear so small a strain was a feeble sentiment? that this little act of eating a fruit showed the man's unfitness for a dominion founded in loyalty to God quite as decisively as a greater and noisier act would have done? Let us beware of flattering ourselves that we will be loyal to God in great issues, even though we may not be in smaller ones. The moral quality which determines the smaller issue will determine the greater one. Our Lord leaves us in no doubt on this point: "He that is faithful in a very little is faithful also in much: and he that is unrighteous in a very little is unrighteous also in much;" and that is the principle which you frankly accept in your dealings with men. Unfaithfulness in the smallest work, in the lowest sphere, is no recommendation for promotion. You do not choose for foreman of your establishment the man who has been doing slovenly work in a lower place. If your clerk has stolen a dime, you will not make him your cashier. It is not a question of quantity, but of quality. You do not consider *how much* he stole, but *that* he stole. It is quite enough for you to know that he will steal, and the dime brings out the fact quite as well as a thousand dollars. In the kingdom of God, nothing is small, nothing is insignificant. The few things take their character from the many things; the talents are of a piece with the joy of the Lord; the pounds and the cities are under one economy. If the joy and the cities are great and significant things, they make the single talents great and significant.

We cannot insist too much on the truth that no act or thought of ours stands by itself. We say, "This is a little transgression, or a little omission;" but we forget how the thing may be magnified by its connections. The handle of the throttle-valve on that locomotive is a small piece of iron, much smaller than the pistons or the driving-wheels; and that reckless lad climbing upon the engine might say, "This piece of iron is so small that it will not matter if I pull it;" but, at the first touch, the steam hisses, and the wheels begin to revolve, and he is carried helplessly down the track. Our contact in this world is not with whole things. We touch extremities, or sides of them; and how far back the things themselves run, how many branchings and connections they have, we do not and can not know. The neglect or the fault which we call little may be as the end of a slow match connecting with a magazine. No matter how little, how few, the things we have to deal with, fidelity is the only insurance.

Hence, the Bible emphasizes small trusts. The tragedy of this parable, and a terrible one it is, centres in the servant who had but one talent. The smaller your trust, the less your ability, the greater is the call for care and watchfulness, because a peculiar temptation attaches to small endowment.[1] There is not even a plausible excuse for neglecting a great trust; but it is one of the commonest of things for people to neglect their gifts, and let them run to waste because they are small. You notice, that, in the parable, the man with the one talent is the only one of the three who is represented as under temptation to neglect. If your boy has a present of ten dollars, he is easily persuaded to put it by as the nucleus of a hundred. It is not hard for him to see that it is a good piece of a hundred. But if he has a quarter of a dollar, he will say, "I may as well spend that." He does not see that the quarter is part of the hundred as well as the ten. The quarter has just as real and definite a relation to the hundred as the ten. Even so, the commonplace man, the man who thinks he does not count, the small talent, the scant power to speak or act or plan, — have just as real and just as definite a relation to the great economy of the kingdom of God as the most brilliant array of gifts. That fact of itself settles the question of duty. That fact of itself enjoins faithfulness. That fact of itself justifies God in rebuking and punishing the servant who hides his single talent in a

---

[1] See Drummond's *Natural Law in the Spiritual World*.

napkin. It has been well said, that, "It is just the men whose capital seems small who need to choose the best investment. It is those who belong to the rank and file of life who need this warning most."

Once more, observe *that the parable fixes our attention less upon the work than upon the worker;* or, perhaps we might better say, upon the work *through* the worker. As we have said, the lesson turns on the question of quality; and the quality, faithfulness, is imparted by the servant. The satisfaction of the master lies, not in the fact that his five talents have grown into ten, but in that the increase is due to his servant's faithfulness. In God's eyes, the best and highest result of work is a good worker. I think, that, in our ordinary interpretations of this parable, we are in some danger of overlooking this, and of laying the emphasis on the development of *power* rather than on the development of *character*. We say, "The servant made the best of his power, and the result was correspondingly large." We draw the practical lesson, "The more faithfully you use your talents, the more you will accomplish." We perhaps tend to forget that it is the moral quality of the user that gives character to the result; that a smaller result, as the outcome of faithfulness, is more in God's eyes than a larger one without it; that to God there is no large result, no good result, without faithfulness; that God demands interest on character no less than on endowment, and that interest on endowment counts for nothing without interest on character; that quality fixes the rate of interest on quantity. We may go into the other world with the reputation of great or brilliant or efficient men. It will count for nothing if we are not also *good* men. But it is also true that the servant's faithfulness sets its own mark upon his work, and gives all results a new and higher character. An engineer puts some pounds of dynamite into a mountain, and blasts open a tunnel. It is a great result, but it is a mere material result. We all know what dynamite can do, and we think only of a powerful material agent overcoming a given resistance. But, when a Washington has conquered freedom for his country, it is more than a matter of cannon and musketry. It is a matter of moral ideas, of holy passion and patriotism and self-devotion and fidelity to a few things, and courage and loyalty — all set their mark upon armies and battles and munitions and glorify them. These fearful material forces, with their ghastly results, are lifted into the moral sphere. In the library of a well-known gentleman of wealth and culture and large social influence, might be seen, enclosed in a glass case, a common brick. It told the story of his first step in life. He was a journeyman bricklayer, and that was the first brick he ever laid; and, from the eminence of his fame and fortune, he had gone back to the old house where he began his career of faithful industry, and had brought back its first result. Only an ordinary brick, like millions of others: but you do not need to be told what it was that made it more than a common mass of clay, that made it a symbol of faithfulness; that took that commonplace thing, and brought it into harmony with all that environment of culture and refinement and religion, and made it seem not out of place in the company of books and pictures and statues, and that linked it with an honorable manhood spent in the service of God and humanity. Faithfulness brings out strange relationships between things apparently most remote, between the material and the spiritual, between the few things and the joy of the Lord. Faithfulness alone glorifies power.

Thus, this parable turns on moral quality rather than on ability. Its keynote is not five talents, nor two talents, nor one talent, but faithfulness to all three. It is faithfulness, and not amount, which links the talent to the joy of the Lord, the few things to the many. The amount of ability is not the first thing for you and me to consider: it is the faithful use of whatever ability we have. To use aright, we must *be* right. Vigorous use of talent is not necessarily right use, for unfaithfulness is vigorous also. Whatever legitimate joy shall ever come to a servant from his talents, will come through the Master's word: " Well done, good and faithful servant." Beware of despising any talent, however small. It comes to you out of heaven. It is God's trust to you. It is linked with the great economy of the kingdom of God by lines which your eye cannot follow. You cannot prophesy a small result from its neglect on the ground that it is a small talent. God turns you persistently away from the question of quantity or amount, and fastens your eyes on one paramount fact — faithfulness. You have but a few things, but one talent; none the less he says, "Be faithful." You will do well to study the fate of him who neglected his single talent.

I am reminded of more than one illustration of faithful service and inherited joy as I call up the faces which have vanished from these familiar scenes of worship, and especially this morning, as my eye rests on yonder beautiful memorial of a beautiful and faithful life,[1] the gift of bereaved love to this church, which shared so largely in the rich ministries of that life. The life itself, it is true, needs no visible reminder to perpetuate its power and memory. It has left its abiding record and its abiding influence in your hearts and on your church-work. It glows there with richer hues than those through which God's sunlight streams to-day; but none the less the memorial will serve through many coming years to point the lesson of to-day, as the sunlight shall bring out the name of a good and faithful servant, who, through simple faithfulness, brought full interest out of large endowment, and, having laid it all at the foot of the cross, entered into the joy of her Lord.

---

[1] A memorial window placed on the north side of the Church of the Covenant to the memory of Mrs. Nancy McKeen Lewis by her husband, Dr. Charlton T. Lewis.

VIII.

EXTRA SERVICE.

VIII.

EXTRA SERVICE.

"But who is there of you having a servant ploughing or keeping sheep, that will say unto him, when he is come in from the field, Come straightway and sit down to meat; and will not rather say unto him, Make ready wherewith I may sup, and gird thyself, and serve me, till I have eaten and drunken; and afterward thou shalt eat and drink? Doth he thank the servant because he did the things that were commanded? Even so ye also, when ye shall have done all the things that are commanded you, say, We are unprofitable servants; we have done that which it was our duty to do." — LUKE xvii. 7-10.

ARE these indeed the words of Him who said, "Henceforth I call you not servants, but friends"? This is a picture of a hard, unlovely side of life, — a slave's life and a slave's service, without thanks or claim for thanks. A slave has been ploughing or keeping sheep all day. He has done his full day's work, and is tired and hungry; but, when he comes back to the house, he finds that his work is not done yet. He cannot sit down, and refresh himself: he must wait upon the master at his meal first. After that he may sit down. Does the master give him any thanks for his service at the table — his *extra* service above his day's ploughing or shepherding? Not so, indeed, says our Lord. The slave is his own; he has a right to his service anywhere and everywhere, in hours or out of hours. Even so, he continues, when ye, servants of God, have done all that is commanded you, say, " We are unprofitable servants; we have only done our duty; we have no title to thanks or reward, no matter how hard we work."

We ask, I repeat, and not unnaturally, where such a representation of Christian service fits into that sweet and attractive ideal which Christ elsewhere gives us under the figure of the family relation, — sons of God, confidential friends of Christ. Does this picture of slavish service, hard duty, and no thanks belong to these?

We hasten to say, No; but it will require a little study to discover why we may say no, and to fix the place of this parable in relation to others of a happier tone.

In the first place, you observe that it is not unusual for our Lord to draw a disagreeable picture in order to set forth his own love and grace. What a type of hard, selfish cruelty is that unjust judge, for example : " I will hear the widow, in order to be rid of her. I will do what she asks me because she troubles me, and for fear that she may weary me to death." Is this like God? No. If the unjust judge can be moved by earnest and persistent appeal, shall not the just God be moved by the cry of his own chosen ones? Or, to take another case, is God like the churlish man who refuses to give his neighbor bread because the door is shut, and he is in bed? Nay, if the churlish neighbor will yield to importunity, and rise, and give his friend as many loaves as he needs, will not God honor the importunate faith which besieges his doors, even though, to test it, he delays for a while? His delay is only the prelude to his rising, and giving like a God.

We must not be repelled by a figure, therefore. But, then, there are the words, "even so ye also," which compel us to recognize in this parable some features of our relation to God. The parable does not say that God deals with his servants as a master does with a slave, yet it may nevertheless express some facts and conditions of Christian service. Let us try to see what these are.

The parable answers to the fact in being a picture of hard work, and of what we call *extra* work. The servant is all day at the plough or in the pasture, and after a full day's work has the extra duty of serving at table, without regard to his own hunger or weariness. The service of God's kingdom is laborious service, — service crowded with work and burdens. Christ nowhere represents it as easy. When Christ says his yoke is easy, he does not mean that there is no pressure from it, and that it is borne without labor. The word "easy" is, rather, "good," "wholesome," "profitable." Daily experience shows us that the highest Christian service involves the most labor, and it also reveals that feature of Christian service to which this parable calls our attention, — the element of extra service, service not limited by times and measures. Its calls come at all times. The master appears at midnight, at morning, or at cockcrow. The servant is to be always ready, with his loins girded. No Christian can shut himself up to a little routine of duty, and say, I will do so much, within such times, and no more. When a flower stands out in the open field, with its great rich petals outspread to the sun, it is not visited only by certain bees which come at stated hours to suck its sweetness. These come, indeed, and fly away loaded with sweets; but the dragon-fly wheels round it with his gauzy wings, the humming-bird thrusts his beak into its crimson cup, the spider fastens his web on the stalk, and swarms of busy flies light upon the petals. Its perfume and its honey are common property. So, when a Christian stands in the field of Christian service, his heart open to God's call, his life distilling the perfume of holy love, he cannot keep his services upon one line or within certain times. Demands for ministry swarm over the lines he may have drawn; outstretched hands are thrust forth from unsuspected corners; voices arise from places given over to silence; his hands are always full. If he begins with a scheme of duties and times, the feeble hands of sickness and want will throw his scheme into confusion, or keep him constantly enlarging it. Take the life of Paul, and see if you can compress it within any lines of routine, or measure out its labors, so much per day, or its rest, so many hours out of the twenty-four. Or look at the life of our Lord, how it abounds in this element of work out of season! It was the hour of rest when he sat at Jacob's well, and we are expressly told that he was weary; yet with what ardor he threw himself into the interview with the Samaritan woman. So, when from sheer exhaustion he had fallen asleep in the fishers' boat, he must rise at the call of the frightened disciples, and quiet the sea and their terror. If he went across the lake to seek for rest, the multitude took shipping, and followed him. When evening fell, he must feed the five thousand to whom he had been speaking. Wherever he walks, some man or woman with a sick child beseeches his aid, some blind man or cripple cries, " Have mercy on me ! " if he sits at meat, some outcast comes, and appeals to his pity.

And this is not peculiar to Christian service. It is a law of all work of a higher type, that it oversteps mere methodical limits. It is only work of a mechanical kind that is confined to specific times and prescribed duties. The nearer you get to machine work, the more this characteristic asserts itself. The machine turns round just so many times in a minute; a cog raises a lever just so often : there are no surprises about a steam-engine or a mowing-machine; we know exactly what they can do in a given time : and, the lower the type of work, the more of the machine character it takes on — so many hours for so much; just such a result for so many pounds of steam. You often hear it said of this or that man, " he is a mere machine : he simply obeys specific orders at given times." The man who makes the fires and sweeps the office of that statesman comes at a certain hour in the morning, does his round of duties, and goes away; comes again at a given hour, feeds the fires, and goes away again. Nothing more is asked or expected of him. There is nothing in him or in his work which carries it over these lines; but the statesman cannot work in that way. To-day a consultation breaks into his routine, a state paper keeps him at his desk until far into the night; to-morrow a cabinet-meeting or a debate takes out a great piece of his time. I have heard a man in this city remark, that, if his regular routine work — which most people would think quite enough — were all he had to do, he should feel quite like a man of leisure. The outside irregular work had assumed such proportions as almost to dwarf the regular duties. So long as a man's work is merely the carrying out of another's orders, it will tend to be mechanical and methodical: but the moment the man becomes identified in spirit with his work; the moment the work becomes the evolution of an idea, the expression of a definite and cherished purpose; the moment it becomes the instrument of individual will, sympathy, affection; above all, the moment it takes on the character of a passion or an enthusiasm, — that moment it overleaps mechanical trammels. The lawyer is not counting the number of hours which duty compels him to work. He would make each day forty-eight hours long if he could. He has a case to gain, and that is all he thinks of. The physician who should refuse to answer a summons from his bed at the dead of night, or to visit a patient after a certain hour of the day, would soon have abundance of leisure. Pain will not measure its intervals by the clock, fever will not suspend its burning heats to give the weary watcher rest: the affliction of the fatherless and widow knocks at the doors of pure and undefiled religion at untimely hours. Times and seasons, in short, must be swallowed up in the purpose of saving life and relieving misery.

I need not carry the illustrations farther. You see that the lower a type of service, the more mechanical and methodical it is; and that the higher types of service develop a certain exuberance, and refuse to be limited by times and seasons.

A second point at which the fact answers to the parable, is the matter of wages; that is to say, the slave and the servant of Christ have neither of them any *right* to thanks or compensation. What God may do for his servants out of his own free grace and love, what privileges he may grant his friends, is another question; but, on the hard *business* basis of value received, the servant of God has no case. What he does in God's service it is his duty to do. The Romish doctrine of works of supererogation — special services or sacrifices meriting special compensation — has no warrant in Scripture. The man's largest services, those which take most from his legitimate leisure and rest, go into the general reckoning as duty. In reading the parable, put the emphasis on the word *servants*. We are unprofitable servants. As servants we can render no service that is not *due*. In the eleventh of Romans we read, "who hath first given to him (God), and it shall be recompensed unto him again?" "God," as Bengel remarks, "can do without our usefulness." God has no necessary men. "Doth he thank the servant because he did the things that were commanded? I trow not. Even so ye also, when ye shall have done all the things that are commanded you, say, We are unprofitable servants; we have done that which it was our duty to do."

Now, then, we reach the pith of the parable. It is spoken from the slave's point of view, it deals with service of the lower, mechanical type; and you find the key to it in the master's command to the slave to do an additional service at his table, after he has already completed a full day's work. Our Lord treats the subject from this lower point of view, that he may warn us away from that type of service, and direct us to a nobler one, in which that which appears to the slave as extra service ceases to be regarded as such, and is taken cheerfully into the larger and more generous conception of duty as part and parcel of it. It is only the servile, mechanical worker, in other words, to whom extra service has any existence. In Christ's real friends, the desire for service outruns the ability. Just as the lawyer and doctor regard their unexpected calls and the infringements on their hours of refreshment or rest as features of their work, never thinking of them as impositions or extra burdens; so the Christian's highest conception of service includes all the calls to the ministry which lies outside any scheme of labor and rest. This exuberance of work, this constant "finding of the hand" interjected into the daily routine, this working "double tides," this bearing another's and yet another's burden beside his own, — all fall under the accepted law of his life. To a man who accepts this view of Christian service, the parable is not addressed. It has no application to him. He is working on a different and a higher basis. The point of impulse is shifted from a mere schedule of duties to his own sympathy with Christ's purposes. Behind service is the trust of a masterful enthusiasm, and not the stricture of a time-table. Overflow is its law. Service on the lower plane of our parable is like that waterfall in the Catskills, shut in by a floodgate, and made to play to order. It is a thing of regulated quantities and intervals. Service on the higher plane is like Niagara, with the pressure of deep, exhaustless Erie crowding it onward without rest. It cuts tracks for itself, it spreads out round the green islands, it boils through the narrow canals, it leaps and races in rapids towards the final plunge, and its mist and thunder arise forever. You might as well attempt to concentrate Niagara upon a single millwheel as to keep the Christ-like impulse to service within the lines of mechanical routine, and of stated times and seasons. That service is as exuberant and varied as it is constant. No jealous floodgates shut down between it and opportunity. Christ's friend does not fence off from the claims of service a section of rights to rest and leisure. He would as soon think of forbidding his neighbor to enter his own house or orchard. He is not his own; his heritage is not his; his life is a practical assent to the truth which Paul so forcibly puts to the Corinthians: "Ye are God's tilled land: ye are God's building." And therefore God's claims have the free and full range of his time and of his powers.

I would that there were more of this rich, spontaneous overflow in the Christian life of to-day. We may not look for the luxuriance of the South-American forest under our colder skies. Our trees and shrubs are cleaner in outline and less lavish in foliage and flower; but our piety need not be subject to any such physical law. The sun of righteousness does not shine obliquely on any part of God's heritage, and we might well have more tropical exuberance in our religious life. I know that enthusiasm, is not necessarily boisterous or demonstrative. The deepest enthusiasm, like deep water, is often the stillest. But when a man is full of true enthusiasm, it will out, though he seldom open his lips. I remember that they used to have in houses what they called an air-tight stove. It was shut up on all sides. You could not see a spark of fire, but you felt it. It was all through the atmosphere of the room. If you touched it, you found there was fire in it; and once in a while it would get red-hot, and show fire. If there is fire, *God's* fire, in a man's soul, it may not sparkle nor roar, but it will make society feel it somehow. I am thankful for all the methodical, well-systematized work of religious societies and of the church; it is doing good. But I wish we could have these methodical lines set on fire. I wish there were more glow in our church-life. As I go about among people, I do not find them any too ready to speak of Christ and of his work. I go into house after house, and I hear all sorts of subjects talked about, but little of the church of Christ, its interests, and its work. Mere order is cold, rigid, and lifeless. You know how, one night in each year, the dome and front of St. Peter's at Rome are illuminated. All over the great curves of the dome, and along the columns and mouldings and balconies, the lines of lamps are drawn; but what a ghastly sight is this skeleton of lamps until, at the signal, every line of the mighty structure, from cross to foundation, leaps into living light! So it will be with our mechanical duties, our well-organized societies, our forms of worship, yea, our creeds and catechisms, unless the Spirit of Pentecost shall touch and set them ablaze. Oh, that there might come, as in Ezekiel's vision, the heavenly messenger, with hand filled with the coals of fire from between the cherubim, kindling all our hearts, and setting every line of our church-order aglow with heavenly love! Sometimes this rigid order, this systematic and punctilious distribution of duty, goes with a worldly half-heartedness, which metes out so much to Christ and his work, and says he shall have this, — so much time, so much money, — but he must not trench on my hours of rest and leisure. He must keep his hands from what I set aside for my indulgences and pleasures. When I have ploughed so many hours in the field, it is my right to sit down to meat, and be served. I must not be asked to gird myself, and serve him.

And the moment a man puts himself on that lower ground, and begins to measure out his times and degrees of service, and to reckon what is due to himself, that moment he runs sharply against this parable. That moment Christ meets his assertion of his rights with this unlovely picture. The parable says to him, in effect, "If you put the matter on the business basis, on the ground of your rights and merits, I meet you on that ground, and challenge you to make good your claim. I made you: I redeemed you, body and soul, with my own blood. Every thing you have or are, you owe to my free grace. What are your rights? What are your claims on me? What is your ground for refusing any claim I may see fit to make upon you? What claim have you for thanks for any service you may render me at any time?" And the man cannot complain of this answer. It is indeed the master's answer to a slave; but then, the man has put himself on the slave's ground. The other kind of servant, as I have said, has gotten out of the way of this parable. He raises no question of rights, claims, or wages. His thought is only of his master's rights. His kind of service involves more labor, and is met by gifts, not wages. That is the service of the widow who dropped her two mites into the treasury. The world would have justified her in holding back her last penny. Christ himself would not have been hard with her: but love gave its last and its best; and not the mites, but the love, has made her immortal. It is the service of her who poured the ointment on Christ's head. Even to the disciples, the gift seemed like waste. Less would have sufficed; but love's impulse could not rest until the flask was broken, and the whole precious contents bestowed on that adorable head: and hence it is, that, whenever this gospel is preached, the story of that woman's love is told.

And, on this higher basis of service, Christ's disciple meets with another class of sayings, quite different from this parable, — sayings which put him in a nearer and nobler relation to Christ, and which lift his work entirely out of the region of moral serfdom. Christ says to such, "Henceforth I call you not servants; for the servant knoweth not what his Lord doeth: but I have called you friends; for all things which I have received of my Father I have delivered unto you." To the servile spirit, Christ asserts his masterdom. He has no word of thanks for the grumbling slave who grudges the service at his table after the day's ploughing; but to the loving disciple, — the friend to whom his service is joy and reward enough, and who puts self and all its belongings at his disposal, — it is strange, wondrous strange, but true, nevertheless, *that Christ somehow slips into the servant's place.* Strange, I repeat; but here is Christ's own word for it: "Let your loins be girded about, and your lights burning." Here is a picture of night-work, you see. "And ye yourselves like unto men that wait for their lord, when he will return from the wedding; that when he cometh and knocketh, they may open unto him immediately." Here are the servants, weary, no doubt, with the day's work, but waiting and watching far into the hours of rest for their master, and flying with cheerful readiness to the door at his first knock. What then? "Blessed are those servants, whom the master when he cometh shall find watching: verily I say unto you, that *he shall gird himself, and make them to sit down to meat, and will come forth and serve them.*" The amount of the matter is, that for him who gives himself without reserve to Christ's service, Christ puts himself at his service. When he accepts Christ's right over him with his whole heart, not as a sentence to servitude, but as his dearest privilege, counting it above all price to be bought and owned by such a master, he finds himself a possessor as well as a possession: "All things are yours, and ye are Christ's." The things which master the slave are mastered by the friend. Fidelity is mastery. "Thou hast been faithful over a few things, I will make thee ruler over many things." Life, with its vicissitudes, instead of a burden to crush the man, or a current to carry him helplessly down, becomes his seat of power; all its chances and changes marshalled upon God's lines, and made to minister to spiritual power and peace and to future glory. "Death is yours." How wonderful! The king of terrors, who resistlessly siezes and carries away whom he will, is no more master but servant, standing humbled and chained as porter at the gate through which you pass to the court of the King Eternal. "Things present," — Christ's touch makes you master of them. They are yours, You are master of each day's trials and burdens. You mount on them a step nearer heaven, instead of being driven by them as with a whip of scorpions. "Things to come," — they trouble the servile heart. His outlook is dark. They cannot trouble him to whom Christ says, "I go to prepare a place for you, and I will come again, and receive you unto myself; that where I am, there ye may be also."

The two lines of service are before us. Which shall we choose? Wretched is he whom *the Lord* calls unprofitable servant. Happy he who calls *himself* so.

IX.

THE PRIDE OF CARE.

IX.

THE PRIDE OF CARE.

"Humble yourselves therefore under the mighty hand of God, that he may exalt you in due time;

"Casting all your anxiety upon him, because he careth for you." — 1 PETER v. 6, 7.

A MAN, digging among ruins, strikes a tile of an exquisite pattern. Its design seems complete in itself. He admires the graceful lines and the charming color, carries away his prize, and shows it with delight to his friends; but, when he goes back to the mine, behold! the workmen have laid bare a broad surface paved with similar tiles, and he finds that his specimen is only a fragment of a larger pattern. If he thought it beautiful by itself, how much more beautiful it is as a part of the larger design.

So it is with Scripture. Single texts it furnishes in multitudes, full of beauty, power, and comfort. But Scripture hangs together. It is a unit, and every text gains by being studied in its connections. The last verse of this passage, for example, is almost always quoted by itself: "Casting all your anxiety upon him, because he careth for you;" and, standing thus alone, it is full of blessed meaning and consolation; and yet, by separating it from the preceding verse, we lose a whole side of its teaching, and a very important side.

Nevertheless, it is not, perhaps, evident at once where these two verses fit into each other, — humble yourselves, and cast your anxiety on God. How does care demand humility?

The two parts of the text, taken together, state this truth: that anxiety carries with it a division of faith between God and self, — a lack of faith in God, proportioned to the amount of care which we refuse to cast on him; an excess of self-confidence, proportioned to the amount which we insist on bearing ourselves. If we refuse to let God carry for us what he desires and offers to carry, pride is at the bottom of the refusal. Therefore, the apostle says, "Humble yourselves under God's *mighty* hand. Confess the weakness of *your* hand. Do not try to carry the anxiety with your weak hand. Cast it all on him. Believe that he cares for you, and be humbly willing that he should care for you."

The revised version has brought out a very important distinction by the substitution of "anxiety" for "care." Anxiety, according to its derivation, is that which distracts and racks the mind, and answers better to the original word, which signifies a *dividing* thing, something which distracts the heart, and separates it from God. The word "*careth*," on the other hand, used of God ("he careth for you"), is a different word in the original, and means *supervising* and *fostering* care, loving interest, such care as a father has for a child. I want to show how the spirit which refuses to give up its dividing anxiety to God is allied to pride, and unbecoming a child in the household of a divine Father who cares for him.

Our Lord's Sermon on the Mount lays great stress on this. Over against the natural tendency to fear and disquietude, it sets the loving care of an almighty Father. He feeds and shelters the birds; he adorns the flowers; he is more ready to bless his children than earthly parents are to give good gifts to theirs. Meat, drink, raiment, — the man says he cannot live without them. "True," says Christ, "God knows that quite as well as you do. Your heavenly Father knoweth that ye have need of all these things. The surest way to have them is to trust in him. These things are included in his kingdom. Seek that, and all these things shall be added."

Yet men will say, and very plausibly, "The anxious man has some excuse." Take, for instance, a man in a position where many are depending on him for guidance or instruction, and where great interests are bound up with his success. It will be said, "It would be strange if he were not anxious." From the world's ordinary point of view, I should say so too. At any rate, he too often *is* anxious, careworn, living in a feverish scramble to overtake his work, haunted by the arrears of work. You honor his conscientiousness. So do I. You say it is unjust to find fault with him. I reply,

God finds fault with him, even while he honors his diligence and fidelity, — finds fault with him because he will not cast off his anxiety on God, who has offered to relieve him of it. Is that unjust on the part of our Father? If so, you are guilty of similar injustice. Your little son is taken sick, and is unable to prepare his lesson for to-morrow's school. He is worried and disappointed; he is anxious to excel; he is high up in his class, and wants to keep his place. You say to him, "Dismiss all care about that. I will make it right with the teacher." And you have a right to expect that the boy will be satisfied with that; that he will take you at your word, and trouble himself no more about the lesson. And if, in the course of an hour, you find him worrying about it, are you not annoyed, and displeased with him? Do you not say to him, "You ought to have more confidence in me"?

Pride, I say, — subtle, unconscious pride, — is at the bottom of much of this restlessness and worry. The man has come to think himself too important, to feel that the burden is on his shoulders only; and that, if he stands from under, there must be a crash. And, just to the degree in which that feeling has mastered him, his thought and faith have become divided from God. Let us give him his due. It is not for his own ease or reputation that he has been caring. It is for his work. And yet he has measurably forgotten, that, if his work be of God, God is as much interested in his success as he himself can be; and that God will carry on his own work, no matter how many workmen he buries. He divides the burden, and shows whom he trusts most by taking the larger part himself, when God bids him cast it *all* on him. God, indeed, exempts nobody from work. We may cast our *anxiety*, but not our *work*, on him. A sense of responsibility is a brace to manhood, and a developer of power; and, because God wants work and responsibility to re-act healthfully on men, he wants them to work with a hearty, joyous spirit. When the joy and the enthusiasm have gone out of work, something is wrong. There is a pithy proverb that "not work, but worry, kills men." God is providing for man's doing his work most efficiently when he offers him the means of doing it joyfully by casting all anxiety on him.

There are few men in responsible positions who have not felt the force of a distinguished Englishman's words: "I divide my work into three parts. One part I do, one part goes undone, and the third part does itself." That third part which does itself is a very expressive hint as to the needlessness of our fretting about at least one-third of our work, besides giving a little puncture to our self-conceit by showing, that, to one-third of our work, we are not quite as necessary as we had thought ourselves. And as to the third, which the God-fearing man cannot do, and which therefore goes, or seems to go, undone, there is a further hint that possibly that third is better undone, or is better done in some other way and by some other man. That does not flatter our pride. I am very sure that it is always true for every faithful Christian worker, that whatever he cannot do, after having done his best, it is better that he should not do. And just there is where the humility comes in, — in the frank and cheerful acceptance of the fact, in casting all care about it on the Lord, and in not worrying and growing irritated over it. Says a modern preacher, "I love to work, but I have carried all my life long a sense that the work was so vast that no man, I did not care who he was, could do more than a very little; that he who could raise up children from the stones to Abraham, could raise up men when he had a mind to, and men of the right kind, and put them in the right place; that, after all, the Lord was greater than the work, and that it was of no use for me to fret myself, and set myself up to be wiser than Providence. All I was called upon to do was to work up to the measure of my wisdom and strength, and to be willing to go wherever God sent me; and that then I was to be content."

A good deal of our energy is expended in planning; and, when our plan is once made, we set our life on that track, and it runs with an ever-increasing momentum. We do not relish a collision or a delay. Insensibly we fall into the way of assuming that success in life means simply the success of our plan. Do we bethink ourselves, that, if our plan is best in God's eyes, he is as much interested in carrying it out as we are? If it is not best in his eyes, surely we do not want it carried out. Either way we may safely and restfully leave it with God. If we are determined to carry it out anyway, and are irritated at obstacles and delays, is that any thing but pride? Are we so sure our plan is right, so proud of our pet project, that we must torment ourselves if God does not pet and foster it as we do? Oh, how afraid we are that our poor earthen vessels will go to pieces! Possibly we have forgotten how God once defeated his people's enemies by means of the breaking of vessels. What fools those three hundred of Gideon would have been if their attention had been absorbed in keeping their pitchers unbroken; and especially if, at the command to break the pitchers, they had said, "What a shame to spoil so much good earthenware!" They would have saved their pitchers, but would have lost their victory. A pitcher for a victory, a plan for a success, fine strategy on paper for conquest, — a poor exchange, surely.

It is right for us to make plans; but we ought to draw them as we draw the first draught of a plan for a new house, in lines that can be easily rubbed out if God so please. Pride gets into these plans before we know it. We think we want God's work to succeed, and so we do; only, we want it to succeed in our way, and on the line of our plan. And yet not seldom God brings about the very result we are working for, by breaking our plan all to pieces. Then comes the test of our humility. Are we content to cast the whole matter on God, and to look cheerfully on the fragments of our plan? Are we humble enough not to feel grieved or angry because God chooses somebody or something else to do the same work? Sometimes God lets us see how much better the work is done by the breaking of our plan. The forty years among the mountain solitudes seemed to Moses, perhaps, lost time; but that slow, tedious ripening gave Israel a leader and a law-giver. The next forty years yielded rich interest on the sad monotony of the previous forty. It seemed to Jacob that every thing was against him when Joseph was stolen away. He could not see that Joseph had been sent to prepare a home for his old age, and to lay the foundations of a nation which should bear his name. It seemed as though the church could not spare Paul when he was shut up in prison, but the church of to-day has the four epistles of the imprisonment from that chained hand.

A young lady had consecrated herself to the work of missions, and was about to go to India. Just at that point, an accident disabled her mother, and the journey had to be deferred. For three years she ministered at that bedside, until the mother died, leaving as her last request that she should go and visit her sick sister in the far West. She went, intending to sail for India immediately on her return; but she found the sister dying with comsumption, and without proper attendance: and once more she waited until the end came. Again her face was turned eastward, when the sister's husband died, and five little orphans had no soul on earth to care for them but herself. "No more projects for going to the heathen," she wrote. "This lonely household is my mission." Fifteen years she devoted to her young charge; and, in her forty-fifth year, God showed her why he had held her back from India, as she laid her hand in blessing on the heads of three of them ere they sailed as missionaries to the same land to which, twenty years before, she had proposed to go. Her broken plan had been replaced by a larger and a better one. One could not go, but three went in her stead: a good interest for twenty years.

But there is a class of cases where anxiety is clearly prompted by self-interest, vanity, and worldly ambition. Self cannot cast such anxiety on God, because God will not take it. When God bids us humble ourselves, he surely will not minister to our pride. He will not stretch out a finger to lighten the burdens of sensitive vanity, or to save pride from a fall. If you are aiming, for instance, merely to make a show in society, without regard to solid worth or usefulness; if you are harassed with care in keeping up your sham, and with fear lest some one may see through it, — you *dare* not cast that care on God. You know very well, that, if you put such a thing as that into his hand, he will break it to pieces. So you will have to carry that burden all alone, if you insist on carrying it. You know that if you cast your care on God, you will have to humble yourself; and to be humbled is the very thing you are most afraid of. If you are making such mad haste to be rich that all the sweetness has gone out of your life, if you are in hot pursuit of the superfluities of this world, and are leaving behind you in the chase Christian charity and Christian duty and Christian worship, do you think God is going to lighten your burdens so that you can go faster after your end? Nay, I challenge you to cast that care on God. You will not do it. You know that God has no sympathy with it. If you will convert yourself into a coining-press, you need not expect God to help it run smoothly when your faith and your domestic affection, and all your best possibilities, are run into dollars. It is hard enough work, as you know, — harder and drier than God would have chosen for you; but you must do it alone. Care which will not humble itself under his hand, he will not touch. It is not an easy thing that the text urges. If it were merely to throw off trouble of all kinds on God, that might not be so hard. But God does not hold out his arms to our burdens unconditionally: he is willing to take the *burden* on his hand, if *we ourselves* will come and stay under his hand, not otherwise. He refuses to take the care without the self. If we will put the self into his hand absolutely, he will take it, care and all. But many a one would like to cast the care on God, and keep the self in his own hand. The text does not mean merely the laying down of *wearied* heads on a fatherly arm, but the voluntary stooping of *proud* heads. Casting all our care on God is casting *self* on God, for self is our worst care. It is not merely coming to God with our failures, and asking him to make them good, but it is confessing also that our unaided self is the worst failure of all, and saying frankly to our heavenly Father, "Without thee I can do nothing."

God has different ways of teaching this lesson. You know how a schoolmaster will sometimes shut himself up with a dull pupil, and hold him down to a problem. So God sometimes shuts a man up with himself and his own helplessness. Even then he does not force the man's will; but he means that he shall for once look squarely at the impotence of self, that he shall for once face and confess to himself the fact that self has exhausted its resources, that the world cannot help him, that he has nothing in heaven or earth but God. That, as men see it, is a terrible blow to pride. The bitterest draught that ever a man is called on to drink is the confession that he cannot help himself. The world says, a man is at his worst then. I am not sure of that. The Bible would say that he is just within reach of his best. I heard a little story the other day, which was very suggestive. An old Scotch woman was on a steamer in the Northern Atlantic, and was in a continual worry lest there should be a storm. The wind and the sea began to rise; and she besieged the captain with questions about the probabilities of disaster, until, becoming a little impatient, he solemnly said, "Well, madam, I think we shall have to trust in the Lord." "Oh!" cried she, "*has it come to that?*" It is the simple, spontaneous utterance of human unbelief, when it is thrown on God alone. Has it come to that? Then, indeed, we are in evil case. Paul did not think so, however. He was in that situation during most of his life; and he really seemed to think that the situation was not only not hopeless, but commanding: "If God be for us, who can be against us?" There was Elijah. God drove him into the wilderness, where, for any thing he could do, he must perish. But he did not perish. God made the ravens his purveyors, and caused the brook to flow for his refreshment. Then the brook dried up. He had no water, but he had God; and, at the critical moment, came God's word: "Go to Zarephath; I have commissioned a widow to feed thee." She was at the gate when the prophet came, but the prospect was not encouraging. She was gathering sticks to bake her last handful of meal, and there was a son to take the small share which the prophet might have had; and what mother's heart could hesitate between her child and a stranger? Elijah might have trusted the evidence of his senses, and have despaired, instead of casting all care for the matter on God; but he can even ask the famishing mother to bring him the first share of the wretched repast, knowing that the barrel and the cruse were in the hand of Him who maketh the valleys stand thick with corn, and the face of His people to shine though the labor of the olive fail. There were those three Hebrews. Look into the blazing mouth of that seven-fold heated furnace, and at those three men lying bound, and tell me what is there for them but death. They needed no mocking king nor courtiers to tell them they could not help themselves. Self and all were in God's hands. The case could not be worse as men saw it; and yet, in fact, the case was at its best. They had nothing but God; but they had in God the best that man or angel could have: the flame burned their bonds, but not them; and they rose, and walked in the fire; and the amazed spectators saw a fourth walking with them, and his form was like unto the Son of God.

But let us give a moment to the latter part of the text. The result of this humbling of self, and throwing it with its anxiety on God, is quite contrary to human logic. The world says, the man who is humbled is the crushed man, the defeated man. The world is right, if the man is simply crushed into submission by overwhelming power; but the world is quite wrong if the man has voluntarily bowed the high head of his pride, and has cheerfully yielded up his will with his care to God. Such humbling, if Scripture is to be believed, is the way to exaltation: "He that humbleth himself shall be exalted." You see something of the same kind in ordinary matters. Now and then you find a man with more conceit than ability, with more self-confidence than resources, who attempts to lead a great movement, or to conduct a great business; and the very position brings out his weakness; and the longer he stays in it, the more useless and dangerous he is, and the more men say he is a fool and a weakling. And yet not a few men have had the sense or the grace to see the true state of the case in time, and to swallow pride, and frankly to confess weakness by retiring from a place for which they were unfit. From that moment they began to rise. They never rose to the high position which they coveted at first, but they rose to a *true* position, which they could hold; and that was really higher than the false position which they could not hold. They became respectable and useful men, doing good work in lower places, and winning esteem and honor; while, if they had held on to the higher place, as pride prompted, they would have won simply contempt and impotence. What is true in some cases in society is true always of men in relation to God. The man is always in a false position, a position he cannot fill, when he ignores God, and tries to take care of himself. He is a larger man, a better man, a more efficient man, by humbling himself under God's hand, and letting God take care of him. He escapes, I repeat, his worst, most consuming anxiety, by escaping from self. In humbling himself under God's hand, care slips off with self; and surely a man is in a better condition to rise when he is lightened of his anxiety: he is in lighter marching-order. All other things being equal, he does better and more effective work when he works joyously. There is a good deal of good, solid work, I know, done by men who work under pressure, and with much burden of care. Sometimes, as I look at such, I am reminded of Dante's vision of those who toiled along their gloomy way, with head and shoulders bent under the weight of leaden cloaks. The leaden cloaks are not for children of God and believers in Christ: "My yoke is easy, and my burden is light." We shall have true exaltation, lighter hearts, better work done, more mastery over the world, less sensitiveness to the shocks of time and change, — by humbly putting our lives into God's hands. While we hold by self, we hold by care. The self which we fondly think is our buoy is really the weight which is sinking us. We lay to circumstances and to providences much that is really the outcome of nothing but our pride.

And note another thing: the exaltation promised here will not come at once: "He shall exalt you *in due time*." This pride of self is a stubborn thing, and will not yield without a struggle; and you may depend that God will bring us sooner or later to a definite issue and a hard fight with self. We shall have to face the question, whether we will trust self, and live in constant irritation and fear because our own plans have come short or our own efforts have failed, or because we have not won the position or the gains we had marked out; or whether we will cut the whole matter short by saying, "I am in God's hands: let him give me and do with me as seemeth good to him." That issue, I say, we have to fight through: there is no going round it. We are like ships in an ice-pack. There is clear and deep water beyond; but there is no reaching it except by breaking through and settling the question, whether we will trust self, or

God. We may stay if we will, and let the ice of pride and self-will draw closer until it freezes out the life of God in us. We may, with God's help, work through into the clear water, and set sail, and look back with triumph as we see the bristling mass of cares lying like a dark cloud on the far horizon: "He shall exalt you in due time." Read on a little farther in this same chapter, and you find that thought again: "The God of all grace, who hath called us unto his eternal glory by Christ Jesus, after that ye have suffered a while, make you perfect, stablish, strengthen, settle you." Ah! that is exaltation indeed: security, steadfastness, mastery over that which burdens the world, peace which the world cannot give nor take away.

If there are any of us here so burdened with anxiety that it has pressed nearly all the sweetness out of life, let us consider. Perhaps we think ourselves subjects for compassion. We may be; but let us look, and see if we may not be subjects for repentance.

Possibly we cannot cast off care because we will not cast off pride. Lay the whole burden of care on God, if with it you will lay self. Ask yourself if you are willing to be any thing or nothing, as God pleases. Only work hard, do your best, consecrate your work with prayer; and then feel that you may be restful and quiet, and leave every thing with God.

So with the care which comes about your growth in grace, comes out of the stubbornness of sin, comes out of your feeling that you make such little headway in the fight with evil. Christ came that you might lay your sin on him. Because of your weakness, he shall lead you to the rock which is higher than you. He bids you do full justice to his tenderness, and prove his mercy. Yes, —

" There's a wideness in God's mercy
Like the wideness of the sea:
There's a kindness in his justice
Which is more than liberty.

There is plentiful redemption
In the blood that has been shed:
There is joy for all the members
In the sorrows of their head.

For the love of God is broader
Than the measure of man's mind,
And the heart of the Eternal
Is most wonderfully kind.

If our love were but more simple,
We should take him at his word ;
And our lives would be all sunshine
In the sweetness of our Lord."

X.
THE PLOUGH AND THE KINGDOM.

X.

THE PLOUGH AND THE KINGDOM.

" But Jesus said unto him, No man, having put his hand to the plough, and looking back, is fit for the kingdom of God." — LUKE ix. 62.

IF you can dismiss from your minds the figure of the modern farmer, with his polished ploughshare leaving the deep, clean furrow in its wake, and put in its place the figure out of which Jesus made this little picture, — the Eastern ploughman doubled over the pointed stick which serves as a plough, — you will see at once how vividly the absurdity of a man's ploughing and looking behind him at the same time would have impressed Christ's hearers. Even a modern ploughman, with the best modern plough, will make sad work if he do not keep his eyes straight before him. Anyway, that is true of ploughing which is true of any other kind of work. One whose interest is half in front and half behind him will be only a half-way man in any thing to which he may set his hand. All good work requires concentration. No good work is done into which a man does not throw himself wholly.

This picture of a slouching ploughman is the

form into which our Lord throws the lesson of to-day, — a lesson which is not confined to the text, but which runs through the entire section, from the fifty-seventh verse to the end of the chapter.

What this lesson is, will appear as we briefly review the contents of the section. Our Lord was about to take his final departure from Galilee. As he walked, a man approached him. Luke says, "a certain man;" and Matthew says he was a "scribe." However that may be, he was, like so many others, moved powerfully by the words and works and personal magnetism of Christ; and he conceived a desire to become one of his followers. Accordingly he volunteered his services: "I will follow thee whithersoever thou goest." I think some of us, at least, have begun to see what a very serious proposal that was. It is no light matter to commit one's self to follow such a master as Christ whithersoever he may go, for the shrewdest man can never predict what direction Christ will take. The most sincere and self-consecrated man will always have an element of surprise in his walk after Christ; for the simple reason, that Christ will lead him in God's ways and in God's kingdom, which is full of surprises, and where he will find out, if he did not realize it before, that God's ways are not his ways.

Evidently no such thought as this had occurred to this enthusiastic volunteer. If it had, he might have hesitated. Peter, Christ's own disciple, after a long acquaintance with the Lord, and knowing that he was going to prison and to judgment, said very much the same thing as this person; but his enthusiasm oozed out by the time he reached the court of the judgment-hall; and he staid behind, and denied his Lord. This man had conceived of no difficulty in the case, — at least, of none which he was not persuaded of his own ability to surmount.

Christ loves enthusiasm, even if it is not wise. Calculation sometimes takes the breath out of enthusiasm. That young man who came to him, asking, " What shall I do that I may inherit eternal life ?" had not counted the cost. Yet Jesus loved him. Christ is drawn to the man who is kindled by him. Even the unintelligent impulse of him who does not count the cost, is in the right direction. That enthusiasm is an invaluable element of Christian power if it can only be somehow perpetuated in a life of steady service and self-denial. If it can be wedded to solid conviction and settled purpose, it will carry every thing before it.

Nevertheless, our Lord will not let a man enter his service without a full knowledge of its conditions. The man shall never have it to say that he was entrapped into sacrifices and labors upon which he did not count. You will all recall our Saviour's words about the building of a house, and the going out to war without counting the cost; and the same thing comes out in his reply to this volunteer: " Follow me if you will; only remember that, in taking my part, you take the part of one who does not fare as well as the foxes or the birds — the part of a wandering, homeless man, with no definite position. The foxes have holes, and the birds have nests, but the Son of man hath not where to lay his head. If you come with me, you identify yourself with my lot, and share the hardness of my life." Nothing more is told us. The account of that interview stops short; and the natural inference, I think, would be, that the man's enthusiasm was arrested all of a sudden by the revelation of such a possibility as this. It was a delightful and inspiring thing, no doubt, to be identified with a man who could speak such words and do such works as Jesus did; but then, the foxes and the birds! No: he must at least think further of the matter; and so we hear no more of our enthusiastic volunteer.

The next man, Jesus addresses with his familiar invitation, "Follow me." He, too, is a ready man, kindled like the first; but he is naturally a more cautious man. Christ seeks all men; but some men go half-way to meet him, others make him go the whole way. This man is ready enough, only he has a filial duty to perform first. His father is dead, and he would pay the respect which a son owes in such a case; and no one would be more ready than Christ to acknowledge the force of such a claim. But this case was peculiar. It is more a representative case than we are wont to think, — representative, I mean, of one of those decisive crises when a man is brought to a choice between two courses, either of which is to give character to his whole life. Going after Christ was a different thing from going after anybody else. He might attach himself to any party-leader, or to a side of any temporary movement, and, as to the rest of his life, go on in the ordinary course; and he might withdraw from such connections at pleasure. But this was a moral issue. To decide for or against Christ was to choose an economy of life. Crises of that kind come to men outside of the religious sphere. When a community, in the old colonial days, was suddenly attacked by the Indians, every man must drop every thing else, and go out to repel the savages. He must leave his team unyoked in the field, his plough in the furrow, his sick wife in the house, his dead child or father unburied, and seize his gun, and take his place in the ranks. You are to remember, further, that this was the man's only chance to attach himself to Jesus. The Lord, as we have said, was going forth from Galilee to return no more. According to the Jewish law, the pollution from the presence of a dead body lasted seven days. By that time the man's first enthusiasm would have become chilled, and Jesus would be out of reach. The man evidently thought that it was only a question of a little delay in following Christ: Jesus knew that it was a question of following him now or never.

Then comes a third. He offers himself also; but he, too, is not ready to go at once. He wants to go home, and take leave of his family and friends. And in this case, as in the last, Christ assumes that there is a moral crisis. He must decide promptly; and, if he decides to follow Christ, he must promptly forsake all, once for all, and follow him. Let him go back to his house, and the tears and remonstrances of friends and kindred would shake his resolution. They would say, "At any rate, if you must go, do not go to-day: let us have one more family gathering. Let us once more sit down to our table together. Go the rounds once more, and say good-by to this and that friend." He never would have gone after Jesus. Christ says to him, in effect, "If you go after me, the course is straightforward. You must give up every thing for me; take me in place of every thing; give me your whole heart: and, if part of your heart is left behind with friends and home and old associations, it is of no use for you to go. You are not fit for the kingdom of God, any more than a man is fit to plough a field who is constantly turning from his plough and his team to look backward.

By this time you have caught the lesson of the text. It is the lesson of *committal*, — the truth, that, to follow Christ is to commit one's self wholly and irrevocably to Christ.

And, before we go farther, observe what Christ means here by the phrase "fit for the kingdom of God." He does not mean that the wavering, half-hearted, half-committed man shall not get his reward in heaven; though that is true. The kingdom of God is not a matter of heaven only. The man enters the kingdom of God from the moment that he engages to follow Christ, or, to carry out the figure of the text, from the moment that he enters his plough. God has a kingdom on earth as well as in heaven, and the sphere of that kingdom is the sphere of Christ's service. One is here under substantially the same moral laws as those which prevail in heaven: so that the question of fitness for the kingdom of God which Christ raises is not a question merely of one's fitness for heaven by and by; it is also a question of fitness to live the life, and to meet the requirements of the kingdom of God, here and now. We are to follow Christ here. The field is the world, and our ploughing is to-day's duty. The kingdom of God involves laws which are to be obeyed here, sacrifices which are to be made here, now, to-day, and every day. The kingdom of God is already set up in the earth, and has a work to do in the world. The question is, whether you and I are fit to do it; and Christ here tells us that we are not fit for it unless we are wholly committed to him.

Again, let me call your attention to the figure in which the truth is set. A man cannot plough, and be looking behind him half the time. Such a man is not fit for a ploughman. You say, Of course not. That is a law of all good work, that a man cannot do it well with half his attention; but why not, then, a law of work and life in the kingdom of God? We have a great deal yet to learn about the words of Christ; and one of the most important things is, that these apparently commonplace truths and familiar laws which he so often cites are merely sides, or ends if you please, of truths and laws which hold in the whole spiritual world. It is not, that, in this little picture of an incompetent farm-hand, Christ gives us something like a law of the kingdom of God. He states the law itself. Good work requires the entire committal of the worker. It is the law of Christian service and of ploughing alike. It is this fact which lifts utterances like our text out of the region of commonplace. They seem commonplace where they touch us, but their line runs out to truths which are not commonplace. The law of the plough followed up appears as the law of the kingdom of God. Now, this law of entire committal is familiar enough to us in its worldly applications. It is the great law of success in ordinary callings. When you choose a calling in life, it is said of you, "He is going to *devote his life* to business or to law or to medicine." And you know very well, that, if you are to succeed in either, the expression is none too strong. If you are going to be a successful doctor, you must give up being a successful merchant. You cannot expect to be a power in science or in letters. You must commit and devote yourself wholly to the thing which you have chosen. And the kingdom of God is a more serious matter than law or medicine or business. Not one of these touches your real inner life. You may fail in business, and yet be the same man you were before you failed,— your real manhood as sound and true as when you handled hundreds of thousands. But the kingdom of God does touch your inmost self. The quality of your manhood turns on the nature of your relation to it. The issue is between the world and your life. You cannot fail in the kingdom of God and be the same man as if you had not failed. Failure there is radical. Moreover, if the variety and magnitude of business or professional interests demand your whole energy, much more surely the interests of the kingdom of God. It is harder to work out a Christ-like character than to make a fortune. It is harder to overcome the world than to outride a panic or to withstand the fluctuations of the markets. It is harder to assert the character of the meek and lowly Jesus amid surrounding worldliness and against the upheavals of passion than to keep your credit unimpaired on 'change. The demands of the kingdom of God admit of no division of purpose, no half interest, no looking back. Ploughing is forward work, — all in advance. Each of us has a furrow to cut through that section of the kingdom of God which includes our lives. There is no call, there is no time, to look back.

And, as a consequence, when you enter your plough in this spirit of entire committal, you agree to take whatever comes in the line of your ploughing, and to plough through it or round it, and in no case to turn back because of it. As I have said before, the kingdom of God is full of surprises; and you will come upon a good many unexpected things, and things as hard as they are unexpected. Your plough will often strike a rock under the greenest turf, and just where you thought the ploughing was going to be easiest. Your ploughing will not always lie on straight lines, either. There are curved as well as straight lines in God's plans, ends reached by indirection as well as directly. A farmer likes to cut straight furrows, and to make a handsome-looking field with the straight parallels; but God is more concerned about our making a *fruitful* field than a handsome one, and will not always let us follow the straight lines of our plans. Any way, straight or crooked, you commit yourself to take what comes. It is no part of your business or mine in God's kingdom to make our conditions. When you give yourself to Christ, and enter your plough in his field, he arranges the conditions, and bids you work them out. If the conditions are to be changed, the right change will develop in faithful working out. I remember once, when travelling among the Spanish mountains in the midst of one of the loveliest scenes I ever beheld, my eye rested on a little tract on the side of a savage height. The patch was literally sown with rocks, and yet it had been most carefully ploughed. I suppose there was not a furrow in it that ran straight for five feet at a time; but the ploughman had not looked back. He had ploughed on, round the rocks and between them. It was a good, thorough piece of work. So God selects the field for us, with its conditions, — rocks in one man's field, stumps in another's. The simple question is, Shall we plough that field? God does not take away the stumps and rocks: what we do with them answers the question whether or not we are fit for the kingdom of God. Last week there came into my study a pastor of many years' standing, — a faithful, able, useful servant of God. I remember when I first heard him, over twenty-five years ago, when he stood before a great audience in the vigor of his early manhood, his hair black as a raven's wing. I remember how he woke the audience from the lethargy of a summer noon, and swayed them with his wise and bright words; and his speech that day stands out in my memory as one of the most telling and brilliant I ever heard. And he sat with me last week, the fire dimmed in his eye, his hair white as the driven snow, and went over a part of his history, — told of sickness and prostration, of burdens lifted in struggling churches, of divisions and dissensions among his people, of final success, and peaceful, happy ministrations in a thriving church saved and established by his labor and sacrifice; and he brought down his hand with emphasis as he said, "I have learned this one thing through it all, *that God's work is bound to go on anyway; and that the only thing for us to do, is to stand in our place, and do our work, whatever comes.*"

And, my brethren, you all know something about this in your own lives. You have all felt the jar when the plough struck a stone. Not one of you has been able to make straight furrows always. Not one of you who has tried to serve God faithfully but has come to something in his ploughing which tempted him to look back; but the only thing for any of us to do, is to stand in our place, and do our work. There is no such thing as failure of faithful work in God's kingdom; and the simple reason of that is, because it is in *God's* kingdom and not man's; and God's kingdom *must* come, and his will *must* and *will* be done in earth as it is in heaven: "He that goeth forth weeping and bearing precious seed, *shall doubtless* come again with rejoicing, bringing his sheaves with him."

The text presents to us a question of the present, a present responsibility. It is not a question whether you will be fit for heaven by and by, but whether, by absolute and entire committal to Christ, you are fit for the service of the kingdom *here* and *now*. Not one of us will venture to say positively that he is fit for the kingdom. God works out the problem of his kingdom on earth by the hands of imperfect men. But Christ puts to us this morning the great essential of unfitness — looking back; a divided interest; a half-way service; an attempt to keep an eye on the world and an eye on the plough. Heaven will take care of itself, and of us if we only plough straight on. The line of the furrow, faithfully held, will lead out inevitably to where

> "Sweet fields beyond the swelling flood
> Stand dressed in living green,"

when the ploughing shall be done; and the redeemed shall walk with Christ by the living fountains of waters. Have any of you unfitted yourselves for to-day's work in God's kingdom by taking back a part of what you gave to Christ, — by looking back? There was a time when, in the first freshness of your consecration to him, you were ready to say, "I will follow thee whithersoever thou goest." There was a time when faith was firm, and love burning, and labor for Christ a joy. Have the heats and languors of life's high noon paralyzed that first enthusiasm? Has the noise of the great world's striving and revelry, borne over the field to your ear, made you loose your hold on the plough, and turn longingly from your appointed work? Have you grown cold toward Christ and his church, sceptical about the outcome of Christian work and the destinies of the kingdom of God, cautious and calculating, and disposed to spare self as much as may be? If that be so, — which God forbid! — the Saviour meets you this day with the warning, "No man, having put his hand to the plough, and looking back, is fit for the kingdom of God."

XI.

JOY AND JUDGMENT.

XI.

JOY AND JUDGMENT.

"Rejoice, O young man, in thy youth; and let thy heart cheer thee in the days of thy youth, and walk in the ways of thine heart, and in the sight of thine eyes: but know thou, that for all these things God will bring thee into judgment. Therefore remove sorrow from thy heart, and put away evil from thy flesh: for childhood and youth are vanity.

"Remember now thy Creator in the days of thy youth, while the evil days come not, nor the years draw nigh, when thou shalt say, I have no pleasure in them." — ECCLES. xi. 9, 10; xii. 1.

PERHAPS you think those opening words are said sarcastically. "Oh, yes, young man! enjoy your life; be merry; have your fling; you will find out to your cost what it all amounts to when the time of judgment comes round." That is the way the words have often been interpreted, and yet nothing can be farther from the truth. Our translators have slipped in a "but" where there ought to be an "and," and have thus made the preacher set the joy of youth and the judgment of God over against each other: "Rejoice in thy youth, *but* know that God will bring you into judgment for your rejoicing." Whereas, in fact, the judgment is put as part of the rejoicing: "Rejoice in thy youth; *and* know that, respecting all these, God will bring thee into judgment."

The preacher, in short, frankly commends to youth a joyful, cheerful life as its natural and proper heritage. He means just what he says. He does not invite youth to a feast, and then set up the skeleton of judgment at the table to make him feast with fear and trembling. There is no covert irony in the call to rejoice. The judgment is brought in, but in a way, as we shall see, which ministers to the rejoicing instead of clouding it: "Rejoice, O young man, in thy youth! childhood and youth are vanity; they pass quickly away; age with its infirmity will come; pleasure will lose its zest; enjoy the beauty, the grace, the pleasure, of the world while you may."

Possibly, these may seem strange words from the man to whom we owe the phrase, "Vanity of vanities; all is vanity!" And, if so, the strangeness may stimulate you to study that old book, from which, it may be, you are repelled by its hard and dry name. There is nothing dry about the book. No book in the Bible is racier. It throbs with life and feeling; it is full of ripe wisdom; it is one of the most consolatory and cheerful portions of Holy Writ.

Let us look at the two parts of the text separately, — joy and judgment; and then we shall see how they fit into each other, and are parts of one great truth. And let me say, in advance, that we need be under no apprehension of finding the stringency of duty relaxed, or a life of sensual pleasure encouraged, by these first, hearty, cheerful words of the wise preacher: —

"Rejoice, O young man, in thy youth; and let thy heart cheer thee in thy youthful days, and pursue the ways of thine heart, and the things which are seen by the eyes." We are not listening to a Christian moralist: nevertheless, the sentiment is Christian. "Childhood and youth are vanity;" that is to say, they are transient, fleeting. "Therefore," say a certain class of religionists, "extinguish their natural instincts as summarily as possible. They are transient; therefore, they are of no account. They are 'vanity'; therefore, to enjoy them is dangerous, if it be not sinful." But the logic of our old preacher takes a different line. Childhood and youth, or youth and manhood, are fleeting; *therefore*, "Banish sorrow from thy mind, and put away sadness from thy body." He evidently does not think that the brevity and transitoriness of a thing is a reason for despising it. Neither do you and I, when we deal with ordinary matters. The rose which you pluck in the morning withers before the next morning, but you delight yourself with its color and perfume none the less while it lasts. A summer morning, with its dewy freshness, is a thing of only an hour or two; but you do not, for that reason, shut yourself up in your chamber, and refuse to breathe the morning scents, and to look upon the sparkle of the dewdrops. Youth and fresh manhood are things only of a few years; but their brevity is, to the preacher, the reason why they should be enjoyed. Those have done infinite damage who have set on foot the notion that youth, from the moment it turns to religion, surrenders all pleasure, lightness of heart, and robust enjoyment; and such teachers have been betrayed into this terrible and fatal mistake through their failure to see that God's training is not to stunt or to crush out human nature, but to develop and elevate it. Our Lord, Christ, you will remember, said some very severe things about those teachers who had made religion a burden instead of a joy and a rest to the people. He called them thieves and robbers, who had stolen away the blessedness from life, and had tried to make it as small and lean a thing as possible; whereas, "I," said he, "came that they may have life, and may have it abundantly." Some people reason as if Christ had come only to reveal *another* life, whereas he came also to teach men how to make the most and best of *this* life at every stage. When a man is rooted and grounded in the love of Christ, Paul tells us he grows up, not into a cherub or an archangel, but into a perfect *man;* and the pattern of this manhood is Christ. What the forces of Nature may do with the rose after it has withered and dropped from the stem, into what new combinations, or into what new forms of life its juices and fibre may enter, is a distinct question. Meanwhile, to-day the forces of Nature are all concentrating themselves to make a perfect rose. What you and I may be after death is indeed an interesting and a vital question; but it does not set aside that other question, — how to make the best and most of this life in all its stages. These successive stages of life are not independent.

Childhood perpetuates its quality in youth, and youth in manhood, and manhood again in age. You realize the divine ideal of manhood to the degree in which you are true to the divine ideal of youth: "Remember thy Creator *in the days of thy youth.*" Youth is pointed back to his creation. What stamp did the Creator set upon it? What provision did he make for youth? What did he mean youth to be? Obedient, reverent, pure, diligent, — all that certainly; yet as certainly fresh, joyous, vigorous. Remember thy Creator, to be in youth what he meant thee to be *then*. God has an ideal for the blossom as well as for the fruit, and the best fruit comes through the best-developed blossom. The work of Christ the Redeemer does not contradict the work of God the Creator. God made man in his own image. Christ comes to bring out that image in men; and Christ set it on childhood and youth no less than on manhood; and God put into humanity, perceptions of beauty, the sense of humor, the love of society, susceptibility to harmony and color; and to develop God's image is not to crush out these faculties, but to learn to use them. God knows that these faculties are freshest and keenest in youth, — that joy is native to youth as blossoms to spring. And the type of youth is not, therefore, the old man, burdened with cares, tired of the world, and saddened by experience. A joyless youth is as unnatural as ice in August: "Rejoice, O young man, in thy youth."

It may be said, "At any rate, this aspect of the

truth does not need pressing in our day, and it were better to warn youth against the coming judgment." And it seems to be assumed, moreover, that there is an antagonism between these two ideas of joy and judgment; that the one excludes the other; that the thought of judgment is enough of itself to quench all rejoicing in youth. But the peculiarity of our text is, that it rejects this antagonism, and makes this coming judgment a cause of rejoicing — a stimulant of the joy of youth as well as a warning: "Rejoice, and know that God will bring thee into judgment. Banish, therefore, sorrow from thy mind, and put away sadness from thy body."

Whenever this book may have been written, we find in it numerous allusions to a state of society which give these words about a future judgment a peculiar meaning and force; for the book depicts a society under a capricious despotism, with all its corruptions and miseries. The grandees revel in palaces, vineyards, and pleasure-grounds; kings are childish, and princes given to revelry and drunkenness; fools are uplifted, and noble men degraded; riches are not for the intelligent, or favor for the learned; to become rich is to multiply extortions; life stands at the caprice of power; sensuality runs riot. "In short, the whole political fabric was falling into disrepair and decay, the rain leaking through the rotting roof; while the miserable people were ground down with ruinous exactions, in order that the rulers might revel on undisturbed." And as the book reveals this fearful social condition, so, likewise, it gives expression to the temper which grows up in men's minds after a long course of such oppressions, — a kind of fatalism and hopelessness which tempts one to yield passively to the current of affairs; to believe that God has ceased to rule, and that order and right have vanished from the world; to snatch at every pleasure; to drown care in sensuality, rather than try to maintain an integrity which is sure to be rewarded with personal and social ruin. That kind of temper, if it once gained headway, would affect all classes and ages. In the nobler and better-seasoned characters, it would become a proud despair; in vulgar minds, a bestial greed, and an untrammeled selfishness; in youth, a prompter to unbounded sensuality.

You can see, therefore, what a powerful antidote to this temper would be furnished by the truth of a future judgment. Once lodge firmly the truth that men are moving on through all the hard and bitter and unjust conditions of their time to a supreme tribunal, and you have made it impossible to believe that the world is lawless. A final judgment implies a law; and a law implies a lawgiver, and an authority to administer and vindicate the law. Thus the truth carries with it both comfort and obligation. There is a divine order in the world; we are not finally at the mercy of chance or of men's caprice: the order will vindicate itself in time, and with itself will vindicate those who hold by it. So long as there is a judgment, wrong is not eternal, and retribution is a fact. Therefore, it is better to do right, notwithstanding the "oppressor's wrong and the proud man's contumely." It is better to live the life of duty and of charity described in this chapter; to cast the bread upon the waters, though it seem to be lost; to share even the few good things of life with seven and with eight; to sow the seed morning and evening, though unknowing whether this or that shall prosper; better for the youth to curb passion, and to hold by purity and truth, and to cultivate duty. There is an order, a divine order, in the world; and an order carries the fact of judgment along with it. So, too, it is better not to give way to despair. One can afford to be cheerful, even amid oppressions and troubles like these, if the time is short, and a day coming in which wrong shall be righted, and worth acknowledged and fidelity rewarded.

The judgment is a fact which confronts us as Christians, — a fact emphasized by the words of Christ and of the apostles, and still further emphasized by the relation in which Christ puts himself to it as the judge of all men. And the attitude of even our Christian thought towards it is largely that of terror and apprehension. Turn over the hymns in our own collection under the head of "judgment," and this will be evident. The key to the popular Christian sentiment is the familiar old Latin hymn, —

"That day of wrath, that dreadful day."

Of course, the terrible element is there in large

measure. The element of solemnity must, in any case, dominate our thought of the last day. It cannot be other than a serious matter to appear before our Creator, and to give an account of the deeds done in the body. And assuredly it will be a day of wrath to rebels against God and to rejecters of Christ. An infallible and final judgment, which shall pronounce a man's life-work worthless, and the man himself a moral failure, must be woe and terror unutterable. But, withal, the truth has another side. It is not mere fancy which sees in the Judgment Day a day of consolation as well as of wrath. That other side is recognized in Scripture. Turn, for instance, to the ninety-sixth and ninety-eighth Psalms, composed during the period of the captivity, probably the same period in which this preacher wrote. What a glorious outburst of praise is this, in which all nature is summoned to join! "Let the heavens rejoice, and let the earth be glad; let the sea make a noise, and all that therein is: let the floods clap their hands, and let the hills be joyful together before Jehovah; *for he cometh to judge the earth.* With righteousness shall he judge the world, and the people with equity." Or turn over to the Epistle to the Hebrews, and hear the apostle comparing the terrors which waited on the giving of the law at Sinai with the delights and privileges which attend the new covenant: "Ye are not come unto a mount that might be touched, and that burned with fire, and unto blackness and tempest. But ye are come unto mount Zion, and unto the city of the living God, the heavenly Jerusalem, and to innumerable hosts of angels, to the general assembly and church of the firstborn who are enrolled in heaven, to the spirits of just men made perfect, and to Jesus the mediator of a new covenant, and to the blood of sprinkling that speaketh better than that of Abel." What a group of joys! what a catalogue of privileges! and into the midst of these is thrown one more: "and to God, the *judge of all.*" It is not a discordant note. It is meant to accord, and does accord, with those sweetest of all sounds, — Jesus the Mediator, and the blood of sprinkling. The Mediator is the Judge, and the blood of sprinkling has taken the terror out of judgment.

Why, then, should a man, young or old, have the work or the pleasure peculiar to his age and circumstances clouded by the anticipation of judgment? Why may not the young man lawfully rejoice in his youth, provided he remembers his Creator? The mistake is in divorcing the Creator and Judge from the joy of life; whereas, God is the true joy of life. "In thy presence," says the Psalmist, "is fulness of joy; at thy right hand are eternal pleasures." That does not mean heaven only. If David, as seems probable, was thinking of the future state when he wrote these words, he was equally thinking of the present life; for he says, "Thou wilt show me the path of life: in thy presence is fulness of joy." And if God is in the life of to-day as Creator and Counsellor and Administrator, he is, by virtue of this, in the life of *to-day* as Judge. If you and I are moral beings, living under a moral order, the element of judgment is in to-day's life as really as it will be on the last day. Every day's life is a test. Every day's life brings us to the bar of that moral economy where conscience sits as God's assessor and deputy. Every day's life is rounded with the approving or condemning verdict of conscience. God is not concealing and hoarding up his judgments, only to let them break forth as terrible surprises at the last day. Conscience anticipates daily the final verdict. The moment we are introduced to the great ideas of right and wrong, that moment we are introduced to the idea of judgment. And, if the fact that God is our Judge is in itself fatal to all joy and good cheer, that fact is fatal to *all possible* joy in God; for God as Judge goes with God as Creator and Father and Friend. He is Judge by virtue of his being all these. Why then, I repeat, should the young man not rejoice in his youth, or a man of any age in the conditions peculiar to that age, provided they remember their Creator? Whence come the pure pleasures of youth, — its hopefulness, its energy, its mirth, its sense of beauty? Do they not come from God? Is he not the Creator of these as well as of bone and muscle? And if these gifts are recognized as God's, are they not at once sweetened, and guarded against abuse by that very fact? Christ tells us that one office of the Holy Spirit is to "convince of judgment;" that is, to show men clearly that all sin deserves and will receive the judgment of God. Is it not, then, a cause of rejoicing, that God guards our pleasures against abuse, that he teaches us what true pleasure is, that he sets up a sign marked "judgment" at the border-line of excess? Is it not a real cause of rejoicing that God restrains us from incurring the judgment of sin? Can that be real pleasure which ends in rebuke and punishment? And, therefore, when we recognize our legitimate pleasures as God's gift, our joy in them is heightened. We may enjoy without fear. God will not condemn what himself has ordained and created; and when we look forward to the great judgment, the eternal life beyond, these very pleasures take on a prophetic character. They are foretastes, earnests of something better beyond. The pleasure at his right hand here, promises fulness of joy at his right hand forevermore. When we have learned that God is love, and is with us lovingly in this world, — *with* us, I say, down here amid these earthly conditions, helping us in every possible way to enjoy what is true, and to do what is right and best, and not far above us, regarding us as a critic, and seeking only to find fault with us, — when we have learned this, I say, are we to conclude, that, in the final judgment to which we are moving on, God is going to throw off this character, and appear simply as an inexorable critic?

"Prepare to meet thy God!" We hear it said in awful tones, as one would say to a convicted murderer, "Prepare for the scaffold!" As if meeting God, the God we name "love" and "father," were the most dreadful of human experiences. But we do not talk in that way about any human object of love. When that wife or child or husband or brother of yours has been long gone across the sea, and the despatch is put into your hand that the ship is down at quarantine, there is no terror nor sorrow in your preparing to meet them. How your feet speed to the wharf! How your eyes are strained to detect among the crowding masts the first cloud of smoke from the steamer's funnel! How you can scarce restrain your impatience until the ship is made fast, and the plank let down, that you may spring on board, and greet the object of your love! And you are the one who sings, —

> "My Saviour whom absent I love,
> Whom not having seen I adore."

And

> "On earth we want the sight
> Of our Redeemer's face."

And you are afraid to meet *Him!*

You see, then, how this wise old preacher, lifting up his voice in the very midst of a horrible and apparently hopeless social condition, found, in the fact of a coming judgment and of a future life, a basis for an exhortation to hopefulness and cheerful discharge of duty as well as a warning against sloth and sensuality. It is for us to find the same, and our doing so depends on one thing simply: remembering our Creator, early and late, in youth and throughout. There is nothing but terror in judgment if God be left out of to-day's life. There need be no terror in it if we take our Creator and our Judge into our life to-day and every day. Our

God, into whose hand we put ours with confiding faith, is not going to lead us to the judgment-seat, only to dash away our hand, and mount the throne, and thunder denunciation at us. If he has ministered comfort and pleasure to us along our earthly way, depend upon it these are only a foretaste of larger comfort and perfect rest by and by. To him who remembers his Creator, the judgment will be fruition and not blight. You profess, my brother, to live your life by faith. Of your own choice you cast in your lot with the unseen Christ, and staked every thing on his promise, against the remonstrances of the worldly wise, it may be, against temptations of worldly policy. The great feature of that day will be the revelation of that unseen Christ, and the consequent vindication of your faith. You have made your decisions in this life according to his tests, — tests which the world has pronounced fanciful and fallacious. You have brought your dealings to the standard of his character and example, and have judged them right or wrong according to these. Then He himself shall appear on the throne of judgment. All these centuries he has been trying to make the world recognize him as Judge : now they shall be compelled to recognize him, and to confess that his judgments are just. You have put your trust for salvation in the blood of the everlasting covenant. You have pinned your faith to a crucified Saviour in the face of philosophy's reasonings against the reality and virtue of the Atonement. Jesus, the Mediator of a new covenant, will then appear as God, the Judge of all: your faith will be vindicated; and the cross, that stumbling-block to the Jew, that folly to the Greek, that symbol to the world of degradation and ignominy, shall stand out brighter than all Heaven's morning stars, as the sign of eternal victory and glory. You have worked faithfully, and have gotten no earthly reward for it. The Judgment will give you your reward. You have been misunderstood, wrongfully accused: the Judgment shall set you right. Your heart has been hot over wrongs and cruelties, cheats and shams, which you could not help. You shall see them meet their due there. You shall see them stand in their naked vileness, blasted with the eternal curse of the Judge of all. You have had sorrow and pain and disappointment here: little of the world's pity has come to you. You have been tempted to think the award of Providence a harsh one. God shall show you then why it all was, and

"Heaven's eternal bliss shall pay
For all his children suffer here."

XII.

SILENT BEFORE GOD.

XII.

SILENT BEFORE GOD.

"I was dumb, I opened not my mouth; because thou didst it." — Ps. xxxix. 9.

THIS psalm is the utterance of a man in trouble. It thrills with a strong but repressed feeling. The writer is striving for resignation, but not wholly resigned; afraid of dishonoring God by a hasty word, yet longing for light from heaven. His heart is hot within him: as he muses over the brevity of life and the vanity of man, as he thinks how all his fathers were strangers and pilgrims as he is, — with the same troubles, the same problems, the same sense of desolation, — the fire burns; his soul is in a ferment.

In a thoughtful man, trouble always doubles itself. Added to the smart of the immediate affliction is the moral problem which it raises, — the great question, raised anew by each successive generation of thinkers and believers, of the reason and the justice of God's administration in the world, of the permission of evil, of the tendency and destiny of this vain show called life. Every special sorrow or disaster is a stream, setting towards this unfathomable ocean of thought with a swift and resistless current.

The psalm, I need hardly say, represents a familiar experience. If the world is not made up of great thinkers, it is full of people who feel deeply; and deep feeling is thought in solution, — none the less so because they are few who can precipitate the thought, and crystallize it.

The psalm, as I have said, indicates strong repression as well as strong feeling. The writer is on his guard against hasty speech: "I said, I will take heed to my ways, that I sin not with my tongue: I will keep my mouth with a bridle, while the wicked is before me. I held my peace even from good." This was the dictate of a goodly prudence. Conscious of the excited state of his heart, he was afraid lest he should say something out of its abundance which might dishonor God in the eyes of wicked men who were watching him. But in our text we get down, I think, to a deeper reason for silence. The man seems to be so overcome by the grandeur and the mystery of God's dealing with him that he is forced to be silent. Ordinary sorrow tends to vent itself in speech. Some mysteries, which present a point of light here and there, we discuss; we find a kind of satisfaction in comparing views, and suggesting possible solutions: but now and then we are brought face to face with a tremendous experience, where we instinctively concede that there is nothing to be said. God has done it: that is all. The thing gives no clew to itself: we stand like a belated traveller before the closed gate of an Egyptian temple, rising, low-browed and grim, under the stars, and no sound answers our knock. We must sit down and wait.

This, then, is the simple, stern picture of our text, — a man in silence before the truth, *God did it!*

It does not seem at first as if much can be worked out from those two factors, yet let us not be too hasty; and let us say at once that this text, and whatever we may be able to draw from it, are not for an atheist. The text assumes God to be a fact, and further assumes faith in God. We are not going to these words for proof of God's being or of God's providence, but, taking both these for granted, to see if we can get out of these two naked facts any light upon the relation between the providence and its subject, between God and the man who is dumb before his stroke, and bewildered by his mystery.

"Thou didst it!" In the first place, then, it is something to have gotten firm hold of a fact. A great deal is gained when the sorrow, however severe, or the mystery, however dark, has been traced up to God. When we can say, not *something*, but *someone*, did it, the matter is greatly simplified. We have no longer to count chances. Whatever we may think of the justice or the reason or the quality of the dispensation, we know its source. Our questioning has no longer to range about the realms of chance, or the possible combinations of natural forces: it is confined to

God. The origin of the thing is fixed. God did it. We know at least whom to question, if we do not get an answer. Though the light for which we are looking may be hidden by clouds, we at least know whither to direct our telescope. If there is any solution to be given, we are on the right road and in the right attitude when our face is turned towards God.

The fact, indeed, reduces us to silence; but let us be sure that we understand the meaning of the hand that is laid for the time over our mouth. It need not mean that God is rebuking our inquiry, or forbidding us to pursue it. It *cannot* mean that God is tantalizing us. It need not even mean that he intends to deny us a solution. It may mean that he is putting us in the way of a solution. A teacher sets for a boy a hard problem in algebra. The boy goes resolutely to work. The day passes, and he cannot solve it. He takes it home with him, and works at it there. He comes back next day, and all day he is busy with his problem; and towards the close of the school-day, with his face flushed, and with perhaps an angry tremor in his voice, he comes to the teacher, and says, "I cannot do it:" and then he begins to talk passionately, to tell what methods he has tried, to hint that the teacher may have made a mistake in his statement, to complain that this or that in his algebra is not clearly defined. The teacher sees the difficulty; and, as the first step toward clearing it up, he quietly says, "Be still! Do not talk any more! I set the problem, and I know it is right." And if he says no more for the time, and the boy goes back to his seat, he has gained something in that interview. There is power in the thought which the lad turns over in his mind, — "This problem was set by somebody that knows. My teacher, whom I have always found wise and truthful, did it." The thought that there may have been a mistake in the statement of the sum goes out of his mind, and the matter is thus far relieved, at any rate: and, under the impulse of that relief, he may attack the question again, and successfully; or, if not, he will gain by silence, by restraint. Let the teacher speak, and let him simply listen. The teacher wisely silences him, not to check his inquiry, but to bring his mind into the right condition to receive explanation.

Just so, we are often, in the presence of our sorrows or of our hard questions, like this Psalmist, — our heart hot within us, our mind a ferment of wild questionings. The best thing for God to do with us then is to silence us, and to set us pondering the naked truth, — God did it! pondering it without argument, without debate, without remonstrance. If he were to give explanations in our heated and confused state, we could not appreciate them. We may think, perhaps, his reducing us to silence is an arbitrary refusal to enlighten us; but we may possibly discover, after we have been silent a while, that a better and ampler explanation lies in the words, " Thou didst it."

The most remarkable illustration of this is found

in the Book of Job. To appreciate it fully, we need to study the entire book, and to follow its wonderful development to its conclusion. Job was confronted at once with the most terrible affliction, and with the profoundest and most perplexing of moral problems. The two were intertwined: the problem grew out of the affliction, and the affliction aggravated the problem. He had been a just and God-fearing man. He had been a prosperous man, and he never had thought of questioning that his prosperity was the reward of his piety. That was the doctrine of the current theology, and he accepted it. Now his prosperity was swept away, his household desolated, his person horribly tormented and disfigured: and the logical outcome of his theology could only be, that he was being smitten for sin, as he had been rewarded for goodness; and this his friends urged with all the weight of their wisdom, and with much bitterness and unfairness. But Job would not admit the conclusion of his own logic. Like many another man who has all his life passively accepted formulas, he found that his formulas would not stretch to cover his case. He was conscious of his integrity, and he would not refuse the testimony of that consciousness. He would not admit that he was being punished for sin. But then came in the other and greater difficulty: "If not for sin, then why? If I have walked justly before God, why does he smite me thus? Is he a just God, who renders to men according to their works? If I have sinned, why does he not show me my sin? Why does he not at least explain his dealing with me, and vindicate his own justice and love?" This is the agony which throbs and seethes through this wonderful poem, — Job trying to understand God, groping in the darkness of his misery for that presence which he dimly feels is behind it all, but which he cannot grasp, and from which he can draw not a word. "Oh!" he says, "if God would but speak, or let me speak to him! He is not a man as I am, whom I might answer, that we should come together in judgment. There is no arbiter between us, to lay his hand on us both, who would remove his rod from me, so that the dread of him should not overawe me. If there were, I would speak, and not fear him. I would address myself to the Almighty. I crave to reason with God. Oh that my words were written down! that they were inscribed in a book, with an iron pen and lead, cut deep in the rock forever! Oh that I knew where I might find him! I would press even to his seat. I would set out my cause before him, and fill my mouth with pleas."

And at last, after he has poured out his soul in bitterness, after he has sinfully impeached God's justice, has fiercely shaken his innocence in the Almighty's face, and has driven his ill-judging friends from the field with his indignant eloquence, the heavens darken. Even while Elihu is speaking, he sees the spreading of the clouds, and hears the crash of the Almighty's pavilion. God clothes his palms with lightning, and flings his flash across

the heavens; and out of the midst of thunder and
wind and great rain comes at last the voice which
Job has been beseeching to hear. The agony of
the great debate has reached its climax; and, as
eagerly as Job, we wait to hear the words which
shall answer for us, as for him, the question why
Almighty love sends suffering upon the good, and
mystery to the honest inquirer. And what do we
get? Magnificent poetry, indeed, in these four
chapters¹—masterful descriptions of God's wisdom
in nature, of his power in the sea, and his beauty
in the dawn; but not a word of explanation; no
answer to the question which has been burning
Job's heart, no telling of the how or why. So
far as that is concerned, God remains silent, and
Job must still be dumb. The only answer is, "I
did it. You must take me at the solution of the
mystery." "But that is no solution," cries one
impatiently. I am not so sure of that. Job found
it a solution. Job was a thinker,—a deeper thinker
than either of his friends. It was because he
thought so deeply, because he appreciated the
magnitude of those awful questions of Providence
and destiny, that his agony was so terrible. If he
could have glossed over those mysteries with certain well-worn sayings, as deftly as Bildad and
Eliphaz and Zophar did, or as some comfortable
people do at this day, he could have borne his
bodily ailments better. But Job, sat there on the
refuse-heap, found out what some of us find out in

---

¹ Job xxxviii.-xli.

our familiar lines of institutionalism, that there are some questions larger than the catechism, — some questions which, when we try to cover them with convenient formulas and familiar oracles, have an awkward way of exposing bare corners: and yet Job, thinker as he was, as anxious to know how and why as any modern rationalist, did find a solution in God's answer. He found God, and that satisfied him. When the whirlwind and the voice are past, Job is another man: he is no longer the protester. He is bowed humbly, penitently, adoringly, contentedly, before his Maker.

Perhaps there is almost as great a mystery to us in Job's satisfaction as in the process of his trial; and one reason why it is a mystery is, that we cleave so obstinately to the position that satisfaction and peace can come only through our knowing why things are. There is a nearer point of rest; but we overlook it, and keep our eyes on the far-off cloud behind which, as we think, lies explanation and consequent satisfaction: and God denies this fundamental position of ours. Firmly and steadily he presses our attention towards the nearer point, which at first seems less promising, — that satisfaction lies in knowing God rather than in knowing the reasons for God's dealings. The compass-needle swings persistently round from the reason why to " I did it," — from the philosophy to the fact of Providence. Job's comfort came out of the fact that he had found God. His friends had been prating to him about God's character and God's laws and God's methods; and it had all gone no deeper than his ear. "I had heard of thee," he says, "with the hearing of the ear, but now mine eye seeth thee." Oh, what a difference there is between knowing about God and knowing God! The reason why the philosophic spirit is so restless, so querulous, so hard to satisfy, is not in the extent of its knowledge, but in the shortness of it. It ranges about God, contemplates God, studies God from without; but it does not penetrate to the Father in heaven. God satisfied Job by revealing himself. The sorely tortured man did not find explanation, but he found something better. There was a wealth of comfort and hope in the fact that God spoke to him. This he had been craving: now God speaks. He is not indifferent to him; he is not alienated from him; he has not been indifferently looking down upon the sufferer from the far-off region of his divine splendor and perfect bliss. He has done this thing; the suffering is of his sending; he is in the heart of the mystery: and so it was with Job as with a frightened child in the dark, conjuring up troops of phantoms, shaken with nameless terrors, — when the mother's voice calls out of the dark, "I am here," the child sinks into quiet, not seeing the mother, not knowing how her presence acts to dissipate the terrors of the night, — knowing simply the precious, all-sufficient fact, that mother is there in the dark.

"Well," it may be said, "all that may do very well for a child; but a reasoning man cannot be disposed of in that way." All I can say is, many a reasoning man has to accept that or nothing.

After all, it may be that the child's satisfaction has something rational at bottom; according to divine reason at least, since the gospel tells us that this great mystery of the kingdom of God, with its hard questions, and its Cross and discipline and tribulation, must be received as a little child if received at all. Reason cannot compel God to answer; and, suppose it could, would man be the better? Would he understand any more if God should tell him all he wants to know? Can there not be a better gift than knowledge? Surely it is not unreasonable to ask; since it is clear enough, that the men who know most are not always, nor perhaps often, the happiest of men. Take a simple illustration. There are certain reasons connected with your child's education or inheritance which constrain you to live for some years in an uncongenial and unpleasant place. Neither climate, scenery, nor society is what you could desire. The child asks, "We are not poor, are we, father?" — "No." — "Could we not live somewhere else?" — "Yes." — "Then, why do we stay here when there are so many pleasant places elsewhere?" You cannot tell him; he could not understand the reasons; but, for all that, the lesson that child learns through your silence, through being obliged to be content with the simple fact, father does it, is more valuable than the knowledge of the reasons. It is the lesson of confidence, of trust in your love and in your wisdom, of unquestioning obedience. Even if he should make a shrewd and precocious guess at your reasons, that would not please you half so much as his cheerful, unquestioning acceptance of the truth that you love him, and will do what is best for him. That moral relation between you is worth infinitely more than any amount of intellectual sympathy. And the very foundation of true character and success lies in dependence on God. God cannot develop the best possibilities of any soul until that soul is first sure of him, — sure that what he does is right, simply because he does it; and that is why God lays so much stress on that lesson. That is why he so often brings his child face to face with the bare "I did it," until he learns to find in it his refuge and his comfort. That kind of teaching may not make philosophers, — when it does, it makes them of a large mould, — but it makes Pauls and Luthers.

But this "thou didst it" has some treasures of knowledge for us. Faith is not ignorance. Some of you remember a story, by a once-popular Irish poet, of a Greek youth who travelled to Egypt in search of the secret of immortality. One night, by the bank of the Nile, he found a little pyramid, seemingly as solid as the rock itself; but, as he examined it more closely, he found hints of a concealed opening, and finally struck a spring, and a door opened, which led him into a region of wonders. And even so, as we go round and round this "thou didst it," which seems so bare and so hard and so unpromising, which suggests at first only relentless will and resistless power, it begins to open: it conceals something, and we begin to make discoveries. God did it. Well, then, I know that *infinite wisdom* did it: these hard problems of Providence, these mysteries of society and of man, — I am not to conclude that they are untranslatable. There is a wisdom which understands the maze, and holds the clew to it. This tangle of society has a thread which passes up into God's hand. If he chooses not to unravel it now, there is a wise reason for it. If the tangle is here, it does not follow that it does not clear itself higher up. Perhaps this mystery has a power of training for me. "If," says a recent writer, "proof were possible; if God could inspire, or man indite, an argument which should once for all interpret our life to us, solve all its problems, dispel all its mystery, — it is still open to doubt whether it would be well that we should have it; for the mystery which encompasses us on every side is an educational force of the highest value. With certainty, we might be content, and we might rust in our content; but with mystery within us, and on every side of us, compelling us to ask, What does this mean, and that; and, above all, what does God mean by it all? we lose the rest of content, to gain a strife of thought which impels us onward and upward, and for which, in the end, we shall all be wiser and happier."

God did it. Then, I know that *infinite power* did it. "Ah!" you say, "we know that but too well. The stroke is on our hearts and homes. It is written on fresh graves, and in the scar of dreary partings." All true. But has power no other aspect than this terrible one? Shall we symbolize it only by a hand hurling thunderbolts? or may we not picture a hand, strong indeed, but open, and pouring forth blessings? "All power is given unto me," says Jesus. Yet he laid his hand on blind eyes, and they saw; on the paralytic, and he leaped and ran. The prophet saw these two meanings in infinite power: "Let us return unto the Lord; for he hath torn, and he will heal us: he hath smitten, and he will bind up and revive us." Infinite power to destroy must imply infinite power to heal. Power to let loose the flood must be also power to say, "Thus far shalt thou go, and no farther; and here shall thy proud waves be stayed." And the power which turneth man to destruction, and sayeth, "Return to dust, ye children of men," is our dwelling-place in all generations, yea, to everlasting, — the power which can stir the dead dust, and say to it, "Return to life!" which can make us glad, according to the days wherein he has afflicted us, and the years wherein we have seen evil.

God did it, and therefore I know that *infinite love* did it. That is a piece of knowledge worth having indeed. Surely, when we reach that, we find the rock yielding water. Ah! we have to creep back for rest into the shadow of love, after all. There is a solution of mystery and sorrow which is not by logic. Just what it is, just how it is, you and I can no more tell than we could tell how a child is comforted, even before it has told its sorrow, by the mere pressure of its mother's arms. Moses knew when he said, "The eternal God is thy refuge, and underneath are the everlasting arms." Logic! How grimly these mighty mysteries smile at logic! Men start with the facts and conditions of their earthly existence, with the things which they see and know, and draw their straight, logical lines, and think they keep on, in undeviating course, straight up to the region of the divine counsels; and they seem to forget, that, just as a starbeam is turned from its direct line by passing into another atmosphere, so the line of their human logic may be strangely refracted when it passes out of the denser atmosphere of man's thought into the high, clear region of the divine thought. No: the way to God is not the logician's way. No man ever reasoned himself to God; no man ever reasoned himself into submission under God's strokes, or into restfulness amid his mysteries. The child's way is the only way, — going direct to him who did it, and resting in silence, if need be, on his divine heart.

And how this truth gathers power when we go to this text, taking Christ with us! How it kindles under his touch! God did it; and I look up into that face of unspeakable love, with its thorn-marked brow, and say, "Thou didst it. He that hath seen thee hath seen the Father. I am in sorrow; the sorrow is driven home by a pierced hand: thou didst it. I am in darkness: the key to the mystery is in the same hand. The hand is closed; it will not surrender the key: but thou didst it; and, if I may only hold that hand, no matter for the key. The pierced hand tells me of the loving heart behind the hand; and, if love hath done it, let me be silent and content.

My brethren, there is not one of us who is not confronted with hard questions in his thought, and with painful mysteries of Providence in his life. These things have a meaning, believe it. Ultimately that meaning may be knowledge; but, before knowledge, their meaning is character. Here on earth their first meaning is not knowledge. That is evident enough from the way in which they baffle our inquiries, and refuse to give up their interpretation to our intellects; but the moment we approach them from the side of love and trust and obedience, they open their lips. God's rightness is our first object of search; and not with the intellect, but with the *heart*, man believeth unto righteousness. God's administration stimulates inquiry. God's dispensations, which break our hearts, will set us questioning. We must question. We shall never cease questioning. God never meant that we should. But you know how, when astronomers erect an observatory, the first thing is to lay a foundation for the great telescope. Deep down in the earth they ground the massive piers; so deep that no jar of passing wheels shall cause the delicately poised instrument to vary a hair's breadth. Let us sweep the horizon of divine truth: let us bring to bear the most powerful lenses which learning and philosophy can prepare; but, first of all, let us have a solid foundation for our telescope. Our intellects will work more calmly, more discriminatingly, to far better purpose, when our hearts are at rest in God.

Over the arched gate of the Alhambra at Granada, there is sculptured an open hand; and over the arch just beyond, a key. It is said that the haughty and luxurious Moors, who held that palace-fort for so many years, were wont to boast that the gate never would be opened to the Christians until the hand should take the key. Many a Providence, like this fortress, contains within its rough walls and frowning battlements fountains of living water; but none the less the gate is shut, and the grim bastions give no hint of shelter or rest. How many of you have been forced to stand silent before one of God's heart-breaking mysteries, and to content yourselves for the time with the simple "Thou didst it"! But, O my friend! stand still a little longer, not in wrath, nor in despair. By and by the hand will take the key, — the hand "which openeth, and no man shutteth." The gate shall open into the heart of the Providence; and, behind the stern "thou didst it," shall stand revealed eternal love and eternal peace.

XIII.

A LEPER'S LOGIC.

XIII.

A LEPER'S LOGIC.

"And it came to pass, while he was in one of the cities, behold, a man full of leprosy: and when he saw Jesus, he fell on his face, and besought him, saying, Lord, if thou wilt, thou canst make me clean. And he stretched forth his hand, and touched him, saying, I will; be thou made clean. And straightway the leprosy departed from him." — LUKE v. 12, 13.

THIS man apparently had no doubt of our Lord's *ability* to heal him: "Thou *canst* make me clean." It was about Christ's *willingness* to heal him that he was in doubt: "If thou *wilt*, thou canst." His coming to Jesus was an act of faith, but of incomplete faith, — a faith which, having grasped the truth of divine saving *power*, failed to grasp the collateral truth of divine saving *love*.

As in so many other cases, we have to deal here, not only with a single incident, but with a representative case and a general principle. The principle is, that true faith grasps alike the power and the good-will of God. The truth is laid down in the words of the writer to the Hebrews, on the nature of faith: "He that cometh to God must believe that he is, and that he is a rewarder of them that seek after him." The leper's imperfect faith represents that of thousands at the present day, who, without any doubt of God's ability to help them, are not convinced of his disposition to help them.

Setting aside for the present the special causes of this doubt in the leper's case, we see, that, as a rule, men do not naturally associate love and power, and that they believe in the existence of power far more readily than in that of love. They know little about the nature or the secret of power, yet there are multitudes who admire and trust it all the more for the very mystery which envelops it. The annals of popular delusions are full of illustrations of this. And such people exaggerate power. Your little child, for instance, places no limit to your power. He will ask you to do an impossible thing just as readily as he will ask you for a sugar-plum or a picture-book. It does not enter his mind that there is any thing his father cannot do. It is the same with the masses of men. They are little more than children in the hands of their leaders. They ascribe to them more power than they have. This leper was an illustration of the same fact: he knew little or nothing of the divine nature of Jesus; he did not know that all power was given to him in heaven and on earth; he had probably heard of some wonderful things that Jesus had done, and hence he leaped to the conclusion, rightly as it happened, but none the less irrationally, that Jesus could take away this most terrible of all afflictions if he would.

On the other hand, there is no such tendency to exaggerate love. That child, — to go back to the illustration, — familiar with love, brought up in its very atmosphere, compassed about with its tender ministrations, — that child, who believes in his father's power to perform the impossible, is sceptical about his father's disposition to pardon his fault, and will hide himself when he hears his father's step, and knows that his breaking of the vase or his upsetting of the inkstand will be found out.

Power, somehow, seems to create distrust in love. Perhaps it is because the world is so used to seeing power used arbitrarily and selfishly that power seems practically to exclude love. The natural instinct of mankind associates power with its deities. That is, perhaps, the fundamental idea in the natural conception of Deity. The African who bows down before his horrible fetich is moved to that act by the belief that it has a strange and terrible power over his life, and his success in war or in hunting; but the familiar Pagan mythologies show us that the gods were expected to use their power in the interest of their passions and caprices, and not, habitually at least, for the good of their worshippers. It was to be expected that a Jove would hurl blighting thunderbolts, or assume human or other form to work mischief and sorrow in the homes of men; that a Mercury should outwit men with his divine cunning: it was not to be expected that all this superhuman power and wit should be concentrated upon human welfare.

Now, it is this very error which the God of the Bible, through all his administration, has been at work to overcome, and to put in its place, and to get lodged firmly in men's hearts, the conviction that God loves them, and "is more willing to give good things to them that ask him than earthly parents are to give good gifts unto their children;" that God, in other words, literally puts himself at the service of those who love him. But this lesson has to make its way slowly against the natural incredulity of which we have spoken. If the question were merely of divine power, there would be much more bold coming to the throne of the heavenly grace to obtain mercy and help in time of need. To all of us, God and power have long since become convertible terms. We all say, instinctively, when our needs, our sorrows, our sins oppress us, "Thou canst." But we are often held back from the throne of power by that little but mighty "*if*," — "If thou wilt." Christ came to break the hold of that "if," and to fill the souls of those who seek him with the conviction, so well voiced in the old hymn we used to hear so often, —

> "This, this, is the God we adore, —
> Our faithful, unchangeable Friend,
> *Whose love is as great as his power,*
> And neither knows measure nor end."

Another reason why men are so slow to associate love and willingness with power in their thought of God, lies in the consciousness of sin: and hence, strange as it may seem, this reluctance to believe in God's love develops along with right conceptions of God as a God of holiness; for the appreciation of God's infinite holiness by man reveals man's own imperfection, tends to make him out of heart with self, and to fill him with self-contempt. When Peter, as the story is told in the verses just preceding this incident, saw the divine power of Christ displayed in the miraculous filling of the net with fish, the first result was not to draw him to Christ, but, on the contrary, to make him say, "Depart from me; for I am a sinful man, O Lord."

And, in the light of this fact, the incident of our text has a peculiar force; for the disease from which this man was suffering was not regarded as the most fearful of *bodily* ills only. As you study the Levitical code, you find that provisions respecting leprosy are more than mere sanitary regulations. They give to this horrible disease a moral and typical meaning, as a representative of sin. It was a decomposition of the vital juices, putrefaction in a living body; and hence an image of death, introducing the same dissolution and destruction of life into the bodily sphere which sin introduced into the spiritual. The leper was treated throughout as a sinner. "He was," as has been remarked, "a dreadful parable of death." He bore the emblems of death, — the rent garments, the bare head, the covered lip; and in his restoration the same instruments and symbols were used as for the cleansing of one defiled by a dead body, and which were never used on any other occasion, — cedar-wood, with its well-known antiseptic qualities, a symbol of the continuance of life; scarlet, a symbol of freshness of life; hyssop, a symbol of purification from the corruption of death. Hence you can understand why the Psalmist, in his prayer for pardon, says, "Purge me with hyssop, and I shall be clean." Moreover, this disease, like sin, was incurable by human skill, and entailed upon the sufferer the penalty of exclusion from the commonwealth of Israel, even as it is said of the holy city of John's vision, "There entereth nothing that defileth."

The case of this leper, therefore, gave our Lord an opportunity not only to do a work of mercy and love upon a diseased man, but also to give a symbolic testimony of his willingness to deal lovingly and forgivingly with a sinful man. Quite possibly one thing which led the leper to doubt Christ's willingness to heal him, was the peculiarly horrible and fatal character of his disease. Christ, as he had probably heard, had healed other maladies, but he had not heard of his healing leprosy; and was it possible that this thing, so terrible that it cut him off from the society of his people, and caused him to be held and treated as a dead man, — was it possible that Christ would be willing to deal with this as he had with other and milder forms of disease?

And, in showing that he was willing as well as able, Christ, I repeat, told the world, that as he was not repelled from the worst form of bodily evil, so he was not repelled from that of which this disease was the type. His word, "I will," his touch upon the leper, said to those who were watching him, and to all who should henceforth read the story, "Nothing stands in the way of my good-will towards those who seek me. No taint, bodily or spiritual, holds back my love or my power from one who needs and wants me. Him who wants me, I want. He who is willing will find me willing. Him that cometh to me, I will in no wise cast out. There is no *if* about my willingness any more than about my power."

Here, then, we see Christ's willingness tested and vindicated by the very worst case which could appeal to it. If his willingness did not stop at leprosy, it would stop at no form of bodily evil; and we need this lesson every whit as much as the men of that time did. The only Christ for us is the Christ who is willing to deal lovingly with *our worst*. And here the doubt comes in. To repeat what I have already said, as men acquire true conceptions of God, they get appalling and disheartening views of themselves. Like the Psalmist, they remember God, and are troubled; and this is all as it should be: only the true meaning of this terrible revelation of self is not to make them afraid of *God*, but only afraid of *sin*, — not to make them flee from God, but to bring them to him. And it is hard to convince men of this meaning, hard to make them believe, when they once fairly apprehend the evil in their own hearts, that that is just what God is aiming at; that that is just what he is anxious to cleanse them from; that that very evil furnishes the best of all reasons why they should go to him instead of keeping away from him, that the very vileness which they deplore is the very thing on which the love and power of God are eager to fasten. Hence you often hear a penitent saying, "Is it possible that God is willing to receive one so deeply stained as I am? He receives sinners, it is said; but will he receive so great a sinner as I am?"

And the same thing is manifest in the Christian struggle after conversion. The Christian *struggle*, I say. No one need tell me that that seventh chapter of Romans describes the experience of an unconverted man, or at least of such as one only. Hear the apostle: "To will is present with me, but to do that which is good is not. The good which I would, I do not: the evil which I would not, that I practise. I delight in the law of God after the inward man: but I see a different law in my members, warring against the law of my mind, and bringing me into captivity under the law of sin which is in my members. O wretched man that I am! who shall deliver me out of the body of this death?" I know nothing of Christian experience if just such a conflict as that is not in active progress in you and me; if you and I cannot say with the French king, "Ah, those two men! I know them well;" if you and I are not distinctly conscious of two forces wrestling within us, the one of which makes for holiness and self-denial and meekness, while the other pushes desperately for pride and self-will and pleasure. And we cry out, like the apostle, "Who shall deliver us?" Is it indeed the will of God that we shall get the strong man armed out of our house? Is it not too great a thing to hope for, that this sin, which dogs our steps, and breaks our peace, and fights every good aspiration, and mines away under every good resolution, shall be gotten under our feet? My friend, Christ is willing. That is just what he is aiming at, — that worst which is in us. Paul answers the "Who shall deliver me?" with "I thank God through Jesus Christ our Lord. Sin shall not have dominion over you."

And now let us see how Christ's willingness comes out in the incident of our text. And, in the first place, you observe that *his willingness is not repelled by an imperfect faith.* This leper believed only in Christ's power: he did not believe in his willingness; he only wished or hoped he might be willing. Christ did not turn him away for that: he did not make him wait until his faith was better developed. It was a good deal for him to have come as far as to believe in Christ's power. That was farther than the possessed boy's father, at the foot of the transfiguration mount, had come. *He* was in doubt about Christ's power. He had tried the disciples, and they could not cast out the devil; and so he turns to Jesus, saying doubtfully, "If thou canst do any thing, have compassion on us." Christ did not say to him, "Go away until you can believe that I have the power." He seized on the possibility which the man's mind had admitted, and sought to develop it into faith. "If thou canst," say you? "All things can be to him that believeth." And the man made a great step forward when he cried out, "Lord, I believe; help thou mine unbelief." Thomas, the Lord's own disciple, was worse than either of these two. He wanted sensible evidence of his Lord's identity, and insisted on it in a most unreasonable and disagreeable way, at which Christ might have been justly offended; but Christ was willing to give him even that, if he could only be brought to believe. You find illustrations of the same truth in the Old Testament; showing how God, instead of being offended by incomplete faith, seizes upon such as there is, and brings every possible appliance to bear, in order to strengthen it. Even Abraham, the Old-Testament type of faith, asked for a sign; and Gideon asked for a second sign after God had given him one, and received it, with a third one in addition. God's willingness is shown pre-eminently in the means which he uses to strengthen faith, so that it may lay firm hold on his love and power. Because, after all, this willingness has a law and a limitation. It is not the reckless, undiscriminating kindness of a foolish father, who gives unconditionally whatever his son asks. God is willing to give us far more than we can ask, or are worthy to receive; but then he makes faith the indispensable condition of his gifts: "Without faith it is impossible to be well-pleasing unto him: for he that cometh to God must believe that he is, and that he is a rewarder of those that seek him." Hence, I repeat, God's willingness is shown first of all in encouraging men to believe in his willingness.

I cannot help thinking that Christ knew of the approach of this poor leper before the multitude did. The man ran a great risk in coming into that company, the more so as his condition was evident to every one. The disease was at an advanced stage. Luke the physician, whose eye was quick to note such facts, tells us that he was *full* of leprosy; and yet his incomplete faith had power enough to nerve him to make the attempt to get to Jesus. I think the gracious Lord must have known that, and must have furthered his effort in some way of his own; for that was a case after Christ's own heart. His compassion made him willing to heal the man's body, but his compassion went deeper than his body. He would fain heal his soul as well; and, in order to that, he must develop in him that faith without which there is no salvation. It was much that he believed in Jesus' power. He must be taught also to believe in his love. The case of the woman who pressed through the crowd, and touched the hem of his garment, resembled this in some points. She believed in Christ's power so fully as to believe that it extended to his clothing; yet, like this leper, she seems to have had some doubt about his willingness. She would make the experiment by stealth. She did not count on Christ's knowing that power had gone forth from him; and she was confused and frightened when found out, as one who had stolen something, but she received that day something of greater value than healing. She learned Christ's heart toward the afflicted. She never again would steal to him, trembling and afraid, after hearing him say, "Thy faith hath made thee whole. Go in peace."

Christ's willingness was shown, further, in *his express declaration*. How striking is the way in which he meets that timid "If thou wilt" with "I will"! The man's only doubt was relieved at once; and not only by Christ's clear, ringing words, but by his extraordinary act in touching him. The leper knew very well, and the whole multitude knew, that to touch a leper was forbidden by the law; that a man contracted thereby a pollution as from contact with the dead. But here is a willing helper indeed, who, in his desire to save me, will break through the ceremonial law, and lay himself open to the inconvenience and the odium of ceremonial pollution. And let it be observed here, that nothing shows the good-will of Christ, his real, deep desire to save and help men, more than his readiness to come into contact with them. It is well for us to look at that fact from the stand-point of our modern habits and tastes. Neatness, cleanliness, order, the concealment of every thing offensive,—these are not merely attributes of *luxurious* living, they are cardinal principles, first instincts of *ordinary* living and of common decency; and it certainly is not open to question, that an exquisitely toned and susceptible nature, like that of our Lord, felt the full power of these instincts. And yet no one knew better than our Lord the power of those very instincts to separate the coarse and ignorant and diseased masses from the cultured and decent who should be their helpers. He knew very well how readily the poor and unclean man caught the impression that the cleanly, well-dressed man despised him, and wanted to avoid him. And the Saviour would never give room for that impression for a moment. Whatever curses the ignorant Jew might vent upon him, he never could say that he avoided him because of his poverty or his uncleanness. He never shrank from the contact of the filthy rabble which pressed round him, thrusting upon his attention their deformities and hideous marks of disease; and Christ's contact with such, Christ's hand laid upon the leper and upon the paralytic and upon the squalid children which poor mothers brought to receive his blessing, has been well-nigh as potent a sermon to the world as the Sermon on the Mount.

And the fact takes on new meaning as a type of Christ's attitude toward moral pollution. As society is constituted, our contact with men is regulated very much by outward decencies. We cannot read each other's hearts; and, moreover, we ourselves are simply imperfect men among imperfect men. But here was the purest moral nature in earth or heaven, one who knew the whole meaning and vileness of sin, one to whom the shadow of evil was horrible; and yet the story of his life is summed up in this, that he laid that pure nature right against the world's polluted heart; that he threw himself into the midst of a society, of which the most outwardly decent part was the most deceitful and corrupt, and touched that moral pollution as really as his hand touched the leper, in order to redeem and save it. This, I say, is the story of Christ's life, the expressive comment on his " I will " uttered to the leper, — " The Son of man is come to seek and to save that which was lost."

And if you will go back to the old Mosaic law, and study the directions for the purification of a leper, as you will find them in the fourteenth of Leviticus, you will see what a beautiful figure they furnish of the provision made by divine love for the purification of a sinful nature. When the priest, on examination, had found the leprosy cured and gone, the patient was bidden to bring two birds. One of these the priest killed over an earthen vessel containing fresh spring-water, so that its blood should mingle with the water; then, taking the other bird, with the cedar (the sign of preservation from corruption), the scarlet (the sign of fresh life), and the hyssop (the sign of purification), he dipped them, with the bird, into the mingled blood and water, and then let the bird fly away. The letting loose of the bird was a symbol that the former leper was imbued with new vital energy, and released from the fetters of his disease, and was now free to go where he would. The slain bird showed that the leper would have suffered death on account of his uncleanness but for the restoring mercy of God. As we look up from this strange rite in the wilderness in the shadow of the tabernacle, our eyes rest on Jesus and the sinner. Tainted with the leprosy of sin, he must die but for the exercise of sovereign mercy, — must die, not from any arbitrary decree, but from the essential nature of sin, which poisons the fountains of life. That mercy is exercised through the shedding of blood: "Without shedding of blood is no remission;" and, as we look upon the bleeding fowl and the stream of its life mingling with the pure water, we turn to the cross, and see Him who came by water and blood, even Jesus Christ, "not with the water only, but with the water and the blood," which we see flowing together from His pierced side. As the symbols of preservation, fresh life, purification, are dipped into the blood; so, as we look at the restored sinner, we see insured to him eternal life, purity, and vigorous power for ministry, through the touch of that blood upon his soul: and, as we mark the bird flying freely and gladly away toward its familiar haunts and companions; so, through the blood of Christ, we see the sinner set free from bondage, called unto the liberty of the children of God, made free of the privileges and the companionship of the household of Christ. This is what Christ's "I will" means. It means a willingness which takes in his descent from the glory of the Father; his taking upon himself the form of servant; his being made in the likeness of sinful flesh. The "I will" speaks from Simon's banqueting-hall, where the sinner meets his tender forgiveness and recognition of her act of love; from Bethany, as Lazarus steps forth from the grave; from the shores of the lake, where the raging demon departs at His word, and leaves the victim at Jesus' feet, clothed, and in his right mind; from under the olives of Gethsemane, and down from the cross in the gathering darkness,— from these, and from every sinful, penitent soul saved, during all these centuries, through faith in his blood, come the echo of that gracious word to the leper, "I will."

In our approaches to God, we must clearly recognize the truth, that God has a will to bless us. The soul that cannot be convinced of God's goodwill by his gift of Jesus Christ, cannot be convinced at all. When God had given the world Christ, he had nothing better to give it; for, in giving Christ, he had given himself: and hence the apostle well says, "He that spared not his own Son, but delivered him up for us all, how shall he not with him also freely give us all things?" If that is true, if we have indeed a Father who is more willing to give good things to them that ask him than earthly parents are to give good gifts unto their children, — why should we not come near with confidence? Why should not our lives be more richly dowered with spiritual gifts than they are? There may be one within the sound of my voice to-day, penitent for sin, with a contrite, broken heart, desiring to find Christ's rest, yet so burdened with a sense of guilt and unworthiness as to doubt Christ's willingness to receive him. Doubt no longer, my friend, as you hear this word from the Saviour himself: "I will:

come, and be cleansed." There may be one almost discouraged with the fierceness and pertinacity of the conflict with inbred sin, tempted to give up the fight, asking, "Shall I ever gain the victory?" Hear Christ this morning: "I will." He wills that you shall conquer. God's good-will is on your side; and, if God be for you, who shall be against you? What excuse can we possibly have for cherishing unwilling hearts in ourselves in the face of such willingness on Christ's part? Depend upon it, if we are cold-hearted, bound down by sin, inefficient, worldly-minded, without power against temptation, it is not Christ's fault. He does not will to have it so. It is our fault that we do not encourage by prayer that faith which he has willed shall overcome the world. Depend upon it, if we live below our privilege, and are content with scanty spiritual gifts and attainments, it is because we have not grasped the riches of meaning in his "I will." You remember what Paul's conception of the will of God toward believers was,—a conception which he evidently thought was no vain dream, since he distinctly asked that it might become a fact in their lives: "For this cause I bow my knees unto the Father, from whom every family in heaven and on earth is named, that he would grant you, according to the riches of his glory, that ye may be strengthened with power through his Spirit in the inward man; that Christ may dwell in your hearts through faith; to the end that ye, being rooted and grounded in love, may be strong to apprehend with all the saints what is the breadth and length and height and depth, and to know the love of Christ which passeth knowledge, that ye may be filled unto all the fulness of God."

XIV.

PRAYER AND PANOPLY.

XIV.

PRAYER AND PANOPLY.

"With all prayer and supplication praying at all seasons in the Spirit, and watching thereunto in all perseverance and supplication for all the saints, and on my behalf, that utterance may be given unto me in opening my mouth, to make known with boldness the mystery of the gospel, for which I am an ambassador in chains; that in it I may speak boldly, as I ought to speak." — EPH. vi. 18, 20.

THE whole of the latter part of this chapter, from the tenth to the twenty-first verse, turns on the fact of Christian conflict. This is a fact about which Paul has a good deal to say in different parts of his writings, and on which, evidently, he feels very strongly. Christians have a battle to fight, an enemy to overcome. The enemy is so strong and wily that no human power can resist him. The Christian must be clad in God's armor. Moreover, he must be armed at every point. Nothing less than the *whole* armor of God will avail. Not only so, the armor itself is valuable only as it is *entire*. It is of little consequence where the soldier is struck, if only he falls. Though his helmet may save him from a wound in the head, the enemy's purpose is gained if, in the absence of the breastplate, he can pierce his heart.

Christ's purpose includes more than the development or conservation of a single virtue in man. It contemplates the salvation of the whole man. God desires and means, not only to keep intact a Christian's faith or hope or zeal, but his *life*, — the Christian *himself;* and a successful blow at either of these is a blow at that life. Moreover, the Christian qualities figured in this picture of complete armor can exist and thrive only in company. Hope is nothing without faith; readiness is nothing without hope; righteousness is of faith only, and is nothing without truth; while truth finds its highest expression in righteousness. Then, as the soldier, however well protected, is useless without his sword; so Christian hope and truth and faith and righteousness get their highest sanction, and are taught their appropriate uses, by the word of God alone, — the sword of the Spirit. The word of God and the armor of God are as necessary to each other as the captain's orders are to the armed soldier; in short, this passage of Holy Scripture will be of little use to us unless we study it entire, and possess ourselves of the unity of all the parts.

Consequently, we cannot understand these words of our text about prayer unless we see how they are related to what goes before. Prayer is the divinely ordained means of intercourse with God. In all that precedes, we get no intimation of the personal contact of the Christian warrior with his divine Leader. This is given us in prayer. We have the word of God to the soldier; but in prayer we have the soldier's word with God, the contact and communion of soldier and general; and it is not without a purpose that the word of God and prayer are brought together here. The word of God gathers up into itself, expounds and interprets Christian truth, hope, faith, righteousness, readiness: but the word of God becomes a living power, something to strike and to slay with, only through the living contact of the Christian with Christ; and this contact is afforded by prayer only. The word of God is to be to us, not simply an object, but an instrument. It represents the aggressive side of our Christian life. The world and Satan are to be not merely *resisted:* they are to be *overcome.* The gospel is to be not only defended and vindicated: it is to be pressed upon men's acceptance. The truth of its principles must be vindicated, but the principles themselves must likewise be made forces in society. As Christians, you and I live to impress. Our Christian character is not merely something to be kept intact: it must also prevail with men, and bring them over into allegiance to the kingdom of God. Hence, it is not enough that we study the word of God, however critically; it is not enough that we hold it in our memory; it is not enough that we are kindled by its poetry, or convinced by its logic. It must pass into our life, be hidden in our heart, shape our character, and inspire our influence; and this no mere word will do. Nothing but life can impart life: nothing but character can mould character. The Bible is chiefly valuable to us as it expresses to us the personal character of God. The Bible leads us to God; but God must take us by the hand, and lead us back through the Bible, before we can gather the best out of it. It is prayer that puts our hand in God's. Those disciples whom the risen Christ met on the road to Emmaus had read the old prophecies scores of times; but they had never seen in them what came out under the talk of that stranger who made their hearts burn as he opened unto them the Scriptures. They knew why it was, when they found out who had been talking with them. And one of the strongest proofs of the need of prayer in the study of the Word is the fact, that so much of the Bible is convertible into prayer. How many of the Psalms, for instance, are prayers of themselves! How many of them you could make, with hardly a change, the forms of your communion with God! Indeed, the best Bible-reading is prayer, in the sense of living contact and communion of the soul with God.

Now, in our text, the apostle describes some of the laws and characteristics of prayer; and these we will touch upon in the order in which he places them.

First, then, we have a suggestion of the *variety of prayer*. All prayer is the same in essence; but it takes on different modes, just as your intercourse with a friend does. One day you will sit down for a long conversation; another day you will simply exchange a word as you pass each other in the street; again, you call at his office on a matter of business, and the thing is settled in a few brief, pointed sentences. So with prayer. It is not all asking. Sometimes it is only interchange, without any petition at all, — talking to God for the pleasure of communion. Sometimes it is a sharp, short cry for help, like Peter's "Lord, save me!" when he felt himself sinking. Sometimes it is merely the aspiration of the heart to God without a word, sometimes a half-conscious sympathy of thought with God, sometimes a formal public petition, sometimes a struggle to climb over self to God. We are to pray with *every* prayer, with *all kinds of* prayer. He is not always the most prayerful man who prays most regularly or most formally or most publicly. Sometimes more prayer is condensed into a sentence than is to be found in a whole series of prayer-meetings. I never can read without emotion the story of the good old German professor who sat studying until far into the night, and then, pushing his books wearily aside, was heard by the occupant of the next room to say, ere he lay down to rest, "Lord Jesus, we are upon the same old terms."

This truth is brought out more clearly in the next sentence, which suggests the *seasonableness of prayer*, — "praying *in every season*," or *on every occasion*. Some persons have been troubled by the familiar version, "praying *always*," and have asked very plausibly how it is possible for one to be always praying, if he is to do any thing else successfully. There would be no real difficulty, even if this rendering were correct. Paul bids the Thessalonians "pray without ceasing," which is even stronger. The difficulty disappears when we take a broader view of prayer as including the habitual contact of the life with God everywhere. But our text adds, to the hint of varieties of prayer, that of *occasions*, which call out these varieties. Leisure gives opportunity for deliberate, meditative communion; public worship, for formal supplication, confession, and thanksgiving; dangerous emergencies, for sharp, short cries to God. A stately liturgical formula would have been of little use to Moses at the Red Sea, or to the Syrophenician woman pleading with Christ for her stricken daughter. Every phase of a prayerful man's life suggests an occasion for prayer; and prayer has varieties enough for every occasion. Take the single fact of temptation, out of which this discourse of the apostle grows, and how many occasions for prayer it furnishes! If Satan tempts in a variety of ways, he must be met with a variety of prayers. The apostle's point, in short, is that life is full of occasions and suggestions of contact with God, and that a Christian is to avail himself of these. Keep that thought of contact with God in mind as the key to the passage. Prayer puts you in contact. The moment that contact ceases, you are in danger and helpless. You have Christ's word for it: "Apart from me ye can do nothing." You want God everywhere; you want his counsel in every thing; your joy is incomplete, yea, empty, without his sanction and sympathy; your sorrow is unbearable without his comfort; your business lacks its one great element of success if God is left out of it; you will as surely fall under temptation as you are human if God does not help you. Pray, therefore, with every kind of prayer, at every season.

We find next in order a statement of the *element and atmosphere of prayer*, — "in the spirit." You know that a great deal of the effectiveness and general quality of work depends upon the element in which it is done. One cannot work equally well under all circumstances. There are certain conditions of the atmosphere, for instance, which seem to paralyze your brain: there are certain close, hot, drizzling days when all your work is up-hill. There are certain people whose very presence freezes you, and makes you question whether you have an average amount of brains or of feeling. What we are, comes very largely out of our surroundings; just as a taper gets much of the material for combustion out of the atmosphere. A light goes out in a vacuum. A swan cannot do his best in the air, nor an eagle in the water. So the power of prayer depends largely on the element in which it works. A man who thinks he has learned to pray when he has learned the forms of prayer, is greatly mistaken. The disciples learned very little when they heard the Lord's Prayer from the Lord's own lips. They had indeed a lesson-book in that prayer, and the lessons were deep as God's own heart; but those men, at that stage of their religious training, could not know what it meant to pray, "Hallowed be thy name; thy kingdom come; thy will be done." The hymn says, Christians

> "Learn to pray when first they live."

So they do, but as a child learns the alphabet. We have to be trained in prayer as in every other department of Christian experience; and one important factor of this training is, to know in what element prayer will or will not work and prevail. The apostle tells us, that the only effective prayer is prayer *in the spirit:* and by this he does not mean prayer when one feels like praying, or, as we popularly say, "is in the spirit of praying;" nor does he mean when one prays *spiritedly*, with enthusiasm and fervor; but he means prayer under the impulse and direction of the Spirit of God. You remember that Paul, in that wonderful eighth chapter of Romans, tells us that we have a natural infirmity in prayer; that we know not how to pray as we ought; and that only the Spirit of God can help this infirmity, and teach us to pray. No wonder, then, that he says in our text, that it is not enough for us to use the varieties and occasions of prayer, but that we must also get into the element of prayer, and pray in the spirit. Otherwise, prayer is only an evidence of infirmity, like the dim burning of a candle in foul air. Let us see briefly what the Holy Spirit does for prayer.

First, it creates *a prayerful heart*. True prayer is the communion of a child with a father; and this Holy Spirit is called the Spirit of Adoption, whereby we cry "Father." That is, the Holy

Spirit creates a son's heart in us: "The Spirit himself beareth witness unto our spirit, that we are the children of God: heirs of God, and joint-heirs with Christ." That is the first thing. We never can truly pray at all until we can pray "Our Father!" You see that we need the Spirit's aid, in order to utter the very first words of the Lord's prayer.

Then, further, the Spirit suggests the *substance* of our prayers: "We know not *what* we should pray for." The Spirit searches our hearts, and lays bare their needs; and these needs in turn drive us to the mercy-seat.

Again, the spirit reveals *the love and helpfulness of God*, and so encourages us to present these many and deep needs to him. We know God through Christ, it is said. True; but we know Christ fully only through the Spirit, which, while it convinces us of sin, likewise convinces us of his righteousness.

The Holy Spirit also *communicates divine love* to our hearts. He reveals God, and gives us the spirit of sons; and we say, "Behold what manner of love the Father hath bestowed upon us, that we should be called the sons of God." "We love him because he first loved us," and this love communicates warmth and enthusiasm to prayer.

And once more, what is most wonderful of all, the Holy Spirit so identifies himself with our case that he makes intercession for us,—intercession so earnest that Paul describes it as "with unutterable groanings." In other words, God's own heart pleads for us; and our mightiest plea is there.

And now, as we move on, we are directed to the quality of *alertness* in prayer. Literally the the words are, "and *being awake* thereunto." Notice that *thereunto*, for it is the key of the sentence. Watchfulness and prayer belong together, even as our Lord put them together; and the word here falls in with what has already been said about occasions or opportunities of prayer. Watch thereunto; that is, unto *prayer*, with reference to prayer. Keep watch over prayer. When Scripture thus puts us on guard, we know that there is either a great danger to be averted, or a great treasure to be defended. In this case, there is both a treasure and a danger. We have already seen what a vital relation prayer sustains to the whole Christian life. Cut that great main which leads the water from the reservoir into yonder city, and how long will it be ere the city is in distress. Prayer is the medium of communion with God, and without that communion there is no Christian living; and so the hymn has not put it too strongly: —

"Prayer is the Christian's *vital breath*."

There is no life without God, and no contact with God without prayer: so that, if Satan can cut that main, the life is in his power; and the danger is linked with the treasure, as always. Value implies danger. The poor man's cabin is safe from thieves. The value of prayer, its vital importance to Christian life, makes it a centre of temptation. A wise general will silence, if he can, the battery which is doing his men the most damage; and, if it be true, that —

> "Satan trembles when he sees
> The weakest saint upon his knees,"

it follows that Satan will leave no device untried to keep that saint off his knees. As a fact of experience, the tendency to neglect prayer is in proportion to its importance. The excuses for such neglect are familiar to you all: the pressure of business, the unseasonable call, the concert or lecture or assembly on the prayer-meeting night, the mood of mind, — all these meet the Christian on the way to the mercy-seat, and delay him, or stop him altogether, until the roads to the closet and the family altar and the place of social prayer are grass-grown.

Hence prayer is a thing to be watched, — watched as a habit to be encouraged by practice, as a pleasure with which the Christian is to grow into a sweet familiarity by frequent communings with Him in whose presence is fulness of joy, as a duty which he neglects at the peril of his spiritual life. We should watch for occasions of prayer, cultivating the habit of associating every detail of our life with God. Often we are so placed that our seasons for prayer must be brief. So much the more need of distributing the communion over the day. Your friend in the adjoining office is as busy as you are. You cannot either of you find time to sit down for a long chat; but there are frequent opportunities in the course of the day, if you are on the lookout for them, to exchange a word, or a sign of recognition. There is a good deal of cheer sometimes in a friend's nod, or in the wave of his hand. We may often exchange a word or a look or a thought with God when we cannot stop for a long interview. Men who are travelling much, and can seldom sit down to a meal, learn to eat by the way. Again, we ought to watch *before* prayer. The best prayer comes out of the best life. We ought to try to live so that prayer shall not come in as something foreign to our life, but rather so that our life shall run naturally up into prayer. Prayer and life should be of one piece. If we watch our lives, to hold them close to God, our prayer will be simply another form of our life. Sometimes we hear the complaint, that social meetings for prayer are spiritless and heavy; and the explanation which is most readily caught at is, that the leader of the meeting does not understand his business. But while this may be true, the difficulty is more likely to lie with those who are led, in that prayer has to overcome the terrible inertia of the prayerless lives which they bring to the house of God.

And we must watch *after* prayer, to see what becomes of our prayers. He would be a strange archer who did not look to see where his arrow struck, a strange merchant who did not care whether his richly freighted ship arrived at her port or not. If we pray, we pray presumably for something; and if that something never comes into our lives, if our prayers never come back to us in the shape of blessings, it is time we were on the watch. David, in the fifth psalm, says, "I will direct my prayer unto thee;" but adds, "and will look up."

That this watching is to be *persistent*, "in all perseverance," follows naturally from what has been said. The conflict with temptation is a lifelong one; the necessity for prayer never ceases: "Long as they live should Christians pray;" and, therefore, the necessity for watchfulness never ceases.

And now, finally, the text directs us to the *objects of prayer*. Prayer must not be selfish. It is the language of the kingdom of God; and the kingdom of God is a community, a brotherhood. Prayer is the expression of the life of God's kingdom, and that life is social. We must pray for ourselves; but we must pray, also, for each other, for the whole brotherhood of God, "for all the saints." Christ himself teaches us to say, "Our Father, give *us* bread, forgive *our* debts;" and it is with our prayer just as it is with our life. We never learn the true sweetness and richness of life until we have learned to live for others, and we never reach the true blessing of prayer until we have learned to pray for others. Such prayer reacts to make our prayers broader and stronger and richer. It gives prayer a wider range, touches it into a quicker sympathy, and pervades it with a deeper emotion.

And while prayer is to be made by the Church for the whole Church, it is also to be made directly and specifically for the *leaders* of the Church, for the ministers of Christ, "and for me," says Paul; and he hints at some of the reasons why special prayer should be made for him and for the class which he represents. They have to proclaim unpopular truths. They preach Christ crucified; and he is to the Jews an offence, and to the Greeks foolishness. Hence they need courage. They are tempted to hold back the truth. They need prayer, that they may make known the truth with boldness. Then, too, the truth they preach is a deep and far-reaching truth. Preaching deals with the infinite; its theme is God in Christ, the mystery of the gospel, — truth which no man can handle unless he be taught of God. To bring that truth home with power to the infinite varieties of mind and character with which he has to deal, he needs the wisdom from above, which God gives only to those who ask in faith. He must ask this for himself; but if the church of Christ is at one with him, in the loving and saving intent of his ministry, they will ask it for him. The strongest bond between a pastor and his people is their mutual prayer. I know that we all preach ineffectively at times. I know that there is a large class of society which emphasizes the foolishness of preaching, and assumes that preaching is nothing but foolishness. But it is too much overlooked, that preaching is a thing in which the people as well as the preacher have a share and a responsibility. When a minister has prepared and preached his sermon, that service is not complete unless to the sermon the prayers of the people are added. Those prayers give a thrust and a momentum to a sermon which all the preacher's intellect and eloquence and piety cannot give. A sermon without the people's prayers is shorn of half its power. And it will turn out, I have no question, when things shall be seen in the clearer light of another world, that a very large part of the ineffectiveness of preaching has been due to the prayerlessness of the people. That eagle, with his strong wings, and his light body framed to cut the air, could not rise if there were no atmosphere for his wings to beat against. Neither will a sermon rise and fly to its lodging-place in men's hearts if the prayers of the people do not bear it up. Paul called himself an ambassador in chains. He spoke literally. He was chained by the hand to a pretorian soldier. But many a minister of Christ is equally an ambassador in chains, hampered and fettered by the lack of his people's affectionate and fervent prayers for him and for the Word he preaches. You remember how Israel prevailed in fight so long as Moses held up his hands; but his hands were weak, and would have dropped, but that Aaron and Hur stood by his side, and held them up.

Pray, therefore, Christian brethren! Pray with all kinds of prayer; pray on all occasions; pray in the power and unction of the Holy Spirit; mount guard over prayer. Pray for all the saints, pray for the ministers of the Word. This will round and complete the Christian panoply. The old fables tell how the gods used to make armor for their favorite warriors, and bring it to them, and set it up for their admiration and encouragement. This armor of God is set up before your eyes by God's messenger. It is no creation of fable. These gifts of truth, salvation, hope, righteousness, faith, are real defences against the arrows of the kingdom of darkness; but they are of little avail without prayer. Without prayer, you and I will be no more to the church of Christ, no more against the wiles of the Devil, than yonder mailed statue on its pedestal.

XV.

THE DAYSMAN.

XV.

THE DAYSMAN.

"For he is not a man, as I am, that I should answer him, and we should come together in judgment.

"Neither is there any daysman betwixt us, that might lay his hand upon us both." — JOB ix. 32, 33.

AT this point of the poem, we are seeing Job at his worst. He has become desperate under his accumulated miseries. His three friends, instead of giving him the sympathy and tenderness which his wretchedness craves, take the attitude of mentors, mete out to him reproach instead of comfort, and, assuming that his trouble is God's visitation for some secret sin, ply him with appeals to humble himself and repent. Conscious that he has hitherto served God faithfully, Job indignantly denies and fights this cool assumption of his guilt; but, in fighting away from this, he is pushed back upon another question, which takes on larger and larger proportions as he confronts it: "If I am not afflicted because of my guilt, as I refuse to believe, why *am* I afflicted?" Why are righteous men everywhere afflicted? The old current theology of his day had but one answer to give, — the answer elaborated by Bildad in the previous chapter,—God is just: therefore he must send prosperity upon the good, and affliction upon the bad. You are afflicted: therefore you are guilty. Job, like many another man, had accepted that answer until he came to apply it to his own case; and then he found it would not work. What an epoch it is in a man's thinking, when he first finds himself compelled to doubt and to challenge the long-accepted, first positions of his thought. How completely at sea he is for a while. The old moorings are swept away: to what can he tie up? The main movement of this poem is the working out of just such a problem as this. In the present chapter, Job answers Bildad. He admits that God is just; but from his infinite justice, holiness, and power, he concludes that the best man has no hope of being approved by him, and runs into a passionate and wicked outbreak against the Almighty, the amount of which is, that God is simply an arbitrary tyrant, laughing at the despair of the innocent, and giving over the earth to the rule of wicked men.

This protest he clothes in the figure of a legal trial. God comes into court, first as plaintiff and then as defendant; first asserting his rights, snatching away that which he has a mind to claim, then answering the citation of the man who challenges his justice. In either case man's cause is hopeless: "He taketh away, and who can hinder him?" If the subject of his power calls him to account, he appears at the bar, only to crush the appellant, and, with his infinite wisdom, to find flaws in his plea.

As we push our way towards the storm-centre of this whirlwind of passion, we find that it is not utterly chaotic. At first feebly, vaguely, timidly, certain lines strike out, growing more firmly drawn and more definite in direction as the poem unfolds. Certain deep-lying instincts begin to take shape in cravings for something which the theology of the day does not supply. The sufferer begins to feel, rather than see, that the problem of his affliction needs for its solution the additional factor which was supplied long after in the person and work of Jesus Christ, — a mediator between God and man.

Let us note, in the first place, the peculiar facts in Job's case which call out this desire. The point of his complaint, as we have already seen, is, that with the natural infirmity and fallibility of his race, for which he is not responsible, he stands no chance in trying conclusions with an infinite God whose wisdom charges even the angels with folly, and in whose sight the very heavens are not pure. As he sees it, plaintiff and defendant have no common ground. God is a being different in nature and condition from himself. He is far withdrawn, in his infinite majesty and holiness, in a realm of pure intelligences, ruled by different laws from those prevailing in this scene of confusion. He sees man's weakness and error, only from this stand-point. If, now, there were a *human* side in God; if his adversary were a man who knew human life and the human heart and the pressure of earthly limitations from actual experience, — then, says Job, I could come into court with him with some chance of justice. Or, if this might not be; if there were only some daysman, some arbiter or mediator who could lay his hand upon us both, who could understand both natures and both sets of circumstances, who should know both the earthly and the heavenly economy; if there were but such an one to stand between us, and interpret, and reconcile the one to the other, and compel whichever of the two is wrong to do the other right, — then all would be well.

It is wonderful, it is most pathetic, this bitter, pitiful wail wrung from a tortured heart in those far-off times, this cry for that better thing so familiar to us, and which we owe to the gospel of the Son of God, — a mediator who lays his hand on both God and man. And this leads us to observe, that this desire of Job's is to be studied, not merely as the experience of an individual under peculiar circumstances, but as a *human* experience, the germs of which are in man as man; in other words, Job's craving for a mediator is the craving of humanity. Natural instincts, indeed, are not infallible guides; but they are truthful suggesters. In the material world, it is a familiar enough fact, that the indication of a want is the indication of a supply somewhere. Supply and demand answer to each other. The channels which run up the trunk of a tree are infallible signs of the tree's need of moisture, and are answered by the streams which run among the hills. A bird's wing implies air; the human tongue, palate, and stomach imply food; the ear is nothing without sound, nor the eye without light. Shall we say that this law ceases to hold from the moment we quit the material world? "Nature," says one, "is true up to the heart of man: shall nature suddenly become a false prophet then?" The cravings of the human heart for love, for sympathy, for masterdom, for an object of worship, for knowledge, — do not these declare that the heart was made for these, and that somewhere in the scheme of things there are answers and supplies for these needs?[1] If not, might we not well ask with the Psalmist, "Wherefore hast thou made all men in vain?" Not a demonstration, indeed; but does not the groping of the human soul in all ages and places for a God, at least suggest that the soul was made for God, and more than hint at the

---

[1] "It is altogether unlikely that man spiritual should be violently separated, in all the conditions of growth, development, and life, from man physical. It is indeed difficult to conceive that one set of principles should guide the natural life, and these, at a certain period, — the very point where they are needed, — suddenly give place to another set of principles altogether new and unrelated. Nature has never taught us to expect such a catastrophe. She has nowhere prepared us for it. And man cannot in the nature of things, — in the nature of thought, in the nature of language, — be separated into two such incoherent halves. . . . After all, the true greatness of law lies in its vision of the unseen. Law in the visible is the invisible in the visible: and to speak of laws as natural is to define them in their application to a part of the universe, the sense part ; whereas a wider survey would lead us to regard all law as essentially spiritual. To magnify the laws of nature as laws of this small world of ours is to take a provincial view of the universe. Law is great ; not because the phenomenal world is great, but because these vanishing lines are the avenues into the eternal order." — HENRY DRUMMOND : *Natural Law in the Spiritual World.*

existence of a being to meet these outstretched hands, and take them tenderly into his own?

Or Christ: has Christ been arbitrarily forced upon the world to make his own place? or is there a place ready for him in the human heart? Is there no *eternal* relation between Christ and the world's need? Why is he called the "desire of all nations?" The need of Christ is not an artificial need, created by conditions of knowledge and civilization: it is a need embedded in the very structure of humanity. Christ meets an *existing* need. Manhood was made for Christ. When antiquarians, digging in the ruins of some old city, come upon the half of a beautiful statue, they are at once stimulated to search for the other half. There are limbs and feet and a body, which want a head and shoulders to complete them. When these are found, it is evident enough that the two parts belong together; so, when Christ comes, it is evident enough that there is a vacant place which it was meant he only should fill. He was meant for humanity; but, equally, humanity was meant for him. And with Christ goes this fact of mediation. Mediation is not a dogma of theologians merely. It is not an invention. It is not an ingenious contrivance to get round or over the two tremendous facts of a holy God and a sinful humanity. It meets a human need and a human craving just as truly as Christ himself does. There is a place for mediation in man's relations to God. There is a craving for mediation in the human heart to which Job here gives voice.

One needs but a moderate acquaintance with the history of religion, to see how this instinctive longing for some one or something to stand between man and God has asserted itself in the institutions of worship. What is the idol but the expression of the Pagan feeling that the Supreme Being, whatever or wherever he be, is too remote from the sphere of human life and suffering to be available? What are all attempts to figure or to symbolize the divine, but confessions that man wants God translated into the terms of his own humanity? What is the lesson of that kneeling figure beneath the cathedral arches, with eyes upturned to the image of the Virgin-mother, but that that heart knows no way to God save through a nature like its own? Men talk as if the incarnation were a thing utterly monstrous, — a miraculous, arbitrary break into the law of humanity; seeming to forget that incarnation is a *demand* of humanity; that, from the very beginning of human history, men have been striving to cast their conceptions of God and of Godlike qualities into forms or symbols which appeal to flesh and blood. Job simply tells over again the old, old story of the human heart; this, namely: God is so remote, the conditions of his being so exceptional, his majesty and power so transcendant, that direct approach to him is impossible unless in something or some one the two lives and the two conditions meet and blend, so that a daysman may stand between, with one hand on weak, ignorant man, and the other touching the divine throne itself, and interpreting the one life to the other.

This demand for a mediator is backed and urged by two great interlinked facts, — sin and suffering.

Job's question here is, How shall man be just with God? While he sturdily protests his innocence of any conscious, wilful sin which deserves this affliction, he never for a moment denies his participation in the common moral infirmity of the race; and his trouble lies just there. He urges that man as he is cannot be just with God as he is. Let him be as good as he may, his goodness is impurity itself beside the infinite perfection of the Almighty. And, really, it is hard to see how, from Job's stand-point, he could reach any other conclusion; hard to see how any man could evade Job's difficulty who should try to solve this problem with only these two factors, — a righteous God, revealed in nature, and a man, imperfect and erring by his own nature. In other words, if Christ, and all that Christ reveals of God, are dropped out of the question, and the question is simply God's approving recognition of man's merit, I do not know that Job puts the case any too strongly. Divine omniscience must detect spots in the best obedience of human hands. It "dares not appear before the throne." God cannot listen to any plea of man based on his own righteousness. It must break down, and the man must needs condemn himself out of his own mouth.

Hence Job's mind, groping round for the unknown quantity in this problem, was feeling its way in the right direction when it struck upon this thought of mediation, as was shown later, when God made that thought the very centre and basis of the Levitical system. Between God and man stood the priest, typically with his hand upon both. No man went direct to God with the burden of his sin. Some one must receive his gift, and place it on the altar, and send it up in fragrant smoke to heaven. Now, the priest turns towards God, entering within the veil with his hands laden with incense, and there, in the awful secrecy of Jehovah's pavilion, making atonement for sin; while the fragrant incense-clouds inwrap the golden cherubim, and hover over the mercy-seat. Again he turns toward the people, and lays his hands upon the head of the scape-goat, confessing over it the people's sin, and sending the beast away to wander in the desert, — strange, unconscious type of a nobler victim, mysterious, unconscious bearer of a nation's guilt. Thus turning now to God, now to the people, himself compassed with infirmity, bearing the names of the tribes ever graven in sparkling gems upon his heart, touched with compassion for the ignorant and for them that are out of the way, yet admitted to the very presence-chamber of Jehovah, — he stands, the first divinely ordained type of the daysman, appointed for men, in things pertaining to God.

You do not need to be told how beautifully the writer to the Hebrews depicts Christ as the reality answering to this type; and a blessed reality we find him when we face Job's old problem, How shall man be just with God? and come with our sins to his bar, to hold controversy with him.

Throw Christ out of the controversy, and we say, "How can I hope for sympathy or compassion at the hands of this terrible holiness? What can it do with sin but condemn it? What with the sinner but punish him? Here am I, weak and erring by nature, compassed about by all sorts of temptations, my mind held down to earth by the necessity of earning my own bread and my children's. I am overworked, overstrained, often sick, irritable, petulant; and I make, at best, but a bungling business of a spiritual life. I might urge these things in extenuation of my case if God were a man as I am; but how can I expect him, a being so infinitely superior, seated on the inaccessible heights of this pure heaven, with a nature to which sin cannot appeal, — how can I expect him to concern himself with these toils and hindrances and burdens of mine?" Thank God! I can say to such an one, "He *is* a man." I point him to God manifest in the flesh. Between God's pure spiritual essence and you stands Christ, tempted and tried like as you are: an High Priest enrolled among men, and, as a man, able to "have compassion upon the ignorant, and upon them that are out of the way." He knows by actual contact the power and seductiveness of evil; he knows by actual experience the hardest and most heavily weighted side of life: and he is touched, not only with the knowledge, but with the *feeling*, of your infirmities. No depth of sorrow so low that he has not been down there; no road so rugged or thorny that he has not walked every step of it;

no agony of pain so intense that he has not been racked by it. And so, as you come to God by him, you learn that your Judge is also your sympathizer. In coming to God, "the Judge of all," you find that you come to "Jesus, the Mediator, the Daysman of a new covenant." You learn through him, the Incarnate Word, what you never could learn so well from any written word, that the God who moulded this dust knoweth the frame which he has made, remembereth that it is dust, cares for every grain of that dust, and pitieth them that fear him, even as a father his children; for even they that fear him — his most reverent, most loyal sons and daughters — have need of pity. This Saviour, this Son of man, in whom thrills the very life of God, is able to come down to where we are, and say to us, "God is just what I am. He that hath seen me hath seen the Father."

So of forgiveness. Clean I surely am not, and never can be, in God's sight. Moral perfection in him I may admire from a distance, as I would some glittering snow-peak of the Caucasus; but it is a different matter when I come to climb, and try to find a refuge for my frailty in that perfect beauty of holiness. Sinful as I am, how can I hope that he will forgive? What can I bring to win his grace? "Will the Lord be pleased with thousands of rams, or with ten thousands of rivers of oil?" Nay, "He hath showed thee, O man, what is good; and what doth the Lord require of thee, but to do justly, and love mercy, and walk humbly with thy God?" What, indeed! Is this a slight requirement? Truly, to fill it out were even harder than to bring the thousands of victims. To do justly, love mercy, walk humbly, — that may seem to some an easy thing; but, when a man has once caught sight of God's holiness, as Job had, and has learned God's ideal of justice, mercy, and humility, he is not unlikely to reach Job's conclusion. What shall I do, then? How shall I bear his hand upon me? Even while I ask, it *is* upon me; and lo! it is a pierced hand, scored with the mark of the nail; and I hear a voice: "What the law could not do, in that it was weak through the flesh, God, sending his own Son in the likeness of sinful flesh and as an offering for sin, condemned sin in the flesh: that the ordinance of the law might be fulfilled in us, who walk not after the flesh, but after the spirit." Thus I learn that this terrible, holy God so loves and cares for me that he is anxious to forgive me, — so anxious that he becomes a man, in order that I may see divine, forgiving love translated into human lineaments and human deeds and human words. Christ says to me, "I offered this life because of your sins. This hand upon you is God's hand; and the voice which speaks to you is God's voice, saying, 'If you confess your sins, he is faithful and *just*.'" Mark that. Not one jot of that awful justice abated; yet still *faithful* to forgive your sins, and "to cleanse you from all unrighteousness." Through him I learn not only how a penitent soul may urge confidently its plea at the divine bar, but how it may be fully justified by faith, and have peace with God through our Lord Jesus Christ. The forgiveness of sins. Every sabbath we repeat it, "I believe in the forgiveness of sins," until it has become a commonplace. But it is well sometimes to look beneath these commonplaces, and see what they cover. Do we realize how much it means for God to forgive sin? Do we realize of what infinite value the revelation and mediation of Christ are in making that an article of faith? Do we realize, as Job did, how hopeless it is to seek to draw from Nature, which never forgives, any comfort or teaching concerning the tender and just dealing of infinite holiness with a finite and erring man?

Again, this craving for a mediator is awakened by human experience of suffering; a fact which is intertwined with the fact of sin. This poor, tortured patriarch! Truly, from the Christian standpoint, he is one of the most pathetic spectacles in all history: no knowledge, no dream, of Christ; no hint of such knowledge of God as is possible only through Christ; no hint of divine sympathy or of loving purpose in affliction. Take up your own bitterest sorrow, and go back with it to the ash-heap on which Job sits, and put yourself as far as possible in his place. Shut out the view of the Christ on whose pierced hand you have dropped your tears, while you have leaned against his heart, and heard him whisper the higher lesson of sorrow, — and will you wonder that Job broke out into passionate despair? Will you wonder that his heart cried out for just that which has been so ineffably precious to you? Take his view of God as his own magnificent words describe him, — overturning the mountains, and sealing the stars, and striding upon the heights of the sea, and bringing this tremendous energy to bear in afflicting a poor, weak son of man, — and do you wonder that he cried out for some one to stand between him and that awful power and holiness? Ah! there was no one to stand by Job, and say, "Look on me. I am purer than thou art, yea, spotless and sinless as God himself; yet it pleased the Lord to bruise me. Behold my hands and my feet. Thrust thy hand into my side. Sit down here, and let me tell thee of Gethsemane and Calvary, of agony such as even you never endured. You cannot understand this. You are shut up within the narrow conception of affliction as punishment and retribution. I can show you, by my life and character, how suffering ministers to perfection. I can show you how, on that hard soil watered with tears, grew up the manhood which is the world's pattern, the world's hope, and the eternal joy and glory of heaven." Christ steps forth from the darkness which veils Calvary, and says to the great host of the suffering, "Here is suffering which is not retribution, suffering which is not the outpouring of divine wrath, suffering ministered by perfect love, and issuing in power and purity." I say again, we need, our poor humanity needs, such a daysman, partaker of both natures, the divine and the human, to show us suffering on its heavenly as well as on its earthly side, and to flood its earthly side with heavenly light by the revelation. The transfigured and the crucified Christ — Christ who had not where to lay his head, and Christ to whom every knee shall bow — are one and the same. Suffering and glory blend in him into greater glory, and through him God's suffering servant learns that he suffers with him that they may be glorified together. In him we have the human experience of sorrow and its divine interpretation.

Job's longing, therefore, is literally and fully met. To the cry which comes from that far-off wreck of earthly happiness, "He is not a man as I am," we can answer to-day, "He *is* a man." To the words, "There is no daysman to lay his hand upon us both," we answer, "There is one God, and one mediator between God and man, — the man Christ Jesus." It is the fashion to decry this doctrine of mediation; to say that there is no reason why man should not go directly to God with his sin and his suffering; that God is loving and merciful, and ready to forgive. But it is sometimes forgotten how much of the knowledge and conviction of God's love and mercy are due to Christian revelation. It will not do for us to receive our ideas of pardoning love through Christ, and then to turn our backs on Christ; and I think that this Book of Job serves, among other purposes, to bring before us the picture of a man with all the moral light of his time, with a moral character indorsed by God himself, and show to us how utterly helpless and hopeless such a man is in his relations to sin and suffering without Christ, how his soul craves just such a mediator as Christ is. "The craving to see God, and to hear him speak to us, is," as has been well said, "one of the primitive, inherent, and deepest intuitions and necessities of the human heart. No student of Job can well believe that any thing short of a supernatural revelation and a mediator both human and divine, can satisfy the needs of such a creature as man in such a world as this." Thus, this oldest of books has its lesson, enforced and confirmed by the gospel, for us of this latter day, — the lesson of the need of a mediator. You need him when you come to face the fact of your own sin. You will feel your need of him more, the more clearly you shall see into the terrible foulness and wide, destructive reach of sin. You will need him to assure you of God's willingness, yea, eagerness, to receive and pardon, when, broken with contrition, you fear to trust a holy God for forgiveness. You need him to accomplish the work of pardon. You cannot bear the burden of your sin alone. You cannot render an equivalent to divine justice. God must be just because he must be true to himself; and so there is nothing for you but either to bear the penalty, or to let some one come in between you and God who can bear it for you, and say to you, "Go in peace." O my friend! talk not of mere morality as answering this deepest need and craving of your humanity. You speak of the Sermon on the Mount and its pure morality, and say that is your model. You need no mediator: you will live by that. Do you remember who gave you that code? and do you not see that the personal Redeemer and Saviour is behind and through that code, and that it is practically ineffective without him? Do you not see, that, if you take Christ's mediation from behind that code, it takes on the semblance of the old tables of the law, that the Mount of Beatitudes without Christ the Mediator is a veritable Sinai clothed with lightnings? That perfect code, so holy, just, and good,— think you, you will dare take your unaided keeping of it into court with the God who framed it, and without the Christ who effectuates it, and be justified? God forbid you should try the experiment!

And you need him in the sorrow of which, sooner or later, all are partakers. Divine love in clouds and hurling bolts is an awful, inexplicable mystery without this Daysman: with him sorrow is interpreted, and what seems to be wrath appears as pure love.

Despise not this Mediator. Seek his intervention. Come and lay the burden of your sin and of your sorrow alike on him; and it shall be with you as in the words of Elihu, — "Thou shalt pray unto God, and he will be favorable unto thee: and thou shalt see his face with joy: for he will render unto man his righteousness."

XVI.

THE LESSON OF RIPENESS.

XVI.

THE LESSON OF RIPENESS.

"For when by reason of the time ye ought to be teachers, ye have need again that some one teach you the rudiments of the first principles of the oracles of God; and are become such as have need of milk, and not of solid food."—HEB. v. 12.

THERE are two clearly defined lines of teaching in the New Testament, which, on a hasty view, might seem to be contradictory. In the one, great stress is laid on being childlike. Our Lord is heard saying, "Whoso shall not receive the kingdom of God as a little child, he shall not enter therein;" and, "except ye be converted, and become as little children, ye shall not enter into the kingdom of heaven." Moreover, he insists on this quality as a condition of spiritual knowledge, and thanks the Father that he has hidden the great truths of the kingdom from the wise and prudent, and has revealed them unto babes. On the other hand, we read such words as these: "That we may be no longer children, tossed to and fro and carried about with every wind of doctrine;" and again, "Therefore let us cease to speak of the first principles of Christ, and press on unto perfection;" and once more, "Till we attain unto the unity of the faith, and of the knowledge of the Son of God, unto a fullgrown man, unto the measure of the stature of the fulness of Christ."

The two are not contradictory, but are, rather, in complete harmony. They are only different sides of one and the same truth. On the one side, a Christian is never to lose the simplicity, the trustfulness, the guilelessness, of childhood. His growth must always be in the direction of these. If being as a little child is a condition of *entering* the kingdom of God, it is equally a condition of *abiding* in that kingdom. If a Christian does not grow in his sense of helplessness, and of dependence upon the power of God and the sympathy of Christ, he does not grow in the right direction. But, on the other hand, Christian life, like natural life, implies progress. No man receives the fulness of the kingdom of God at once. There is an infancy and a childhood of Christian experience; a feeble grasp of faith before the stronger grasp; an imperfect spiritual seeing before the clearer vision; ignorance of the weakness of the human spirit and of the devices of Satan, which gives way before the results of larger experience; superficial conceptions of the word of God, which are slowly replaced by firm apprehension of that Word as spirit and life. As in the family, the child, from being taught, gradually grows into a position of authority, from being directed by others, becomes self-determining, and has a voice and an influence in the counsels of men; so, in the great family of God, Christian maturity and its accompaniments are recognized facts, — attainments which the gospel treats not merely as privileges, but as obligations. There is a Christian manhood, in short, which is expected and *required* of the child of God, in which, from being a recipient of gospel influences, he is to become their defender, their illustrator, and their propagator. This is the truth for our consideration. It is embodied in these words of the text, addressed to those who had been for a good while under gospel training: "Ye ought to be teachers." Let us look at —

The duty of being Christian teachers;

The reason for that duty;

Some specific features of that duty.

Ye, as followers and disciples of Christ, ought to be teachers. One reason why Christ found it expedient to go away in person from the world, was, that the number of teaching-centres might be multiplied. If he had remained in the world, and depended upon his own personal instructions for success, he would have reached comparatively few. Instead of this, he sent the Holy Spirit, not confined to place, but working simultaneously at many points, in order to inform the hearts and minds of men, and to make every Christian, in some sense, a teacher. As plainly as words could speak, he laid the burden of diffusing the gospel upon his church. "Ye," he said to his disciples, "*ye* are the salt of the earth. *Ye* are the light of the world." Men are taught by the gospel that their responsibility does not cease with their own salvation; that they cannot live out their Christian lives simply with reference to God and to themselves; that, from the fact of their being members of society, they exert power for good or for evil over other lives; that they cannot be Christians, and not teach.

And that which is a necessity, growing out of the laws of human contact, Christ wants every Christian to take consciously into his life as a principle, and conscientiously to use and improve that necessity for the extension of Christian truth and the development of Christian life.

Thus the position and duty of each Christian, as a teacher, are laid down among the very rudiments of the gospel. "Ye ought to be teachers."

But this duty is here urged by one consideration merely, to which we may confine ourselves. The familiar rendering, "*for the time*, ye ought to be teachers," entirely obscures the force of the passage. One would naturally draw from it the sense of "for the time being;" as if the duty of Christian teaching were a temporary matter or a thing of special occasions, instead of being of permanent and universal obligation. The meaning is, rather, "*by reason of* the time;" that is, because you have been for a long time under Christian influence, listening to Christian doctrine, versed in Christian experience: by reason of the time which has passed since you became Christian disciples, you ought to be teachers. Here there is the plain statement of a general principle: *that*

Christian knowledge and Christian experience ought to be so developed by time as to become instructive and helpful to others.

Time is an element of all growth; and, wherever there is growth, we expect fruitage as the outcome of time. We are surprised and disappointed if the man who has been for a score of years engaged in business remains the mere petty shopkeeper he was at the first, and does not become a power in trade, a creator of new industry, a maker of wealth. We do not expect the apprenticed mechanic to be always an apprentice or an underling. Time is needed to teach him how to handle tools, and to make him acquainted with the capacity of materials: but, with the time, we expect to see him a master-workman; we look for him to develop new resources out of his material, and new methods of treating it, and thus to become a teacher to his craft. The man who through all his years is merely acquiring knowledge, and does not come in process of time to give it out, may be a prodigy of learning, but he is also a prodigy of uselessness, no better than so much lumber. And the same principle runs up into the moral and spiritual realm, and prevails there. There is, as I have said, an infancy and a childhood of Christian life in which we may expect to see uncertain walking, crude conceptions of truth, unwise zeal, and undisciplined character; but we have a right to be astonished and dismayed, if, after years of experience, that character is no less crude than at the beginning. When time brings to Christian character nothing but childhood, we are entitled to regard it as we regard the second childhood which waits upon human age. We have a right to expect, as the result of years, larger and clearer views of truth, better defined conviction, more self-mastery, more practical efficiency, and more consistency of life. I know that the mere passage of time does not bring all this to pass. Age and maturity are not the same things; but the gift of time in the Christian economy is accompanied with a charge and obligation to *redeem* the time. Time is a trust. You remember Peter's words: "If ye call on him as Father, who without respect of persons judgeth according to each man's work, pass the time of your sojourning in fear: knowing that ye were redeemed with the precious blood of Christ." In other words, the time of life is to be passed in godly sobriety and activity, because life has been redeemed at the price of Christ's blood; and life thus redeemed is a sacred trust to be accounted for to our Father, God, who is a strict judge of every man's work. The same truth is brought out in the parable of the talents. The element of time enters there. Time is given to the several servants, as well as five and two talents; and time enters into the general reckoning. The time given is an element of the responsibility: "After *a long time*, the lord of those servants cometh, and reckoneth with them;" and then it appears that time, in the Lord's mind, meant business, exchange, investment, profit. The servant who had failed to catch this meaning, and had given his time to something else than his talent, found himself in sorry plight at the end. The man who represents mere time is one of the most pitiable of spectacles. The simple fact that he is old entitles him to no respect beyond that which common humanity pays to weakness. Old age is one of the loveliest things in this world when it stands in front of an earnest life, during which it has gathered sweetness out of sorrow, charity out of contact with men, and wisdom out of experience; but old age divorced from character is not even respectable. And, if that is true in general, it is pre-eminently true in the Christian sphere. It is a sad thing when a man has been before the world for long years as a professed follower and disciple of Christ, and when all he has to show for it is that he is very old. Length of days, be it remembered, is in the right hand of wisdom.

And now let us look at a few of the points in which, by reason of time, a Christian ought to be a teacher.

He ought to be a teacher by reason of *a matured faith*, and that under three aspects: —

1. In respect of *his own assurance of Christian truth*. A man, in this age, who does not encounter much that is fresh and even startling in this department, can hardly be said to be alive. One who, in the course of an average life, has not changed or modified some of his views of Christian truth and doctrine, can hardly be said to have grown. A great deal of the truth of Scripture is given *germinally*, as a seed which keeps throwing out new

growths in the course of years. The Saviour said that there were things which his disciples could not understand at the time, but which would be clear to them later. God often gives a central core of truth, and then leaves it for human research to formulate the truth. For example, he lays down the truth, that all things were made by him; that the universe is ultimately the result of his creative will. Science investigates, and attempts to explain the physical facts of creation. The Bible gives us no information about God's methods. Science may discover the method if it is able; and it is reasonable, that science should give us new light on these methods, and should modify or change our views concerning them. To all that new light, we may rightly open our windows. All that we are asked to hold by as Christians is that core of truth, that our Creator, and the world's Creator, is the ever-living God. So the integrity of the Bible, as the word of God, is a distinct thing from certain questions about the Bible. It is not affected by the showing of biblical criticism that Solomon did, or did not, write the Book of Ecclesiastes, or Paul the Epistle to the Hebrews, or that the Pentateuch was, or was not, made up of a series of documents. On such questions, we have a right to hold ourselves open to all the light which earnest scholarship can give us; and it would be strange indeed if some of our traditional views were not greatly modified, or even entirely changed.

But we profess to be Christians, and by that profession we avow our faith in a certain body of truth. Its elements, indeed, are few and simple, but they are fundamental; and our Christianity takes all its character and all its meaning from them. Our Christianity, if it has any meaning at all, means Christ, the divine Son of God, and not a mere man like ourselves. It means Christ taking our human nature on himself, Christ living in our world, Christ crucified, Christ risen from the dead, Christ ascended to heaven and living there forever, and Christ the Judge of quick and dead. It means God, our Creator and everlasting Father, and the presence and energy of the Holy Spirit. It means salvation through faith in a crucified Redeemer. Whatever leaves this out is not Christianity. To the world, these may still be open questions; to us as Christians they cannot be open questions, any more than the foundations of a house can be left to be finished while the superstructure is going up. The whole superstructure takes its shape and its security from the foundations; and whatever Christ may be to others, if he is not the chief corner-stone of our moral and spiritual life, that life has no settled basis and no consistency. And if our Christian profession during all these years has been any thing more than a name or a form, if it has been, as our very profession implies, a living, genuine experience of the saving power and daily grace and sympathy of Christ, we ought by this time to have reached settled convictions on these points. We cannot be teachers otherwise. True, effective teaching is bound up with the teacher's conviction of the truth. Teaching is something more than repeating lessons from books. In every kind of teaching, success is measured by the degree in which the truth has become a part of the teacher himself. A truth suffers even by the advocacy of a man whom it does not possess. And this is pre-eminently true of Christian teaching. The instructive power of the gospel resides very largely in the lives which it shapes and pervades and propels. The *life* is the light of men. Ye ought to be teachers, but ye will not be if the gospel is still an open question to you. Ye will not be if your attitude towards its foundation-truths is that of suspense.

You know and acknowledge the power there is in profound conviction. In the discussion of social or political questions, you know how deeply you are often moved, even by a man who represents what you do not believe, but who himself believes it with his whole heart, and speaks out of the abundance of his heart. Conviction carries power. And, I repeat, this is not a matter of words only. Most of you, if you teach at all, will do it more by your life than by your words; and you cannot keep your life apart from your conviction of Christian truth, or from your want of conviction. If your basis of Christian life is an open question, the uncertainty and suspense will get into your living. The New Testament recognizes a direct relation between faith and conscience. Paul writes to Timothy that "the end of the charge is love out of a pure heart and a good conscience and faith unfeigned;" and Peter told the council at

Jerusalem that God cleansed the heart by faith. And therefore faith which purifies the heart and the conscience is the mainspring of right living; for out of the heart are the issues of life; and weakness or vagueness of faith will get into the conscience, and will issue in weak and vague living, and therefore will take out of the life its great power of witnessing. Paul, in that same letter to Timothy, tells us how well such faith as that worked for teaching. — "The end of the charge is love out of a pure heart and a good conscience and faith unfeigned: from which things some having swerved have turned aside unto vain talking; desiring to be teachers of the law, though they understand neither what they say, nor whereof they confidently affirm."

2. Again, time ought to develop faith, in the sense of *spiritual discernment*, — clearer perception of the things of the unseen world. That is something different from a man's feeling that he is growing old, and realizing that his friends are dropping around him, and that he must soon die. Any man will be made to feel that in the course of nature. The seaman may see the rocks and shores fast falling behind, and hear the roar of the surf, and yet have no outlook ahead. The outlook is one of the great things in Christian experience. As by reason of the time the old scenes and the old friends fall into the background, we ought to be getting clearer views of the great moral and spiritual truths which have their roots in the unseen world, and a deeper sense of their impor-

tance and power. It is not strange if a young Christian simply *believes* in the things which are not seen. It is strange if the older Christian does not *feel* the power of the world to come. It is one thing to *assent* to the truth that "the things which are not seen are eternal;" it is another thing to *apprehend* that truth, and to take it into life as a working principle; to realize that the things on which heaven stamps a value — love and faith and purity and truth and good conscience — are the paramount things, and to make every thing give way to these.

That kind of spiritual seeing has a teaching power. It is of the very essence of all teaching that the man who sees what we do not see, brings us to his feet to learn. When we want to know about the stars, we go to the scholar who has the telescope. And the life which one lives by faith in the unseen, teaches. It does what all true teaching must do, — it excites attention, it awakens inquiry, it communicates enthusiasm. Paul says, "Our conversation, or our citizenship, is in heaven." The stranger who tarries among us for a little while, born of another race, subject to another government, clad in another costume, receiving his instructions from beyond the sea, all his hopes and interests centring in that country which he sees with his mind's eye, all his expectation converging towards his return thither, — that stranger is a marked man. He awakens our curiosity to know something of his country and institutions; and, as we talk with him, we catch something of the flavor of that land which we never caught from the descriptions of our geographies. A ripened Christian, with his citizenship in heaven, brings to us in like manner the flavor of the heavenly world. The world learns how a man may live and thrive on meat which they know not of; learns the power there is in those heavenly qualities of meekness and faith, and poverty of spirit, which seem to it so puerile; learns how he can endure as seeing Him who is invisible. A quality steals into his life and words which gives the worldly man hints of a country strange to him, and a subtle attraction gets into his life which affects the most world-hardened heart.

3. And time ought to have ripened faith in the sense of *restfulness*. We count it strange if natural manhood does not bring with it increased composure, tranquillity, balance. Shall we count it any less strange if, with the lapse of time, Christian manhood does not become better poised, more restful and quiet, less easily thrown off its balance? Have we not had experience enough of God's strength to make us settle down on it, and trust it? Have we not found out so well how much better he can take care of us than we can take care of ourselves, that we have learned, not only to put ourselves in his hands on occasion, but to stay there all the while, and to be uneasy only when we do not feel the pressure of the Everlasting Arms? That kind of restfulness has a teaching-power. You know how naturally, in any time of danger or

confusion, all eyes turn to the man who is calm and self-poised. Even the gay, dissolute heathen poet had learned to admire the man just and firm of purpose, and eloquently pictured him as one whom neither mobs, nor the frown of tyrants, nor the wrath of storms, nor even the world falling in ruins, could disturb;[1] but a higher lesson is taught by him who can say, " Who shall separate us from the love of Christ? shall tribulation or anguish or persecution or famine or nakedness or peril or sword? Nay, in all these things we are more than conquerors through him that loved us. For I am persuaded, that neither death, nor life, nor angels, nor principalities, nor things present, nor things to come, nor powers, nor height, nor depth, nor any other creature, shall be able to separate us from the love of God, which is in Christ Jesus our Lord." We are seeking rest. These men who have come to Christ, and have found rest, have power to teach us, and to tell us where to find it. We Christians, who by reason of time should have entered deeply into this rest, ought to be teachers.

By reason of the time, a Christian ought to have been confirmed in *the habit of communion with God.* Our hymn says, that "prayer is the Christian's vital breath," and that he learns to pray, as to breathe, when *first* he lives. That is true. But you know that an infant's breath is feeble. Prayer is a subject of discipline. No man learns all its resources at once. No man learns how

---

[1] Horace, Ode 3, b. III.

to pray as he ought all at once. To a young Christian, prayer is commonly a matter of systematic observance; and that is a good thing. It is a part of his training in the art; but it usually takes time to make prayer the atmosphere of the life, and communion with God the habit of the soul. A young Christian is very likely to call in God after he has done his very best in something, and has found his own strength fall short. A ripened Christian begins by assuming that his own strength is perfect weakness, and so calls in God at once. I have somewhere seen a little story of a king who had employed some people to weave for him, had supplied them the materials and the patterns, and had told them, that, if they were ever in trouble about their work, they were to come to him without fear. Among those at the looms was a child; and one day, when all the rest were distressed at the sight of the tangles in their yarn, they gathered round the child, and asked, "Why are you so happy at your work? These constant tangles are more than we can bear." — "Why do you not tell the king?" said the little weaver. "He told us to, and that he would help us." — "We do," replied they, "at night and at morning." — "Ah!" said the child, "I send directly whenever I have a tangle." Brethren, we ought to have reached that point by reason of time, — that habit of referring everything *at once* and *directly* to God; just as, when we are walking with a friend, we naturally refer to him every matter of interest as it comes up. That habit of communion with heaven sets its mark on the life and invests it with a teaching-power. If one draws from cultured associations a quality which impresses itself on other minds in a way they cannot understand, surely familiar converse with heaven will impart its quality to a Christian. Cowper's lines are worth quoting: —

> "When one who holds communion with the skies
> Has filled his urn where those pure waters rise,
> And once more mingles with these meaner things,
> 'Tis e'en as if an angel shook his wings:
> Immortal fragrance fills the circuit wide,
> And tells us whence these treasures were supplied."

By reason of time, a Christian should have become a teacher in the matter of *habitual consistency of life, obedience, and docility.*

Surely, surely, though the patience of God is wonderful, and the grace of God abounding, we should not continue in sin that grace may abound. True, we shall be erring mortals to the very end, compassed about with infirmity. True, no day will ever pass but that, to the prayer, "Give us our daily bread," we shall need to add, "Forgive us our debts." But certainly, by reason of time, we should have gained some power over temptation in the course of our experience of temptation. We should have learned to keep habitually away from the paths where we have stumbled and fallen. It is strange, something is wrong, if we are still committing and repenting of the same old sins which we began to fight long ago. As the lines of that living epistle which we began writing when we entered Christ's service creep farther down the page, they ought to be more fairly and evenly written. In short, though we shall never be *perfect* men and women, though the nearer we get to Christ, the less we shall be pleased with ourselves, — yet we ought to be *better* men and women by reason of the time, and, by our better living of the gospel, be teachers to those about us.

And, by reason of the time, we ought to be *broader in our charity*. Our own experience ought to have given us an insight into our own weakness and fallibility, and to have made us correspondingly tolerant of the weakness and fallibility of our brother men. Where we have stumbled so often, we shall not jeer when a brother stumbles. It was to those very Christians who had made the greatest attainments in the Christian life, that Paul referred for restoration those who should be taken in a fault: "*Ye which are spiritual*, restore such an one in the spirit of meekness." He knew that real spiritual maturity, so far from making one censorious and self-righteous, turned him upon his own heart to consider its weakness, and made him the best and most sympathizing helper to his fallen brother.

Ye ought to be teachers. There ought to be more fruit of Christian maturity in the church of Christ. How a church, made up largely of Christians who have tasted the good word of God and the powers of the world to come, and in whom years have wrought, along with God's processes of discipline, to compact and balance and ripen character, — how such a church ought to tell on the community! — a church of teachers as well as of learners, teaching by godly life and conversation: teaching by the poise and symmetry of character; teaching by calm courage and steady persistence; teaching by the power of a faith which links their life with the principles, the motives, the joys, the aims, and the hopes, of heaven; teaching by their solid grounding in the word of God, and in the great truths of redemption: this is no fanciful ideal, no chimera of a religious enthusiast. It is the pattern of a Christian church held up by inspiration itself. The word of the apostle comes to us this morning (God grant it may come with fresh meaning under the power of the Spirit!): "That we may be no longer children, tossed to and fro and carried about with every wind of doctrine, by the sleight of men, in craftiness, after the wiles of error; but speaking truth in love, may grow up in all things into him, which is the head, even Christ."

XVII.

STRENGTH, VICTORY, AND KNOWLEDGE IN YOUTH.

XVII.

STRENGTH, VICTORY, AND KNOWLEDGE IN YOUTH.

"I write unto you, young men, because ye have overcome the evil one. . . . I have written unto you, young men, because ye are strong, and the word of God abideth in you, and ye have overcome the evil one." — 1 JOHN ii. 13, 14.

COUNSEL is the prerogative of age. Christianity is pre-eminently an experience. That which is most quickening in it is born of experience; and experience, in its turn, is born of years.

It is not strange, therefore, that the venerable John should assert the privilege of his age, no less than of his position, in writing to young men. These are Christian young men whom he addresses. They have overcome the Evil One, and the word of God abideth in them. Nevertheless, they are not, for that reason, beyond the necessity of wise counsel. Youth may, and does often, serve Christ loyally; but it cannot fully appreciate the quality and reach of Christ's mastery. Youth may be taught, and may believe, that Christ's person and truth are the very core and kernel of all life and of all history; but time alone makes them realize that Christ not only fits everywhere, but gives the law everywhere. Youth may be told, and may acknowledge, that the world passeth away; but it does not feel it, and especially it does not feel that *the desire* of the world is passing away. Age knows that it is passing away, because, for it so much of the world has already drifted out of sight; and therefore the claims of the will of God, as against the love of the world, come with no such emphasis as from the lips of age.

But we are concerned this morning, not so much with the counsels of this aged and beloved apostle as with the assumptions which underlie them, and which, as it seems to me, are quite out of the line of our popular Christian sentiment.

For we commonly look upon youth as a season of tutelage. Whatever we may concede to it, — and we concede very much, as will shortly appear, — we regard it as unripe. Even from the religious stand-point, we look upon youth as militant, rather than as victorious. The fight with the Evil One is upon them; but the victory, we take for granted, is in the future. We are disposed to be lenient when the Evil One gets the upper hand for the time. We do not expect them to have the word of God abiding in them, to be possessed by the spirit and power of the Word. We accept the partial and remittent influence of the Word upon them as a necessity of their age. We know they are strong; but we do not expect them to be strong in God, and in the power of his might.

Are we right in this view of the religious possibilities of youth? Certainly not, if our apostle is right; for this assumption of ours directly contradicts his. He addresses the young men as strong, as having overcome the Evil One, as having the word of God abiding in them. Is he thinking of a few exceptional young men? He does not put the matter in that way. He writes to the Christian youth of the Church generally. If he had said only, "Ye are strong," we might have construed his words to mean merely the native freshness and vigor of youth; but his words are of spiritual strength, spiritual knowledge, and spiritual victory.

The question, therefore, is very pertinent, whether we are justified in looking for only a crude, feeble Christian development in youth; whether we do not set the standard too low, and therefore encourage them to do so.

Now, in fact, we reason just as John does, when we look at youth in its relations to society. On that side, we frankly recognize their strength, victory, and susceptibility to truth. As for strength, young men are accepted as important factors in the active and aggressive relations of life. They are invited to posts of responsibility; they occupy positions of trust in business; they come to the front in politics; men put their legal tangles into the hands of young lawyers, and intrust their own and their children's lives to young physicians.

In like manner we assume their ability to receive and apply the teachings of human wisdom. They come under the power of the great masters of thought; they are set to study Plato and Aristotle and Kant in the schools; they discuss among themselves the theories of political leaders; they read with zest the writings of great scientists; the word of a Huxley, a Tyndall, a Spencer, abides in them, and shapes their thought. They are trained by the masters of painting and music; they appreciate the pictures of Murillo and Raphael, and the harmonies of Beethoven and Wagner.

So of victory. Youth overcomes. It wins victories in the world of mind. It gains the world's ear, and helps to shape the world's opinions. The history of great literary successes is largely a history of youthful triumphs; it displays an intellectual vigor equal to its physical power; it faces great problems of practical life, and solves them; it makes a place for itself in spite of obstacles. In the secular sense, it does overcome the world. Youth exhibits a strong individualism. There is no parent who has not at some time awaked, as out of a dream, to the fact that the children, whom he had been wont to regard as mere reflectors of his opinions and practice, have developed a quality of self-assertion and self-determination; that they have formed opinions of their own, and are moving upon lines of life and thought quite different from his; that they are no longer integral parts of his life, but distinct units. And, as time goes on, he finds that these self-determinations are not mere caprices, but that they have direction and consistency, and work themselves out to definite results. In short, we admit that strength, victory, mental receptiveness, and power of assimilation, are characteristics of youth, as such, apart from all its moral relations.

After we have thoroughly taken in this fact, we may be disposed to look again at John's words, and to ask why the fact should not hold equally on the moral and religious side of youth: in other words, why youth, who are susceptible to the best thoughts and principles of masters in science and art; youth, who win intellectual and social and material victories; youth, who are strong on every other side, — should be only half-mastered by the word of God, devoid of all spiritual definiteness and force, and mere defeated weaklings in the greatest of all battles, — the battle with temptation and sin.

The text, then, does certainly assert two things: first, That youth is a power; second, That it is a power for holiness. And I hold its teaching, therefore, to be, that we have a right to expect of our Christian youth, Christian vigor, Christian knowledge, and Christian victory. Let us look at each of these points.

I write unto you, young men, because ye are strong. There may be strength without maturity. People act upon that principle everywhere. A man who wants a good horse looks out for a young horse. A lady who wants an active and useful servant does not seek for an old man or woman. Not only so, but we expect real and telling service from youth. The business man who employs a young man as cashier or book-keeper gives over those departments of the business to him, and expects that the books will balance, and that the finances will be kept in order. He does not expect him to be a weak, nerveless, unreliable element in his business, always making mistakes, and requiring to be helped on by older men. He takes him as a power. Ought the case to be any different in the church of Christ? Young men, I know, cannot fill all places in the church, even as the book-keeper cannot fill the place of the capitalist; but there are places which they can fill, and where we have a right to expect that they will be powers. The work of instruction and of counsel may be left to maturer Christians; but the work of the church is not confined to instruction and counsel. It has an aggressive side, where strength is in demand. The work of pushing the gospel into new fields, of bringing other youth under its influence, of carrying on benevolent and missionary enterprises, is work which young men and women can do. You show that you can do it when you undertake it. An organization, formed and sustained by young ladies in this city, has issued in a reading-room for messenger-boys, which harbored something like a thousand of these little fellows in one year. There were heathen scattered along this avenue and elsewhere in the city. You young men were urged to try and bring them under Christian influence; and you went out, and sought the Chinaman in his laundry, and brought him here, to teach him to read, and to speak our tongue, and to tell him of Christ. You have done it, and you are doing it; and I doubt if even yet you wholly appreciate the reach of your work, or the fact that you have quietly addressed yourselves to the practical solution of a problem which has occupied the attention of the church councils, without waiting for them.

There is a small hospital in this city where little or no provision was made for religious services. Last winter I found that two or three young men — one of them, at least, a member of this church, and I am not sure but all of them — had quietly taken the matter in hand, and were regularly holding services there; and I learned, too, of the ability and efficiency with which they were doing that work, and how eagerly their coming was looked for each week by the inmates of those wards.

Yes, you are strong; and the church of Christ lays claim to your strength. You came into the church to serve, not to be entertained. When you came before these altars, to profess your allegiance to your Lord, he met you there, and asked you to put your strength at his disposal; and, if you do not recognize that claim, you are blind to your duty. If you do not respond to it, you are untrue to the Christ whom you profess to serve. Service is not to be an incident of your Christian life: it is to be its law, as it was the law of Christ's life. The sooner you accept the truth, that as Christians you live for other people, the sooner you will be down upon the firm, hard base-rock of the gospel theory of life. Some one once said, that a highwayman demands your money *or* your life; but Christ demands your money *and* your life. I would have you recall the words which were read to you when you professed your faith before the church: "We are now receiving you to take part with us in maintaining the honor of the church of Christ, and in the defence of the faith once delivered to the saints." I beg that you will not think those words meaningless. We conceive that Christ and his church do you honor by inviting you, not as children to be pleased and amused, but as strong to help us in our fight against the Devil.

But the question is not only of Christian work: it is also of Christian character lying behind the work, and inspiring it. There can be no good work without good character. Here we see, that the strength of which John speaks is the strength which comes of the abiding of the word of God in the heart, and of victory over evil. He assumes that youth may have fixed principles, positive, religious character, and victory over temptation: "Ye have overcome the evil one." Youth's record may include moral victory. And here we are dealing with fact, and not merely with theory. Youth, as we very well know, is not characterless. Strong traits, positive, definite tendencies, emerge in the very child. A moral bias in one or the other direction reveals itself very early, and often with a force which neither discipline nor punishment seems able to control. Youth is susceptible to bad influences,—takes them in, is shaped by them. Is it not likewise susceptible to good ones? Bad character in youth is a positive and acknowledged fact. Is not good character in youth equally a fact? Evil in youth overcomes good influences. Is it impossible that good in youth should overcome evil influences? So far as religious principle is a matter of knowledge and training, the great truths of morals and religion are as easily comprehended by the child as the principles of arithmetic and grammar which he learns in the school. The child of five years may, and often does, learn them, and apply them successfully to the conquest of his little temptations, which have as much moral significance as the mightier and subtler allurements addressed to the mature man. As a fact, we see that young people, very young people, do develop positive religious character. With all the sneers at early piety, early piety is a blessed fact. And why not? It is very evident what youth can do in the way of victory over self and temptation, when a great worldly end is to be gained. How many young enthusiasts in art will deny themselves to the last pinch, in order to go abroad, and, when there, will resist temptations to self-indulgence, and live in a garret on a pittance, while they are studying music or painting! How many a young man, in order to acquire a college education, will stint himself in the very necessities of life, and imperil eyes and health, and bear the sneers of fops at his poor clothes! He gets his education, he overcomes; and are we to say that the young Christian, with Christ's inspiration in his heart, and Christian influences around him, and God behind him, shall not take up the great crosses of Christian service, and practise its grand self-denials, and resist and overcome the world, the flesh, and the Devil? Shall not his youth already have scored some victory over evil, and have developed some determinate character and some fixed principles against which the floods of temptation shall break in vain? Are we to assume that youth must be always weak and vanquished on its moral side? Must we admit that the Devil is always stronger than youth, and weaker than ripe manhood only? To do this is to give the lie to Christ's words about Heaven's interest in the little ones. It is to say, that, while God suffers the *fight* with temptation to come with all its fury upon youth, he gives the *victory* only to ripe age. And the Bible biographies, at least, do not tell us that story. A large proportion of the great moral slips recorded in Scripture have been made by middle-aged and old men: Noah, Job, Lot, Moses, David, Solomon, Elijah, Peter, are startling comments on the truth that moral weakness is peculiar to no age; while, on the other hand, young Joseph, young David, young Saul, young Samuel, young Ruth, young Josiah, young Timothy, — all testify that moral strength and victory are peculiar to no age. No: John is right. He does not assert too much when he says, "Ye have overcome the evil one." If youth can be Christian, it can overcome. If it is truly Christian, it *will* overcome; for Christ is victory.

And once more, what of the Word abiding in the young? "The word of God abideth in you."

In the order of the text, this comes before the conquest over the Evil One, and rightly; because the Word in the heart stands to conquest as means to end. John's thought here centres in the word "abideth." His emphasis is on the permanent power of the Word over youth. This means more than the pleasant memory of old Bible-stories carried by youth from childhood. It means more than the transient interest in an eloquent sermon. It means, rather, the Word's mastery of the young; the Word in the heart, no less than in the memory; the Word as the law of the life; the Word as the well-wielded weapon of moral victory, — the sword of the spirit, with which Christ, in the freshness of his manhood, met and vanquished Satan in the wilderness.

This mastery by the Word, John assumes as a fact in addressing the young men: "The word of God abideth in you." Paul assumes the same thing with reference to Timothy. He calls to mind the unfeigned faith which dwelt in his mother and in his grandmother, and adds, "And I am persuaded that in thee also." Young people have, many of them, come to think that such mastery by the Word is impracticable. They think they must master the Word before they are mastered by it. They get hints, and sometimes more, of grave discussions which are going on over the Bible; and they come to think of the study of the Bible as a labyrinth of hard questions which must be left to theologians, and with which they have nothing to do. The consequence of this is, that the Word gets no hold on them, even as they get no hold on the Word. The Bible, it is true, cannot be mastered, if mastering it means understanding all that it contains and suggests. Divine truth must always have a side of mystery, from the very fact that it is infinite. If you and I could perfectly master the Bible, we should not need it. But if the difficulties of the Bible are a reason for neglecting it, they are equally a reason for neglecting God and Christ. We cannot find out God by searching, and yet we pray to this God whom we do not wholly know. Enough can be known to call out our adoring love and our implicit trust. We do not deny God because we cannot perfectly understand him. Why should we refuse his Word? In science and art and philosophy, the difficulty of a subject does not repel youth. They study, and that intelligently, the works of master minds. They comprehend difficult subjects. They work out hard problems in engineering and astronomy. And what I complain of in a certain class of young people is, that they will not apply to the Bible the same amount of attention and labor which they bestow on other things. When they meet a hard question in physics or mathematics, they go to their teachers, and discuss it: but they will read, and brood over, the words of infidel philosophers and lecturers; they will take up the cheap, superficial objections against the Bible, and never examine for themselves how much they are worth, or consult their religious teachers, who could enlighten them.

What great book does not present difficulties? There has been as hot discussion over the authorship of Junius' letters, as vigorous cross-firing on the Homeric question or the worthless epistles of Phalaris, as subtle criticism on Shakspeare, as there has been over the Pentateuch or the Gospels. And yet young people read Homer and Shakspeare, and enjoy them. Why not the Bible also? There is enough in the Bible which the child can understand, enough which the youth can grasp. — fully enough to give it the mastery of the young life. Whatever mystery may attach to the Bible, the materials for character-building lie on its very surface. If there are parts of this great divine map which we must still mark "unknown land," the track to goodness and to heaven is sharply drawn. The wayfaring man, though a fool, need not err therein. It is enough for the seaman that his compass points to the north, even though it does not lead him into strange seas, which he is curious to explore. You may not know all the rich ore which lies buried in this mountain of God, but its duty side is out in the sunlight; the very children can climb it towards heaven, and gather fruits and flowers on its massive sides. The young men and strong men can move upward over its rocks into the pure atmosphere of the high lands, and see from its lofty outlooks the rich pastures of the kingdom of God, and the far horizons of divine truth. We have inspired authority that the young may live a clean and godly life by the use of God's Word: "Wherewithal shall a young man cleanse his way? by taking heed thereto according to thy word."

You are, then, as young men and women, bound by your Christian profession to have the word of God abiding in you, as a permanent impulse and formative force in your character and life. It is for you as well as for age. You can appreciate its calls to faith in God and Christ, to purity of life, to industry, to patience, to consistency, just as well as I can. The Holy Spirit is as ready to make its precepts a living power in you as he is in me. It is not a question of your familiarity with theological problems, but of your reception of plain, practical truths. It is indeed knowledge that is bound up with personal character. The Bible instructs you, that it may form you. It gives you knowledge, that you may translate it into goodness and spiritual power. If you can grapple with current questions of science and politics, you can take in the truth that there is a God, your Creator, who claims to be remembered in the days of your youth; that there is a Christ, your Saviour, and that you can come to him as he invited even the children to do: that Christ gives the law to life; that duty is better than sin; that Christ points towards unselfish service. And you can appreciate the point of warnings, the comfort of promises, the inspiration of noble examples, the stir of calls to duty. You know, in other spheres, what it is to work on a principle and for a purpose; and it is no harder to know this when the principle is laid down by Christ, and when the purpose is holiness and heaven. The word of God abideth in you. O young Christians! can you say this morning that this is true of you? Has the Word which godly parents and teachers instilled into your childhood been welling up in your lives ever since with a fuller flood? Has that Word, which you promised to study and cherish when you confessed Christ before the church, been a steadily working and growing power in your life? Have you kept this heavenly guest with you by constant questioning and communing? Has the power of the Word over you become stronger, more steady, more direct, since you began to follow Christ?

This, which the apostle assumes of youth, is, therefore, to be your ideal. You ought to be, as *young* Christians, strong and victorious, under the mastery of God's Word; and that, not only for your own sakes, but for the sake of the Church and of the world. Vagueness, wavering in the character of our Christian youth, menace great interests of the future. You are back one or two ranks: you do not see what is coming, as we do who are at the front. We would not have you brought suddenly to face dangers for which you are unprepared, and against which the great defence will lie in your pure and Christ-like character, your thorough mastery by the power of the Word. A few years more, and our heads will no longer be between you and the enemy's advance. We shall be down, and carried off the field; and the brunt of the battle will be on you. A fight is coming on from many points. The thoughtful, the studious, the educated among you, will have to face religious and social problems which are daily rolling up complications. If the next age is to be a victorious age for the gospel, its professors must go into the fight with settled convictions, with established moral principles, with a steady enthusiasm for Christ, with a faith that can remove mountains. Whatever your education, whatever your culture, you can all alike compass the apostle's ideal of godly character; and character, quite as much as knowledge, is going to decide this conflict. You can have the word of God abiding in you, and be thoroughly under its power, and shaped by its precepts. You can overcome the evil one. You can be strong, — strong in God and in the power of his might. May he give you the victory!

XVIII.

GOD AND THE TIMES OF IGNORANCE.

XVIII.

GOD AND THE TIMES OF IGNORANCE.

"The times of ignorance therefore God overlooked; but now he commandeth men that they should all everywhere repent."
— Acts xvii. 30.

THERE are few scenes in Scripture or elsewhere of more profound interest and meaning than that of Paul on Mars' Hill. In the Athenian people and civilization, the heathen intellect and the heathen faith attain their climax. Athens represents the very best and most that either of these could effect. The outcome was artistic beauty, false philosophy, and idolatry. These are now confronted with a new faith in the person of Paul. Standing in the public tribunal, surrounded by the representatives of the great philosophic schools, and with the beautiful objects of Pagan devotion on every side, he puts into one broad statement the representative thought of Pagan idolatry: "The godhead is like to gold, silver, and stone, graven by man's device." He briefly and sharply characterizes the error as a mark of ignorance. The stamp upon all the splendid artistic paraphernalia of worship is that of ignorance, — the ignorance of the past perpetuated in the present. It was a severe thing to say to a people who cherished the past so fondly, who deified its great men, that all the old worship of their fathers, all the dear old stories of gods and heroes which it was still their delight to embody in gold and ivory and gems and marble, were but marks of ignorance, — especially severe to a people who boasted of their culture; and perhaps not the least irritating thing was the attitude in which Paul represented his own God — that God so new and strange to his hearers — towards their religious history and worship. He had tolerated it, overlooked it, as a matter which in no way concerned his own honor. Truly, it was not strange that Epicurian and Stoic sneered, and asked, "What will this babbler say?"

This is the point for our study to-day. Paul's words bear one, and but one, simple construction: that God tolerated and permitted, or, to use his own word, "overlooked," the follies of an ignorant and idolatrous age: "The times of ignorance therefore God overlooked."

This raises, as you at once perceive, the very difficult question concerning certain things which God has permitted to run their course in past ages, — things which will not for an instant bear the test of even the lowest Christian morality. It would be the height of folly to underrate or ignore this difficulty. I certainly am not presumptuous enough to think that I can wholly resolve it. But we can face facts, we can grasp general principles of God's administration as revealed in the facts, and we can walk together as far as the Bible and history give us solid footing. And thus I think we shall obtain some light at least, and get upon lines which, though they may not carry us as far as we might desire, certainly bear in the right direction. We shall never be the worse Christians or the worse theologians for acknowledging real difficulties when they arise. It would be the strangest of things if the economy of an infinite God did not present some real and some insoluble difficulties to the finite understanding.

As we study the Bible history, we see two movements or currents in progress simultaneously. One of these we may call the natural historic movement; that is to say, the progress of a history, like that of Israel, for example, according to the natural laws, the ordinary physical influences under which nations mature, such as climate, soil, migration, conquest. There are those who refuse to see, in the history related in the Bible, any thing more than this. When, for instance, Abraham goes out from his country, it is merely the ordinary migration of a Semitic tribe beyond the Euphrates. The Hebrews go down into Egypt because of its fertility, and under the pressure of famine. The same results ensue as always where a stronger and a weaker race come into contact. The law of the survival of the fittest holds. The stronger race subdues and enslaves and oppresses the weaker. The natural revolt against oppression follows. There is another migration, and the oppressed people find the way at last to Canaan.

Then comes, naturally, a long period of confusion. Two hostile races are side by side, like the Normans and the Saxons in England. The civil polity of Israel is struggling to shape itself to the new conditions, and this struggle throws to the surface the strange characters and incidents of the Book of Judges. Gradually the need of an absolute head develops: the popular voice demands a king, and the monarchy is instituted. This, I repeat, is the only aspect of the Bible story which some will allow; but another, and let us hope a larger, class detect another influence and another movement in this history; and to them this is the *controlling* movement, the influence which gives character and direction to the other. That is the *providential* movement, the outworking of a divine purpose. In other words, the Bible is, to such readers, a record, not only of the great national changes of nations and men, but of these changes as shaped and guided by a superintending Providence toward the fulfilment of a divine purpose. Thus, where the philosopher sees only the migration of a tribe under some physical pressure, the religious historian hears the Lord say unto Abraham, "Get thee out from thy kindred and from thy father's house." Where the one sees Abraham blindly conforming to the fierce Syrian ritual which bade him slay Isaac, the other hears God say, "Take now thy son, thine only son, and offer him on the mountain." Where the one sees only the natural uprising and emigration of a slave people, the other sees God beginning to mould a nation to preserve and transmit his truth.

And to us, at least, the Bible ceases to have any special moment or meaning if this element is left out of it. If the Bible is not the record of God's saving and educating purpose in the world, if God is not behind and through its historic movement, then the Bible is unworthy of our special reverence.

Now, our difficulty arises out of the fact that these two movements, the natural and the providential, are mysteriously intertwined; that God's design works itself out through much which, to an educated Christian sense, is cruel, selfish, and even brutal, and by means of men who fall below even the lower types of the social morality of our day. Certainly, if we were called on to select types of devout servants of God, we should not choose Samson nor Barak nor even Gideon. They are passionate, revengeful, superstitious, sometimes loose in morals; and yet they are placed by a New-Testament apostle among the heroes of faith. Take, for instance, the story of Jael. She is represented as acting under a divine impulse. She is praised by the prophetess Deborah as the Lord's deliverer of Israel; but, after all, say what you will, it was a brutal thing to drive a tent-pin through the temple of a sleeping man. It was a treacherous thing to allure even an enemy with hospitable invitation and with promise of safety. Or Samson, announced as devoted to God from his birth, and of whom we keep reading at intervals, "The spirit of the Lord came upon him," — can you commend him to your children for imitation? Or, there is that horrible business of the Canaanites, which, in some aspects at least, must, I fear, continue to be a puzzle, — the divine mandate to exterminate man, woman, and child. These are terrible facts, and facts which lie in our way as inevitably as the crossing of the Red Sea or the birth of our Saviour.

Take the matter of genealogy. Take that genealogical line which we should naturally suppose would have been kept absolutely pure along its whole length, — the line of our Lord's human descent. And yet it is not so. He was of the tribe of Judah, but you find some strange episodes in the history of Judah. He was of the stock of David; but the Book of Ruth and the Book of Chronicles will tell you that Salmon was the father of Boaz, and Matthew will tell you that the mother of Boaz was Rahab.

Such illustrations — and they are but specimens of a great number — show us that, in the Bible, the natural and the providential currents do not run side by side like the Rhone and the Arve, where they issue from Lake Geneva, each preserving its own distinct color, but, on the contrary, mingle; so that, to human eyes, God's work in history seems discolored by human passion and infirmity.

Now, as I have already said, these facts involve difficulties; but we can nevertheless discover, running through the mass of facts, some straight tracks leading us to three general principles, which we will do well to have clearly in mind always when we read our Bibles.

The first principle is one with which you are already familiar; namely, *that there is a progress in the divine revelation in the Bible,*— a progress from limited to fuller revelation, from smaller to larger knowledge, from more contracted to expanded views of God and of truth. The Bible is a record of a revelation given, as we are told in the Epistle to the Hebrews, "at sundry times and in divers manners." Take, for example, the truth of the incarnation, the very heart of Scripture. There is a fulness of time which must come before the Redeemer can be revealed; until then there are foreshadowings, types, symbols, prophecies. Now, after Christ has come, the same law holds. He plainly tells the disciples that larger and richer developments are to come after him: "I have many things to say unto you, but ye cannot bear them now. Ye shall see greater things. When the Spirit is come, he shall guide you unto all truth." God's earlier revelation is confined to an individual, a family, a tribe. He appears as a God of the Jews, a national God. The idea of the Father of all mankind comes later. Or, take the doctrine of immortality. How imperfect its revelation in the earlier Scriptures! How dark and chaotic the picture of the future life drawn by Job! It has no sanction in Jewish law, no symbol in Jewish worship: it is never appealed to as a motive to exertion, nor upheld as a comfort in trouble. What a step to the revelation of life and immortality in the gospel! Or, take the matter of spirituality in life and worship. Is there not a distinct progress from a religion which required the complicated apparatus of altars, ark, candlesticks, curtains, incense, shew-bread, sacrifices, to that which intelligently accepts the truth that God is a spirit? So, too, there is a progress from the morality which must be held in leading-strings, kept to duty by specific rules and minute precepts, to the freedom with which Christ makes his disciples free, throwing them upon the guidance of the conscience enlightened by his Spirit. All these illustrations, with a multitude more, show us clearly that the revelation of God and the unfolding of character in Scripture are as the progress from starlight to the brightness of noon.

But this principle necessitates a second, — *the principle of accommodation.* We must never forget that we, as Christians, read the Bible from a New-Testament stand-point; and that, consequently, if we read the Old Testament expecting to find New-Testament standards and principles in operation there, we shall be constantly disappointed and puzzled. As a recent writer has most aptly said, "We must leave our own position amid the worked-out results of revelation; and we should divest ourselves of our Christian associations, which are the results of the whole educational work of God in history." When you read the Book of Judges, for instance, you cannot help saying, "These characters are not for my imitation. These deeds are not such as I ought to do. These words would not become my lips. How is it that men who say and do such things are marked as the servants of God, and endowed with his Spirit? Or, here are certain things permitted, even commanded, by God. They seem inconsistent with what the gospel teaches me to believe of his character: what am I to think?"

You cannot help thinking that there is a terrible inconsistency if you do not recognize the fact of progress in revelation, and the consequent fact of the accommodation of revelation to the actual condition of mankind. You cannot make the full tide of the Hudson at the Tappan Zee run in the channel of the little brook among the Adirondacks, though the brook may grow into the river. No more can you expect the full tide of Christian revelation to fit the moral conditions of Israel when it stood before Sinai. And therefore, as a fact, we find that God does adapt his mode and measure of revelation to men as he finds them, instead of miraculously fitting the men to his highest revelation. For example, take the Israelites at the Red Sea, and let Christ have come in the flesh, and have uttered the discourse in the fifteenth and sixteenth of John, or the Sermon on the Mount, — would it not have been as an idle word in their ears? Could they have received those sublime truths? Therefore, he gave them symbols and rites, — the ark and the altar, the pillar of cloud and of fire. What was the revelation of God in human form but an accommodation? Man would not understand God by hearing that God was a spirit; and so the Infinite took upon himself the form of a servant. Why did he not make man by a miracle fit for his latest revelation? All that can be said is, he did not do it. For reasons of his own, he adapted his revelation to men as they were. And we ourselves stand upon the same basis. There is more in revelation than we have yet seen; there is a glory to be revealed; we might as properly ask why God does not fit us at once to receive the full weight of glory as it comes down upon a heavenly nature. We know simply that that is not his way; that we could not bear it if it were revealed.

But this principle goes farther. It is impossible to deny that God gives temporary sanction to certain things which will not stand the test of Christian morality. There is polygamy, for instance. The New Testament refuses to recognize it. The Christian sentiment of the age abhors it. The civil law of the Christian community punishes it. And yet it is among the accepted facts of the primitive times, and God blesses the offspring of polygamous marriages, as in the case of Joseph. Abraham was no less the friend of God and the father of the faithful because he had Hagar as well as Sarah to wife, and Jacob was called a prince with God, though Rachel and Leah shared his conjugal affection. Slavery was incorporated into the Mosaic law. God might have brought the ages of Deborah and of Samson up to the level of the Sermon on the Mount, but he did not. He might have worked out his purpose by new methods specially devised; but he took men's crudity and cruelty and savage passion, — the practice of war and all its attendant miseries, — took them as they were, and let these things work themselves out according to their natural law, according to the spirit and the methods of their age.

Christ recognized this fact clearly enough. When the Pharisees appealed against him to Moses on the question of divorce, he said, "Moses, because of the hardness of your hearts, suffered you to put away your wives: but from the beginning it was not so." That is to say, the standard of true marriage was fixed in the beginning in Eden: "Therefore shall a man cleave unto his wife, and they shall be one flesh." What was Christ's baptism by John but a temporary adaptation to crude religious conceptions? What else did he mean by "suffer it now"? Or do not his words in the Sermon on the Mount point back to a similar accommodation? "Ye have heard that it hath been said by them of old time" — and those sayings were in the law too; they were not mere popular proverbs: "but I say unto you" something different and better. Surely the pure utterances of God do not repeal each other.

We have, thus far, two principles. First, that there is a *progress* in divine revelation; second, that there is an *accommodation* in divine revelation. To these we must now add a third, without which the whole question would be left in worse confusion than before.

The principle is this: *that through this partial, growing, and accommodated revelation, God is continually working toward his own perfect ideal.*

You can easily see, that if you once admit this fact of a progressive revelation, — and you cannot deny it, — the character of the revelation must be judged by its general tendency and by its outcome. Suppose, for example, I should give a peach-stone to a man who had never seen a peach, and tell him, that, if he would plant it, it would yield a delicious fruit; and if, after a few weeks, he should dig it up, and, finding the seed just sprouting, should come jeering, and saying, "Do you call that a delicious thing?" you all see what the proper answer would be. Back of the fruit is a *process*, a long process. Why God did not make the peach to spring in an instant fully ripe from the ground, is not the question. It is enough that he did not, but subjected it to the law of growth; and you cannot pronounce upon the meaning or the quality of that process until the tree is grown, and the fruit hangs ripe and blushing on the bough. Then all becomes plain. So, back of the perfect law and the perfect manhood of the gospel lies this slow, moral growth of humanity. You cannot understand God's meaning in it until you see its consummate result. When you once perceive that the Bible means Christ, that the history recorded in the Bible moves steadily toward Christ, then you may begin to understand that the imperfection of the early time means perfection in the later time; that God's toleration and accommodation are simply parts of the process which is to issue in the cheerful subjection of a man in Christ to the perfect law of the gospel. Hence, "The morality of a progressive dispensation," as Canon Mozley remarks, "is not the morality with which it starts, but that with which it concludes." When you want to form a judgment of some great historic man, do you study carefully the first ten years of his life, marked by his crudeness, passion, and waywardness, and stop there, and decide that the man was a hasty, weak, passionate man? Do you not rather read his life backward in the light of his glorious prime? Do you call his father weak, inconsistent, corrupt, because he bore with the boy's childish folly, and accommodated his own higher wisdom to the lad's ignorance and crudity? As, therefore, we study God's economy in the Bible history, we find that there is a continuous upward movement in it. Toleration is exercised, not as a compromise with sin, but with a view to making toleration unnecessary. With all its accommodations, God's economy is never content to leave the man or the people in the condition to which it accommodates itself. It accommodates to raise. Its testimony against sin is clear, unvarying, trumpet-toned throughout. Its punishment of sin is terrible. Side by side with the record of the call and approval of such agents as Samson and Deborah, goes a faithful record of divine retributions. But, through all, God's purpose is clearly defined to lead men up to a higher level of morals and faith. The polygamic ideal of marriage moves upward toward the Christian ideal as embodied in Paul's beautiful words to the Ephesians. Christianity finds slavery spread over the Roman world; and it does not begin a crusade against slavery, which would have rent society asunder and defeated its own ends, but takes Roman society as it finds it, and infuses the spirit of the gospel into the relation of master and slave: and yet Paul sends Onesimus back to Philemon. Gradually the great Christian truths of the dignity of the human soul, of the personal right and responsibility of the individual, of the law and spirit of love, are gathering force and leavening society. It was a little gain when it gained strength enough to make a law forbidding a slave to be crucified. It was a further gain when Constantine forbade the separation of the families of slaves. It was a further gain when Justinian abolished all the old restrictions of the Pagan laws upon manumission, and granted to the freed slave nearly all the privileges of the citizen. In the old city of Ravenna, lying down amid the marshes of the Adriatic, stands a noble church, built in the sixth century; and as one stands amid its graceful arcades, its richly carved capitals, its costly slabs of Greek marble, its blazing mosaics, his mind runs down a long perspective of history, as he remembers that this church was dedicated by a Roman emperor to the memory of a slave who was buried alive for exhorting a brother martyr to fidelity under his tortures. That was a gain upon Nero's time. And so the leavening process went on, until, in the fourteenth century, slavery had ceased in Europe; and still on, until, in its last stronghold, the institution was honeycombed, and fell to pieces, and not even the appeal to the law of Moses could save it. That was just what God had meant all the while. Elijah was a prophet of fire, harsh and stern. None the less God used and honored him in his own generation, — yea, so much as to say, "There shall not be dew nor rain these years, but according to thy word." And yet Christ rebuked the disciples who wanted to do the very same thing that Elijah did, — to call down fire from heaven on those who had insulted him. God had sent the fire at Elijah's call. Christ told the disciples they were of another dispensation, where the spirit and deeds of Elijah were out of place. "Ye know not what spirit ye are of. Ye are ignorant." The time of Elijah's ignorance, God had overlooked; the Christian disciples' ignorance, Christ rebuked and corrected; and yet the God of Elijah, and the Christ who reproved James and John, are one and the same. There is no inconsistency between the sending of fire and the forbidding of fire. Elijah is first understood, and his place fixed by the spirit and the deeds of Christ. There is a very significant passage at the close of the eleventh of Hebrews, in which these Old-Testament saints are ranked among the heroes of faith, — a passage which groups them all under the general law we have been discussing: "God having provided some better thing for us, that they, apart from us, should not be made perfect." What does this teach but that God's purpose in the education of men does not fulfil itself in any man or generation of men, but in the whole history of mankind. According to this, we are not to view Abraham and Moses and Gideon and Samson merely with reference to their own time, but as parts, along with ourselves, of God's great movement in bringing the race to the measure of Christ's manhood.

But we must not leave this subject without alluding to the practical conclusion which Paul draws from God's forbearance in past ages: "The times of ignorance therefore God overlooked; *but now He commandeth men that they should all* everywhere repent." In other words, God's tolerance in the past is a warning against presuming on his forbearance in the present. So far from being an encouragement to sin, it is a most pregnant warning against sin, a most imperative call to repentance. God bore with the crudeness and ignorance of the men of olden time, in order that men of a later and more enlightened day should have no excuse for claiming his forbearance. A very different conclusion this from that which certain men at the present day draw from this Old-Testament record, making it a ground of attack upon God's character, and a reason for rejecting his later revelation in Christ. As we in happier times read of those old days of brutal struggle, cruelty, character tainted with human passion, our proper sentiment is that of wonder at the patience of God through all these ages, of admiration at the wisdom of his forbearance, of congratulation that he has provided some better thing for us. Let me repeat, that, through all these ages of patient forbearance, God's testimony is uniform, unmistakable, terrible against sin: and the true course of every man who studies this record is, to turn his face toward the cross; to seek in Christ's sacrifice deliverance from the power of the evil passions which wrote their mark so deeply on the olden times; to find in Christ's character the model for the spirit and the deeds of the man of to-day. In the light which is thrown backward from the cross, Barak, Deborah, Samson, Jephthah, — yea, Jael with her cruel hammer and nail, — stand, saying to the men of this generation, "Repent, repent! we acted but according to the light we had. That we were God's instruments was not the result of our virtue, but of his wisdom and tolerance, which used the agents at his hand. But you, under the light of the gospel, with our errors on record to warn you, with the example of One who knew no sin to beckon you to purity of life and sweetness of spirit, — repent ye! the kingdom of heaven is at hand."

My friends, this history is reproduced, on a smaller scale, in your individual life. You have had your times of ignorance and crudeness, your times of the dominion of passion; and though you have had less excuse than they had, yet how your life has been marked by the forbearance of God! How much he has overlooked and pardoned in every one of us! What is the practical result of this forbearance in your case to-day? Has it led you to a true estimate of sin? Has it made you afraid of sin? Has it led you to the Lamb of God, which taketh away the sin of the world? or are those terrible words of the apostle verified in you, "Or despisest thou the riches of his goodness and forbearance and long-suffering; not knowing that the goodness of God leadeth thee to repentance? but after thy hardness and impenitent heart treasurest up unto thyself wrath against the day of wrath and revelation of the righteous judgment of God; who will render to every man according to his deeds"?

XIX.

THE PROMISE OF INCOMPLETENESS.

XIX.

THE PROMISE OF INCOMPLETENESS.

"And these all, having had witness borne to them through their faith, received not the promise, God having provided some better thing concerning us, that apart from us they should not be made perfect." — HEB. xi. 39, 40.

THERE was a plain mechanic in a little town in Scotland, who feared God, and built houses for a livelihood. He never had more than three months of schooling in his life. Let us draw a circle round the seventy-five years of that life, and look at it merely by itself. Measured by the ordinary standards of the world, how cramped it is! how short in its range! how insignificant! What does one builder of peasants' cottages, more or less, matter? But, then, *can* we look at that life in that way? Can we look at *any* life in that way? It is plain to us all that we cannot; for every life everywhere establishes connections and creates consequences. The statement of Scripture, "No one of us liveth unto himself," may be said to be self-evident; and, therefore, no man's life-account can be made up at his death. It is with a life as it is with a large estate. It cannot be closed up at once upon the death of the testator.

Certain obligations have a given time to run. Certain outstanding amounts of capital may not be paid in for years. Certain lands or houses cannot be sold until certain other persons die. And we all know, moreover, that an estate may depreciate after the testator's death. His investments may not turn out well in the end. Indeed, it is doubtful if the real sum total of any man's life can be stated until the end of all things. This humble mechanic, for instance, was the father of a son whose name is known and honored wherever the English language is spoken. To James Carlyle's narrow life in the village and in the kirk and in his own cottage, must be added the sum of Thomas Carlyle's life, and the influence of his writings, and the influence of the men whose thought has been stimulated or shaped by those writings. And so the son himself says, "Let me not mourn for my father; let me do worthily of him: so shall he still live even here in me, and his worth plant itself honorably forth into new generations."

I have taken this familiar illustration as containing in itself the substance of my text to-day. The truth it gives us is, that no man's life can be estimated by itself, but helps to complete the past, and is completed by the future. No man's life can be judged as an isolated unit; it must be judged as part of a whole: and therefore every man is a debtor to the past and to the future.

This is a peculiar text. These people — Abraham, Jacob, Moses, and the rest — were the spiritual heroes of an earlier time, representing the nation's moral high-water mark. They were powers, and society acknowledged and bore witness to their power. Yet there was a good in store, which, though they contributed to it, did not come to them. There was a promise infolded in their life which was not fulfilled to them, but to those who came after them. We should naturally say, that, if there were any large and healthful result to follow the sacrifice of home, the surrender of royal splendor and culture for the desert and the society of a slavish rabble, the dangers of the lion's den and of the fiery furnace, it ought to have fallen to the lot of those who made these sacrifices, and faced these dangers. But it was not so. They bore themselves, in these hard conditions, in such a way as to call forth the admiring witness of their time, and of later times; but "they received not the promise," and the better thing provided was for those who came after them. If their life is to be estimated only in itself, if its record is to cover only the sum of its years, then this state of things seems unjust and cruel, and the life itself of little account.

But you at once see that the writer is taking a far wider view than this. He is contemplating these early heroes, not only by themselves, but as links in a great succession of men of faith. He is viewing the results of their life as parts of the great development of humanity at large. What they received or enjoyed of ease, pleasure, or success is not the question: but in what relation did they stand to the world's welfare?

Now, the recognition and acceptance of this as a law of life has a vast and decisive influence upon any man's character. It shapes a man of a different type from one who regards his life as an end to itself; and it is here set down to the credit of these Old-Testament heroes, as an element of their faith, that they apprehended this larger law, and lived by it; that they put mere personal considerations out of sight, — were content to be merely stages, and not finalities, in the great growth of human history. They saw that there was a richer future, which they were not to share personally. Moses had to be content with the wilderness, and to forego the promised land, to which he had brought the people. Jacob was not to enjoy the brilliant future which his dying eyes saw. Joseph could provide only for the resting of his bones in Canaan: he was not to see it. And hence the writer says of these men, that they saw the promises as sailors see dimly the shore of a desired and beautiful land, where they may not disembark. They "confessed that they were strangers and pilgrims on the earth." "Now," he continues, "they that say such things make it manifest that they are seeking after a country of their own," — a place beyond this world. "Now they desire a better country; that is, an heavenly." In other words, all this matter of success and reward and happy fixedness is transferred to another realm. They forego these on earth. So far as this world is concerned, their life goes to minister to other lives, and is simply a factor in the progress of mankind as a whole.

This is a far deeper and wider conception of faith than we commonly form. We are disposed to make faith exclusively personal, to trust God mostly for what he will do for *us*, or for those most closely bound to us. We say to ourselves, " We must trust God for daily bread, for provision for old age or sickness, for a place in heaven ;" and so we must. So Christ commands us to do ; but, at the same time, he teaches us to give faith a much wider range. Let me illustrate simply. You and I are citizens of this republic. More than twenty years ago its existence was menaced. War was in the land, public sentiment was divided, disaster was imminent. Every man knew what significance lay in the issue of that conflict for a long future. There were two ways of looking at the matter. A man might consider simply the possible effect of the war upon his property, — whether his securities would be depreciated or not; whether he was to be left in comfort and luxury, or thrown upon his daily toil for his daily bread, — and that view would determine his attitude towards the whole conflict. He would embrace the side which promised best for himself. There were such men, and they met with the contempt which they deserved ; but there were other men, and more of them, who saw something larger than their own fortune. Their faith and hope and desire took in the whole great question of the nation's welfare. The dominant thought with them was not, " What will become of me and of my fortune ?" but, " What is to become of the country ?"

And this was the thought which made them joyful over victory, and despondent over defeat. This was what made them pour their money into the nation's treasury, and put themselves into the ranks. It was the merging of the individual man's interest in the interest of the State and of millions yet unborn. Similarly, in becoming Christians, we become citizens of heaven. If we are loyal citizens, our thought must include the interests of the kingdom of heaven: and these must be the *dominant* interests, rising above all selfish considerations; for the very first condition of citizenship in the kingdom of God is, as Christ very plainly tells us, to deny self. We are parts of a great divine economy, of a great march of ideas and character; builders on a great building of God, each carving his stone, or laying his few courses of brick; husbandmen in God's vast domain, each tilling his few acres, — one sowing, another reaping; one planting, another watering. No man's faith is perfect which regards merely his own salvation; no man's prayer is according to Christ's standard which leaves out, "Thy kingdom come. Thy will be done on earth as it is in heaven."

Thus identifying ourselves with the interests of God's kingdom, — the whole development of our race, — we find ourselves identified with a process. The perfect man, the perfect society, are not created out of hand. They have not come yet; but they are slowly coming, and coming through much crudeness and imperfection by the way. Thus, then, the kingdom of God is no exception to the law which obtains in other kingdoms,—that growth involves imperfection and destruction. Take the law as it holds in nature. Growth comes through death. The corn of wheat brings forth fruit only as it dies. In nature's processes, we find much which serves merely as the step or the scaffolding to something better and greater and more beautiful, and which, when its purpose is accomplished, passes away. Where are last year's leaves? They came forth in freshness and beauty last spring, as they are coming out this morning; they waved and rustled through the summer heats; they served their purpose of shade; they gathered the influences from the atmosphere for the nurture of the tree, and gave them back again in moisture; they sheltered the growing fruit; and then, when the fruit was ripe, they faded, and fell like dropping gold through the autumn haze. They had done their work: they were no more needed on the branch. If they had a further mission, it must be under new forms and conditions. There is the worm. It crawls in the sun, and lies upon the leaf, and then wraps itself in the cocoon; and then springs forth the butterfly in all the glory of gold and purple: and the worm-life and the cocoon-life have done their work, and have given that beautiful creation to the air and the flowers, and they pass away.

Go higher up, into the life of man. A perfect, healthy child, how beautiful it is! how winning, how innocent! how natural and graceful its attitudes! What parent has not found himself looking back to the years of infancy with a feeling that the years which have made his children men and women have robbed him of something ineffably sweet and precious? Childhood is only a stage: so is youth, with its flush of hope, its high aims, its fulness and vigor of life; and so manhood, with its strength and achievement. In a normally developed life, each stage, as it passes away, hands over to its successor something better and stronger. Does the process end with old age? Is there not something better beyond the line which we call death? Scripture itself breaks out into praises of the human body, so fearfully and wonderfully made; but the charnel-house tells you what becomes of this divinely ingenious mechanism: "Thou turnest man to destruction; and sayest, Return, ye children of men;" and a new generation comes to the front, only to run the same round, which ends in the sepulchre. A wondrous waste it seems to us.

So of society. It passes through crude conditions, which give place to higher and better conditions. There is a race which does not enjoy, and is not fitted to enjoy, Raphaels and Shakspeares and Dantes, but which plies the sword and the axe, — a rough-handed and rough-mannered race. The delicate touch of the harp-string, the cultured intercourse of the saloon, are for the later generations for which these have made the standing-ground. One here and there, some prophet of his time, catches glimpses of these higher possibilities, but only sees them afar off. One life is spent in evolving the powers of electricity: the man who comes after reaps the full benefit of the telegraph and telephone. A Columbus discovers America: we enjoy it.

Go still higher, into the region of religion and worship. The same law holds. Religion is not given to man full-grown. The true faith works its way into shape and power out of a mesh of false faiths. One by one these fall off, and die, leaving only what is essentially true to be taken up into the new and higher form. The history of religion is indeed a history of the march of eternal truths; but it is also a history of accommodation and temporary provision, of the breaking of types and the fading of shadows: "He taketh away the first, that he may establish the second." God tolerates stages of crudeness and imperfect moral development: "The times of ignorance God overlooked." He holds back from one age forces which come into play later. He left out, for instance, from earlier methods of moral training, the stimulus and discipline which we get from the revelation of a future life. Why? I do not know. Why did he not send Christ at once to Eden's gate to meet the banished inmates? I do not know. I know only that all the generations from Abraham to David are fourteen generations, and from David unto the carrying away into Babylon are fourteen generations, and from the carrying away into Babylon unto Christ are fourteen generations. Therefore we have dark hints of a race of giants, of an age of brute force, out of which flash the sparks from Tubal Cain's hammer; and the notes of the wild "song of the sword" are heard, and the huge bulk of Babel rises through the mist. A chaos of wickedness, and then a chaos of tumbling waters. Then the patriarchal history, with the faith of Abraham, indeed, but with the worldliness of Lot, and the trickery of Jacob. Then the seething transition period of the judges,—Shamgar with his ox-goad, Jael with her hammer and tent-pin, Samson with his gigantic strength and grim humor and childish passion and gullibility, Gideon with his lamps and pitchers and trumpets,—and so on, down through the monarchy and the prophetic age. Not one of the men mentioned in this catalogue in the eleventh of Hebrews can be held up as a perfect model of character for the men of a Christian age. The New-Testament morality is higher than that of the old. The sabbath-school child of to-day has richer spiritual revelations than Abraham had. The humblest Christian believer has what Samuel and Elijah had not.

And as to worship, we say, "God is a spirit: and they that worship him must worship him in spirit and in truth." *We* come to God without priest or victim or symbol; but what a stretch between our stand-point and that of the Israelite! — a stretch strewn with broken types. What a carefully arranged ritual for the Jew! What solemn charge to Moses to make all things according to the pattern drawn up in heaven, and shown him on Sinai! What minute, specific directions about the details of ark and altar, fringe and curtain, material and workmanship! and yet only that all might pass away: "He taketh away the first, that he may establish the second." Prophet, priest, king,—one after another, God breaks these types in pieces as the fulness of time draws on, when Christ, the Teacher, the great High-priest, the Lord of lords, is to come into the world.

We come, then, to the second truth of our text. Having seen the fact of imperfection, we see that along with the imperfection goes a promise. You notice the peculiar word here, "received not the *promise*." It is noted as a mark of the faith of these good men, that they saw a promise of something better in the imperfection of their own age. Christ bears witness to this in the words, "Your father Abraham rejoiced to see my day; and he saw it, and was glad." In like manner, Moses saw a nation in the rabble which went out of Egypt. To him the desert meant Canaan. So in nature, the seed, even in its falling into the ground and dying, utters the promise of the corn: the blossom, as it is borne down the wind, promises the fruit. Even the falling leaf, as it settles down to its new task, promises next spring's juices and leaves. So in the moral progress of our race. Paul tells us, that "That is not first which is spiritual, but that which is natural," that "The first man is of the earth, earthy;" but in these he sees the promise of something better. "*Afterwards*, that which is spiritual. As we have borne the image of the earthy, we shall also bear the image of the heavenly. It is sown in corruption: it is raised in incorruption." Society, in its best development to-day, is imperfect: the ideal form of government is yet to be revealed: but, as we turn over to the vision of John on Patmos, we see a perfect society, a holy city, a heavenly Jerusalem, a faultless administration.

Now, the practical question for us is, what is our true attitude toward these two facts of imperfection and promise? Our text tells us, by the example of these men of old. They were imperfect men; they lived under imperfect conditions; they saw a possible good which was not for them: but through faith they accepted the imperfection, and made the best of it, and cheerfully gave their energy, and endured their suffering, to make the coming man and the coming time better than themselves and their time. Hence the peculiar expression of the text: "they, *without us*, should not be made perfect." Abraham, Isaac, Jacob, good men in their time and way, were not complete either in themselves or in their work. They went to the making of better men, like Paul and James and John. Nor were they completed in Paul and James and John. We see from this chapter that their work did not end with their death; for they are taken up into the New-Testament economy, and used here as examples and helps to the faith of New-Testament times. Nor will the character and work of these patriarchs be complete until the perfect man in Christ shall stand forth as the ripe fruit of the Christian centuries, — until the kingdom of Christ shall have come, and his will shall be done on earth as it is done in heaven. In that man, Abraham and Noah shall be made perfect. In the fully ripened social economy of that time, the ages of the patriarchs and judges and prophets shall be completed.

We are on the same line. We and our time are simply a stage toward something better. With all our boast of high civilization, elaborated jurisprudence, rich spiritual acquirement, and vast knowledge, there is something better for the men of the coming time. They will know more, and enjoy more than we do. They will be better men than we are. They will have greater riches of spiritual culture. The life of every thoughtful Christian is full of pain because of what is unrealized and unfulfilled; because he discerns greater possibilities of Christian knowledge and Christian efficiency: "We ourselves, who have the first fruits of the spirit, groan within ourselves." We are chafed by the hardness, the ignorance, the obtuseness, of men. We mourn over numberless cruelties and neglects. We are indignant at the corruption and trickery of politics. We weep in secret places over the coldness and apathy of the church. But the simple question for each of us is, what are we going to do with it all? What will faith do for us in this condition of things? We may sit down with folded hands, and say, "The world is going to destruction; happiness is impossible; perfection is an idle dream; and we will give ourselves up to the tide, and be carried down." That course will not mark us as men of faith. Or, we may take the stand-point of faith, the stand-point of the men of this chapter. If perfection is not for us nor for our time, it need not follow that perfection is impossible. If perfection cannot attach to any one age, it may come out as the resultant of *all* the ages. The question is simply this: are we willing to accept the imperfection of our own time, and to do our utmost and our best in it, knowing that we shall not reap what we sow with tears and toil? knowing that the perfect man and the perfect time are to come in hereafter?

It is a high test of faith for a man to do his best under temporary conditions, as a mere fraction of a great whole, as a mere means to the development of some better thing in a future which he is not to enjoy; and yet that is the lesson which God's administration teaches us. How much care and skill and beauty go into merely temporary things! Take a wheat-corn, that very thing which is to fall into the ground and die, and split it open, and put it under a microscope, and what a perfect and beautiful organism it is! Look at that apple-blossom, which in a few days will be blown away by the wind, and what perfection of form, what delicacy of texture and tint! Each one of those living motes which dances for an hour in the setting sunlight is finished with all the nicety of your own anatomy. Nature is prodigal in her apparent waste of beautiful and perfect things. So, when God gave a temporary system of worship to carry men over to Christ, how carefully selected were the types; how stringent the insistence on details which seem trivial to us! Does it not seem strange to us to find the Almighty giving directions about the dimensions of the tabernacle, the weaving of fringes, the color of curtains, the cutting of priests' robes? Did it matter if the tabernacle or the ark or the table of shew-bread were a foot longer or shorter? Did it matter if there were one row more or less of knops and flowers on a cornice or a pillar? It *did* matter in God's eyes. He would let no imperfect nor haphazard work go out of his hands, though it were only to serve the purpose of a day. Cannot we read this lesson? Shall we refuse our best, because our best is to be merged into something better? Or shall we not rather feel ourselves at once stimulated and honored by being allowed to contribute our best to the great result which is by and by to gather up into itself the best of all the ages?

You have read how, in the old border-wars of Scotland, the tidings of invasion and the summons to arms were carried by the fiery cross. One runner took it, and went at full speed to a certain point, telling the news as he went, and then gave it to another, who ran on in like manner. It was not for the messenger to whom that summons came to sit down and prepare for the defence of his own house and the protection of his flocks and herds. He must take the cross, and run for the next stage. Brethren, the message of Christ's cross points us beyond ourselves and our own interest and our own time. It lays on us the charge of the coming time. It bids us do our best in our own time, as a means to making that cross the central fact of the future time. "After us, the deluge" was the motto of debauchers and sensualists, who cared only for what the present might yield them, and who were willing to leave the future to work out its problem, and struggle with its suffering, as best it might; who would not give a thought nor lift a finger to make that problem easier and that suffering lighter. That is no motto for Christians. True manhood means more than eating and drinking, and dying to-morrow. Our stage of life contains a promise for the next stage, that it shall be better and higher for our faithful toil. Our problem is, to push that promise nearer to its fulfilment.

Thus, then, let us take the promise of the better thing into the inferior, incomplete conditions of to-day. Let us accept the fact of incompleteness: not passively nor idly. That were to exclude faith, and faith is the very keynote of this lesson. Nor, on the other hand, despairingly nor angrily. That were presumptuous, and useless as well. But let us recognize in it a promise of completeness, a stage towards it, and a call to promote it. No one of us can be more than a factor in the world's history. The power of each factor will appear only when the whole column shall be cast up. The sum total will be greater than any factor; but, for the very reason that it will include *all* the factors. "We must be slow," as one remarks, "to judge unfinished architecture." Truthfully said the old Greek poet, "The days to come are the wisest witnesses." If there be truth in that theory of development, so widely accepted in this day; if we are living in an incomplete physical universe, no less than in partly developed moral and spiritual conditions, — that fact goes to show, that one law holds from the natural up to the spiritual. That holds out the hope that all the apparent waste in nature will one day be accounted for, and shown to be no waste : —

> "That nothing walks with aimless feet;
> That not one life shall be destroyed,
> Or cast as rubbish to the void,
> When God hath made the pile complete.
>
> That not a worm is cloven in vain;
> That not a moth, with vain desire,
> Is shrivelled in a fruitless fire,
> Or but subserves another's gain."

That points again to the larger hope, that the imperfect work of true men, the imperfect teaching of half-taught men, the imperfect moral development of primitive men, and all the disappointed aspiration and seemingly fruitless toil and rejected testimony of God's workmen in all times, will be found again, revealed in its true value and power, at the unfolding of

> "That one far-off, divine event,
> To which the whole creation moves."

It was a profound remark of a modern essayist, that the continual failure of eminently endowed men to reach the highest standard has in it something more consoling than disheartening, and contains an "inspiring hint that it is *mankind*, and not *special men*, that are to be shaped at last into the image of God; and that the endless life of the generations may hope to come nearer that goal, of which the short-breathed three-score years and ten fall too unhappily short." The present, for each of us, bears the sign of the cross. The crown is in the future. The true suggestion of incompleteness now is faith and duty, not reward; sowing, not fruition. Only, with the cross, Christ is in the present; and the future shall see his own men and his own work complete in him.

XX.

ONLY A LITTLE WHILE.

XX.

ONLY A LITTLE WHILE.

"But this I say, brethren, the time is short: it remaineth, that both they that have wives, be as though they had none;

"And they that weep, as though they wept not; and they that rejoice, as though they rejoiced not; and they that buy, as though they possessed not;

"And they that use this world, as not abusing it: for the fashion of this world passeth away." — 1 Cor. vii. 29-31.

THERE is no difference of opinion about that first statement, "The time is short." It has passed into a commonplace.

But there is a difference between the admission, and the practical recognition, of a fact. Even in a case like this, it may fairly be asked, What is the practical bearing of our admission? There is little, if any, difference here between ourselves and the men to whom Paul wrote. They knew that no long time, at the longest, remained for them on earth; they believed that the old order of things was soon to give place to a new and different and better order; yet the apostle evidently thought that a reminder of the fact was necessary, even to those within the Christian circle. Evidently he was impressed with the fact that men were marrying and giving in marriage, weeping and rejoicing, buying and selling and laying up possessions, as if the time were not short.

And the state of things now, I repeat, is not materially different. Paul's warning is not superfluous. Whatever men believe about the permanence of the present order of things, multitudes of them act as if it were permanent.

The time, then, is short. The world, for us, is fast passing away. Death cannot be far off, and death is going to introduce us into new conditions. We, as Christians, profess to believe that the new order of things is to be better than the present order; that it will clear up what is now dark; that it will resolve what is now confused; that it will adjust and correct what is now wrong; that it will rectify and explain what now seems unjust. Our one question is, What is our proper attitude towards the present temporary, brief life which remains to us, in view of the new and larger life to come? What is the practical bearing of that single fact of brevity upon our doing, enjoying, and suffering here?

As a fact of common life, we see that the attitude of people towards a temporary and transient state of affairs is very different from their attitude towards something permanent. No man fits up the room at the hotel where he is to stay for a week or a month, as he does the home where he expects to pass his life. When one is waiting in the vestibule of a public hall where he is to hear some great orator, or witness some spectacle, he does not give much thought to the inconveniences of his situation. There is no place to sit down comfortably; the vestibule may be chilly; there may be a good deal of pushing and crowding, and he may be obliged to come in contact with disagreeable people: but he takes very little note of these things. The thing for which he has come is behind those doors; there his seat is secured; there will be warmth and light and comfort: and he says to himself, if he gives any thought at all to the matter, " The time is short. This is but for a few minutes: it will soon be over; it is not worth troubling myself about." When a man rides down from the central station in a street-car, of course he would rather have a seat, and the crowding is rather annoying; but he never thinks of making a serious matter of that. His object is to get down to business. The great interest of the day is in his office; and so he holds on by the strap, and occupies his mind with the plans of the day, and dismisses all care for the temporary annoyance.

We all agree that this is right, reasonable, sensible. We laugh at the man who invests temporary and transient conditions with the importance of permanent ones. But do we recognize the larger applications of the same principle? Suppose we simply enlarge the spaces a little, and set this life of sixty, seventy, or fourscore years over against the eternal life of the future. The two spaces are related to each other as the vestibule to the hall, the transit on the car to the day's business. Well, then, can we bring ourselves practically to recognize this relation; really to regard this life as the ante-chamber, the time of transit, the room in the inn where we stay until our house is prepared? Can we bring ourselves to regard our real life as commencing only when this life shall be over; to look for our real, permanent interests, for all fixedness and perfection of condition, in the life beyond; and to treat the affairs of this life accordingly?

This is very clearly the drift of the apostle's words; and not only here, but all through his writings, one cannot read without seeing how very slight the hold of this life is upon him. Not that he has any morbid, sentimental desire to die, not that he is indifferent to the duties and opportunities of this life; but his whole mode of looking at it and speaking of it indicates that it is to him merely a preparatory stage, a period of transit. He is quite willing to abide in the flesh as long as God wills, and he proposes to occupy himself during that period for the furtherance of his brethren's faith; but he does not hesitate to say plainly, that to depart and be with Christ is much the better thing, and that he sometimes has to struggle between the claims of the present duty and the overmastering desire to enter upon his new and better life.

Now, following the order of our text, we find Paul bringing this idea to bear in certain special directions, and intimating how it ought to affect Christians in certain departments of their life and work. But, before speaking of these in detail, let me say, what perhaps hardly needs to be said, that neither here nor elsewhere does Paul, nor any other inspired writer, use the fact of the shortness of life to encourage a sense of indifference to life's duties. The teaching of Christ and of his apostles is clear and sharp, that life, however short, is a time of work, of duty, of ministry. If the world is not to be abused, it is none the less to be used. Short as the time is, it is long enough for much weeping and rejoicing; and, because it is short, we are not to cultivate indifference to the joy and sorrow of our brethren, but rather to rejoice with them that rejoice, and weep with them that weep. Buying and selling must go on, even in this short space: we are none the less to be diligent in business because the time is short. There may be in the ante-chamber not a few beautiful pictures, a marble column which has blossomed under the sculptor's chisel, or a fountain of sweet waters. These things are for us: we may and ought to enjoy them. Life, however short, has its joys and its means of giving joy. We cannot afford to be indifferent to its sunny side, nor escape our duty of making it just as sunny as we can. We are not excused from the courtesies of life, even on a street-car; and if we can grasp the hand of an old friend with our unoccupied hand, and interchange a few hearty words, so much the better. The other world may be, and is, the *prime* fact; but this world is a fact, too, though a secondary one. If Paul says, "It remaineth that those who have wives be as though they had none," we are not to conclude, that, because a man expects to depart for heaven in a short time, he is therefore to treat his wife as though she were not.

This being premised, let us now follow the apostle into some of the details of his application.

"The time is short: it remaineth, that both they that have wives be as though they had none." By this we may assume that the apostle represents the whole class of domestic relations. These are the nearest and dearest of all the ties which bind us to earth; these relations call out our deepest affections, our best energies; they are the things which make life most attractive to us, and death hardest; there lie the possibilities of our worst heart-breaks. And God himself instituted these relations, and Christ adorned and beautified and sanctified them by his presence and first miracle at Cana; and Paul chooses the love of husband and wife as a figure of the love of Christ for the church. Yet it remaineth, that they that have wives be as though they had none.

It is very easy to see, in the light of familiar social facts, the side on which the apostle would guard us. If our earthly homes crowd out the attractions of the heavenly home, if we use them to foster our worldliness, our pride and vanity and self-indulgence, we are misusing them; and we need the apostle's caution. When that side of our life becomes so attractive as to shut out the fast-approaching life of eternity, when home tempts us to lounge and enjoy while life's short day is ringing with calls to God's work, when home ceases to be the nursery of consecrated power, a temple of worship, a training-school for Christ, a scene of preparation for heaven, and becomes, instead, a base for fashion and for shallow pleasure, — then it is time to consider the temptation and danger which lurk even in so holy a thing as domestic life, to draw aside the tapestries, and see how fast the sun is hastening towards the west, to face the hour when a voice shall call us forth from these beloved doors, to return no more.

And then, too, we know that often the family relation is unfortunately not the earthly type of heaven. We know how men make it the instrument of fostering their pride of birth, and of perpetuating some insignificant fact of lineage; and how, for the sake of preserving a family name, loveliness and innocence are constrained into alliance with senility and debauchery. If England's laureate had never written another line, he would have earned the eternal gratitude of every true soul by the brand he has left on that monstrous fiction of long descent, in his poem of "Aylmer's Field." Even more bitter is the quiet satire of the Psalmist: "Their inward thought is, that their houses shall continue forever, and their dwelling-places to all generations; they call their lands after their own names."

On the contrary, we find that, in the New Testament, domestic life is always treated with special reference to the life to come. The institution of the family, beyond any human institution, points up to God. God himself takes the name of the family head; marriage is to be in the Lord; children are to be trained in the nurture and admonition of the Lord. Domestic life is regarded, first of all, as a link between this short life and the long future; as a means to godly affections, godly living, godly training, godly working. And thus, in its Scriptural aspect, as a preparation and not a finality, it emphasizes the words, "The time is short." The apostle's injunction is met when the home is treated as a means to holy and useful living here, and as a preparation for a better home hereafter.

The apostle next takes up the bearing of this fact upon the joy and sorrow of this world: "The time is short. It remaineth that they who weep should be as though they wept not, and they that rejoice, as though they rejoiced not."

Let us confine ourselves to one element of the world's pain and sorrow, — injustice. There is the fact, patent enough to the most careless, that multitudes of people fail to get their deserts. The innocent suffer; the good do not succeed; the bad prosper; honesty and fidelity go to the wall, while villany rides by in triumph. It is not always so; but why is it so at all? Away back in the far past we find Job wrestling with the question. It furnishes, as it always has furnished, not only a theological problem, but a practical problem. On the one hand, the reasoner asks, "How did it come to pass? Why is it allowed?" On the other hand, the man who is trying to live rightly and to save his soul asks, "What shall I do with it? How shall I adjust myself to it?"

And it is interesting to study the various answers which are given to the latter question. Here comes a Rousseau, who tells us it is all unnecessary. It is all the result of false training. Human nature is good; and, if you only educate it properly, its good will have free play, and its evil will be checked, and we shall have a reign of peace, liberty, equality, and fraternity. You can read history for yourselves, and can study the value of Rousseau's answer by the side of the guillotine and in the lurid light of the French Revolution.

Or, here comes the communist, saying, "Only do away with all private interest, and merge all individual right and difference in the public, and all will be well." Doubtless, if you could only be sure of universal love and disinterestedness among men; but, unfortunately, the commune of Paris and the history of Nihilism have some significant stories to tell of that experiment.

Or, there were earlier answers. There was the Stoic, who steeled himself against injustice, treated feeling as a disease, and cultivated insensibility to pain, anger, and pity alike. Or, there was the Epicurean, saying, "Yes, pain and sorrow from human wrong are facts; but I will evade them. I will keep out of all such relations with men as will engender injustice or cruelty. I will have no friendships, and therefore no misunderstandings. I will have no zeal, and therefore I will have no disappointments. I will espouse no cause, and therefore I will suffer no defeats. I will confer no obligations, and therefore I shall expose myself to no ingratitude.

And now you will observe one fact, common to all these views, — that they are strictly bounded by this life. The evil, if it is to be corrected, must be corrected here; and this is the real cleavage-line between these views and the New-Testament view which Paul represents in our text.

For you perceive that the New Testament shows no sympathy with the sentimentalist view, that all that is needed to prevent injustice is proper education. It treats it as a necessary evil. It is a fact, and will be a fact so long as human society is not under the power of divine love.

Further: the New Testament does not give us a picture of any favored man who escapes the world's injustice. On the contrary, it is a portrait-gallery of martyrs. The better its men, the more they suffer at the world's hands. Christ gathers up into himself all virtues and perfections; and the cross is the world's practical comment upon the man in whom no fault could be found. His name, given by prophecy, and countersigned by his life, is "Man of sorrows." His great service to the world is through crucifixion.

And the New Testament, moreover, gives us no men of iron, insensible to suffering. The victims of the world's cruelty are real sufferers. If the New Testament is full of the triumph over pain, it is equally full of the human sense of pain. The perfect Man shows us his natural recoil from suffering when he says, "Save me from this hour," and, "If it be possible, let this cup pass from me." Paul is no stoic, but thoroughly a man in his keen sense of cruelty and wrong. He never affects any other sentiment. His body is a body of humiliation, — a tent, flapping and straining in the winds of time, which he will be only too glad to have taken down, so that he can break camp, and go to the fair city where Christ is.

Once more: the New Testament puts every Christian in a positive attitude towards this fact. He cannot ignore it; he cannot evade it; he must feel it; and he must feel towards it in the right way: and that way is not to live under protest, and let the world's injustice eat all the sweetness out of life. There are people who have gotten to brooding over the misery and inequality and cruelty of this life until they are literally filled with cursing. The world will not take them at their own value: therefore they hate the world. The world deals unjustly by them and theirs: they stand aloof from the world. They see certain things wrong in the church; they mutter in secret places, and can see no good in the church: all is formalism and hypocrisy. You find no warrant for any thing of this kind in the New Testament: you find the true bearing of a Son of God towards the world's evil summed up in our Saviour's words. "Resist not evil." This is really the essence of this part of our text: "They that weep; they that feel keenly the world's cruelty and sorrow, as if they wept not:" not acting as though all of life consisted in the world's being just and kindly to them, as if to live were only not to weep; not wasting time in idle lamentation or impotent scolding; not consuming themselves in the effort to prove to the world how great or how good they are: but, on the contrary, feeling that it is far more important to be right than to be thought right; far more important to be sweet and loving and tolerant, and cheerfully busy about God's work, than that the world should give them their due.

Look at Paul's words about love. They imply throughout an element of evil and injustice upon which it is to exert itself. In that thirteenth chapter of First Corinthians, the very keynote is struck by Christ's words: "If ye love them that love you, what thank have ye?" It is against hatred, evil, injustice, that the quality of love proves itself. "Beareth all things:" love, the best thing in this world or in heaven, is none too good for a burden-bearer, — nay, bears the heaviest burdens of all. "Believeth all things:" love, which is most wounded by faithlessness and treachery, is the last to lose faith in humanity. "Hopeth all things:" love is set hopefully over against the multitude of facts in man, and in society, which tempt to hopelessness. And so with the rest. The very principle of the divine life, love, most warmed by sympathy, most sensitive to coldness and injustice, most deeply cut by cruelty, is the very principle which is not provoked, and which thinketh no evil, and which never faileth. You find the same thought underlying Paul's words in the Epistle to the Romans about "the powers that be." How kind and just those powers were he knew who had felt the scourge at Philippi, and had known the horrors of the inner prison; yet, "Let every soul be subject under the higher powers. Servants, obey your masters according to the flesh." And so Peter: "It is thankworthy if a man, for conscience' sake, endure grief, suffering wrongfully;" for Christ, our great example, suffered not only *from* the unjust, but *for* the unjust, esteeming his suffering of little account if he might but bring us to God.

Now, all this is the purest sentimental nonsense if this life ends all things. If the wheat and the tares are to grow together, and no separation is to be made; if love is to hope and bear, and no time is to come when that which is in part shall be done away, — let us eat and drink and resist evil, and assert ourselves; for to-morrow we die, and are as the beasts. But if, as the gospel everywhere assumes, this state of things is passing away, to give place to a larger and better and more permanent one, then let the injustice and cruelty and sorrow be measured by the proportions of that larger life. They seem to be much in themselves; but Paul puts the proportion for us in one of his graphic sayings: "This light affliction, which is but for a moment, worketh out a far more exceeding and eternal weight of glory." The only difficulty with Paul's statement is on the side of the glory. It is so great and transcendent that it will not go into any formula that even he can devise. But even the statement which he does give makes the sorrow and trial of earth look very small.

Suppose we must be sorrowful to the end of time, — and many a man and woman has to face that necessity, — there is something else in life besides our sorrow. We can be as though we wept not; that is to say, we can be as useful and as helpful and as kindly and as sympathizing and as busy as if we had no cause to weep. We may have lost what was ours; but the time is short, and heaven will give it back with interest. Hard words, unkindness, neglect, — we all get our share; yet we need not be made thereby hard or bitter or neglectful. We may be to the world, in our spirit and ministry, just as if these things were not. The time is short. The day is coming when Christ's children shall pass into a realm of perfect love, where no unkindness shall ever make the cheek flush, and no ingratitude ever wound the spirit.

And so of our joys: "They that rejoice, as though they rejoiced not." Not that we are to pass this life in gloom and sullenness because it is short, and another life is coming. When the train goes through the tunnel, the lamps are kindled, and the carriages made as bright and cheerful as possible. We shall not sit down, and resign ourselves to gloom, and go to sleep if we can. No. The time is short. Let us be cheerful, — all the more cheerful because the sunlight will pour in by and by. But if there is grander, richer, more enduring joy in the life beyond this, it is not the part of wisdom to be too much absorbed in earthly joy. When a boy is going on his first journey to the city, which has been in his mind the sum and ideal of all splendors, you may find him playing his game of marbles or ball an hour before the train starts, but not with the same abandonment which marks him on the ordinary school holiday, when he has nothing to do but play. He plays as one who is ready to drop the bat at a minute's notice, and go upon his journey, to enjoy his greater pleasure : and so the comparison of the familiar hymn is not extravagant : —

> "This life's a dream, an empty show;
> But the bright world to which I go
> Hath joys substantial and sincere."

You can easily follow out for yourselves the applications of the thought to the buying and selling, the possessing and use of the world in general. All these things, in New-Testament thought, have their value determined by two facts, — the shortness of this life, and the overshadowing, transcendent grandeur of the life to come. Does it not become us to hold this world lightly in view of these two truths, — so little time left, and eternity approaching ? Does it not become us to guard ourselves against being too much absorbed in business, too much engrossed by pleasure, too much fretted and irritated by the trouble and sorrow and injustice of this life ? Such things do not become those who are passing through this temporary stage to an eternal home. An old woman sat one day beside her apple-stand in a great thoroughfare. A well-known judge walked up, and stopped for an apple. "Well, Molly," said he, "don't you get tired of sitting here these cold, dismal days?"—"It's only a little while, sir," was the answer.—"And the hot, dusty days?"—"Only a little while, sir."—"And the rainy, drizzly days, and your sick, rheumatic days?"—"It's only a little while, sir."—"And what then, Molly?"—"Then, sir, I shall enter into that rest which remains for the people of God; and the troublesomeness of the way there don't pester nor fret me. It's only a little while."—"But," said the judge, "what makes you so sure, Molly?"—"How can I help being sure, since Christ is the way, and I am his? Now I only feel him along the way: I shall see him as he is in a little while, sir."—"Ah!" said the judge, "you've got more than the law ever taught me."—"Yes, sir, because I went to the gospel."—"Well," said he, as he took up his apple, and began to walk off, "I must look into these things."—"There's only a little while, sir." My whole sermon is in that story.

www.ingramcontent.com/pod-product-compliance
Lightning Source LLC
Chambersburg PA
CBHW030356230426
43664CB00007BB/612